The Book of DŌ-IN

The Book of DŌ-IN

Exercise for Physical and Spiritual Development

by MICHIO KUSHI

Japan Publications, Inc.

© 1979 in Japan by Michio and Aveline Tomoyo Kushi

Published by
JAPAN PUBLICATIONS, INC., Tokyo and New York

Distributors:
UNITED STATES: *Kodansha International/USA, Ltd., through Harper & Row, Publishers, Inc., 10 East 53rd Street, New York, New York 10022.* SOUTH AMERICA: *Harper & Row, Publishers, Inc., International Department.* CANADA: *Fitzhenry & Whiteside Ltd., 195 Allstate Parkway, Markham, Ontario, L3R 4T8.* MEXICO AND CENTRAL AMERICA: *HARLA S. A. de C. V., Apartado 30–546, Mexico 4, D. F.* BRITISH ISLES: *International Book Distributors Ltd., 66 Wood Lane End, Hemel Hempstead, Herts HP2 4RG.* EUROPEAN CONTINENT (except Germany): *PBD Proost & Brandt Distribution bv, Strijkviertel 63, 3454 PK de Meern, The Netherlands.* GERMANY: *PBV Proost & Brandt Verlagsauslieferung, Herzstrasse 1, 5000 Köln, Germany.* AUSTRALIA AND NEW ZEALAND: *Bookwise International, 1 Jeanes Street, Beverley, South Australia 5007.* THE FAR EAST AND JAPAN: *Japan Publications Trading Co., Ltd., 1–2–1, Sarugaku-cho, Chiyoda-ku, Tokyo 101.*

First edition February 1979
Sixth printing: January 1988

ISBN 0–87040–382–6

Printed in U.S.A.

Dedication

With our endless dream of one peaceful world arising from the infinite ocean of the universe, this book is dedicated to all brothers and sisters who have come to this earth, manifest as human beings at this time, sharing the same social and natural environment for our health and happiness as well as physical, mental and spiritual development.

This dedication is shared by the ancient spiritual macrobiotic people who developed and practiced the various ways of Dō-In, and by the many people who have passed away who devoted their lives to human development, including George and Lima Ohsawa. This dedication is also shared by my ancestors and family: my parents, Keizo and Teru Kushi; my brother, Masao, and his wife, Kayoko and their children; my wife Aveline Tomoko Kushi and children, Lillian, Norio, Candy, Haruo, Yoshio, and Hisao; together with all my friends throughout the world who are learning and pursuing the order of the universe to be realized upon the earth among mankind, in one peaceful world.

We Are One Forever

We have come from the infinite ocean of the universe.
We have manifested from endless oneness into millions and billions.
We have realized ourselves into human beings upon this planet at this time.
We are playing, with endless dream, enjoying the vicissitudes of relative
   waves upon this earth.
Our human life is ephemeral, yet our dream is endless.
We live with day and night, health and sickness, misery and happiness, sad-
   ness and joy—rise and fall, continuously;
Yet our dream never changes, our universal origin never ends.
Let us enjoy together with everyone else while we are on this planet.
When we return to the infinite universe, let us say to each other:
      We are always one in the infinite ocean,
      And let us meet again
      When we manifest in this relative world.

MICHIO KUSHI
March, 1978

Editor's Comment

Dō-In has its origins in the ancient traditions of the Far East, but today it is practiced by increasing numbers of people in both the Eastern and Western worlds.

The introduction of Dō-In in the West is largely due to the teaching of Michio Kushi and his contemporaries and students. Mr. Kushi's practice of Dō-In and a natural, macrobiotic way of life for over twenty-five years, along with his study of the traditions of healing of many cultures, has given him a profound comprehension in this field; and his remarkable ability as a teacher and consultant has enabled him to spread this ancient oriental understanding among modern people of many nationalities.

While practicing Dō-In and the macrobiotic way of life for the past nine years, I have consistently experienced its value in developing sound physical health and a sense of mental well-being. As an assistant to Mr. and Mrs. Kushi in their educational activities, I have been impressed with the beneficial changes not only in myself, but also in thousands of people who have come to them for advice, attended their classes and read their publications.

The Book of Dō-In, with Mr. Kushi's original drawings, offers a clear explanation of the basic exercises of Dō-In and the natural and traditional way of life within which Dō-In may be most effectively practiced. The already-experienced student will find a wealth of new and advanced material for further studies.

I would like to thank Mr. Kushi and Japan Publications, Inc. for the opportunity to assist in producing this book. I hope that many people will enjoy reading it, and will find their lives enriched through the practice of Dō-In.

OLIVIA OREDSON
Brookline, Massachusetts
September 1978

Acknowledgment of Sources

In the creation of *The Book of Dō-In: Exercise for Physical and Spiritual Development*, I wish to extend my acknowledgment and gratitude to those whose studies and teachings have contributed to certain parts of the contents:

1. In Part One of the book, the general introduction on the order of the universe, the macrobiotic way of life, and the physical and spiritual constitution of man, I appreciate the inspiration received from various discourses, articles, books, and teachings of ancient wisdom from many parts of the world including Japan, Korea, China, India, and Egypt as well as ancient Europe and America. I also appreciate the inspiration received over the past many years through our own practice of the macrobiotic way of life, from the Infinite Universe—the source of memory and dream, the beginning and end of our life.

2. In Part Two, the Exercises of Dō-In, I wish to dedicate my appreciation for the following teachings:

A. Special Exercises
Traditional teachings and exercises descended from centuries ago as the heritage of ancient human customs, including those religious and spiritual practices of Shintoism, Buddhism, Hinduism and Taoism remaining mainly in the oriental countries. Some of these are still being exercised within a comparatively small group of seekers for spiritual development in the Far East and other areas of the Orient.

B. Daily Spiritual Exercises
Teachings and exercises practiced mainly in Shintoism, Hinduism and Taoism, as well as other spiritual practices, still remaining in some oriental countries· among an inner circle of religious training.

C. Daily Exercises
1. Morning and Evening Exercises: The teachings of basic Dō-In exercises as daily practice by 仙道連, Sen-Dō-Ren (Association for the Study of the Tao of Free Man, Tokyo, Japan). For further studies of these practices. it is recommended communicate with this association.

> Sen-Dō-Ren
> 1-27-12 Kaminoge
> Setagaya-ku
> Tokyo 158
> Japan

[7]

2. Meridian Exercises: Various exercises related to meridians, developed and practiced during many centuries; and among them, especially those introduced by Mr. Shizuto Masunaga as Meridian Exercises in the book, *Zen Shiatsu*, published in Tokyo, Japan by Japan Publications, Inc., pages 122–124. In order to study further, it is recommended to communicate with the following:

Shizuto Masunaga
5-9-8 Tokiwa, Urawa-shi,
Saitama-ken 336
Japan

I-O-Kai Shiatsu Center
1-8-9 Higashi-Ueno, Taito-ku
Tokyo 110
Japan

3. Additional Exercises: Various teachings and exercises traditionally practiced in connection with breathing, which have appeared in the way of health in the ancient physical training of Shintoism and Buddhism.

D. *General Exercises*

Major classics of oriental medicine from 3,000 years ago up to the present, beginning with 易経, *I Ching*, the *Book of Changes* and 黄帝内経, the *Yellow Emperor's Classic of Internal Medicine*, and ending with modern books related to diagnosis and physiognomy, meridians and points, sicknesses and treatments in the field of oriental medicine.

MICHIO KUSHI

Preface

During my life of one-half century, I have experienced and observed the miseries of world war, together with the misery of present-day society—the various diseases and poverty, greed and selfishness, failure and difficulties, anger and hatred, discrimination and prejudice.

In my youth, I was inspired with the dream of realizing world peace through many possible measures, including the establishment of a World Federation. However, through the process of maturing, I have become able to see that world peace can be achieved only through the reconstruction of humanity, or the resurrection of man, from current degenerative trends which have prevailed throughout the world, increasing with the development of modern civilization.

At the same time, I was able to have an enlightening experience during meditation, which revealed universal and eternal life. I have also had the opportunity to deepen my understanding of ancient oriental philosophies and religions, which should be combined together with the modern occidental thought and way of life. In this regard I am grateful for the inspired teaching of George Ohsawa and many other present-day philosophers, as well as ancient spiritual, philosophical and scientific thinkers.

All miseries in human affairs come from our personal incomprehension of the order of the universe, or we may say, our ignorance of ourselves. From this ignorance we misguide our daily way of life in our dietary practice, social relations, and mental attitude as well as spiritual comprehension.

Life is one infinite universe itself, and our way of life should be simple and practical, according to the order of the infinite universe. Realization of health and happiness is the easiest and simplest way. On the basis of this understanding, I have begun to spread the way of life which everyone can practice at any time as the simplest means to achieve health and happiness, freedom and peace—known as the macrobiotic way of life.

Together with the spread of the way of life for humanity for one peaceful world, I have encouraged the adaptation of several traditional ways of physical, mental and spiritual development, namely, oriental medicine, acupuncture, moxibustion, shiatsu massage, palm-healing, meditation, and mental and spiritual exercises. In order to reinforce our own development, I also began to introduce an ancient macrobiotic practice, Dō-In, in the United States about ten years ago. I am grateful to Mr. Jacques DeLangre and Mr. Jean Bernard Rishi for their respective books on Dō-In, which introduced part of these exercises. However, the Dō-In which I introduced was a partial exercise, mainly related to energizing our physical and mental vitality, and did not fully explain other aspects of Dō-In which are more spiritually oriented. I have been obliged for the past several years to introduce the general scale of the entire scope of Dō-In exercises.

It has been necessary to rediscover and reconstitute the Dō-In exercises because these ancient macrobiotic exercises were largely lost in many areas, although some of them have been practiced among a limited society of seekers in the Far East. The entire scale of Dō-In exercise is not limited to the several series of exercises introduced in this book. These ancient macrobiotic exercises were actually the origin of all physical, mental and spiritual exercises which are currently differentiated into various kinds of meditation, chanting, yoga exercise, physiopsychological training, the martial arts, as well as other methods of self-development.

The origin of Dō-In exercise is simply our intuitive self-adjustment to maintain and develop ourselves, within the ocean of universal life or the infinite universe. Therefore, the beginning of Dō-In exercise is historically unknown, but it has always existed with human life, throughout all generations of mankind. However, it was over 10,000 years ago when Dō-In exercises were actively adapted in the ancient way of physical, mental and spiritual development to produce free man—the *Tao of Shin-Sen* (神仙道), the Way of Spiritual Free Man.

The uniqueness of these exercises is that anyone can practice them at any time as daily exercises under ordinary circumstances, without requiring any partner or special technique. In this sense, all races, all ages, man and woman, can practice them easily for health and happiness. Some of the exercises introduced in this book are my own modification in the hope that they may benefit everyone.

I sincerely hope that everyone throughout the world will freely practice these exercises for his or her own physical health, beauty, and spiritual happiness.

I am grateful to the publisher, Japan Publications, Inc., for extending to me the opportunity to introduce these exercises. I am also grateful to Miss Olivia Oredson, who is a dedicated senior and friend in studying and introducing the macrobiotic way of life to many hundreds of people, for her assistance in the preparation of the book.

The models who performed the various forms of the Dō-In exercises are my long-time friends and students who share the same dream through the macrobiotic way of life. The lady in white is Miss Laura Knudson of Boston, Massachusetts, who has been studying yoga exercises in addition to assisting in my work in macrobiotic studies. The lady in black is Miss Lynda LeMole of Brookline, Massachusetts, who has been teaching the macrobiotic way of cooking and way of life, working as editorial assistant for the *East West Journal*, and as my personal assistant for studies.

The photography has been done by Mr. John Fogg, who is currently a staff member of Erewhon Natural Food Distributing Company in Boston, Massachusetts, and has been practicing and teaching the macrobiotic way of life. Mr. William Spear of Middletown, Connecticut, teacher of the East West Center there, has assisted in drafting a part of the General Exercises. Peter and Bonnie Harris of Koi Graphics in Brookline, Massachusetts have made the drawings on pages 60 and 73.

I wish to extend my thanks to these friends as well as to all teachers, seniors, friends and students, who are some millions throughout the world, seeking together the realization of our common endless dream of one peaceful world.

March, 1978

MICHIO KUSHI
Brookline, Massachusetts, U.S.A.

Contents

Part One

Introduction to Shin-Sen-Dō: Physical, Mental and Spiritual Development

Chapter 1

The Order of the Universe and the Macrobiotic Way of Life

1. The Creation of the Universe

In the beginningless beginning, the infinite universe did not manifest as phenomena. There was no time nor space, no light nor darkness, no form nor dimension. From this oneness, there was only endless motion which moved with infinite speed in all directions. Because of this infinite speed, there was no past nor future, nor any relative phenomena whatsoever.

However, whenever and wherever the infinite motion, which moves in all directions, intersects, spirallic movements begin to form in a process of differentiation. Forces producing spirals from the periphery toward the center, and forces decomposing spirals from the center toward the periphery, are the two primary forces in the world of spirals, the world of all relative phenomena.

From the motion of galaxies to the motion of preatomic particles, from invisible spiritual movement to visible physical constitutions, all are spirallically formed and governed by two antagonistic, complementary forces: yin ($\triangledown$), the centrifugal and expanding force, tendency and direction; and yang ($\triangle$), the centripetal and contracting force, tendency and direction.

All phenomena manifested in this infinite ocean of the universe are governed, directed and destined by these two forces. All change and movements are either more yin, centrifugal, or more yang, centripetal. There is nothing that is not governed by these two tendencies and directions. All phenomena differ from each other because of the different degrees of these two forces working within and without them.

Accordingly, yin and yang manifest into everything—every phenomenon within the universe as well as upon the earth. The relation between these two forces, tendencies and directions can be figured as Fig. 1 at next page.

The yang force, the course of contraction and physicalization, is the course of materialization; while the yin force, the course of expansion and dephysicalization, is the course of spiritualization. When the yang course accelerates, matter is formed. The molecules composing matter move faster, generating a faster spinning motion of preatomic particles such as electrons, resulting in the production of higher temperatures (Course A). Conversely, the course of spiritualization expands and decomposes matter, making the speed of the motion of molecules and preatomic particles increasingly slower, producing a lower temperature (Course B).

When the course of materialization produces a high temperature, matter starts to expand, turning its course from materialization to spiritualization (Course C);

[17]

Fig. 1   The Eternal and Universal Cycle of Change

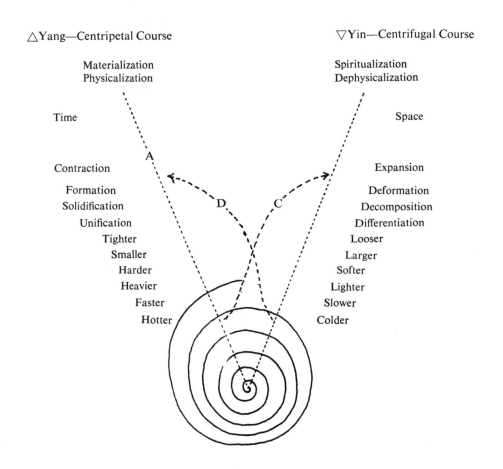

and when the course of spiritualization produces a cold temperature, matter begins to contract, turning its course to materialization (Course D). That yang ($\triangle$) course of contraction changes into a yin ($\triangledown$) course of expansion, and the yin ($\triangledown$) course of expansion changes into a yang ($\triangle$) course of contraction, alternating between yin and yang perpetually.

Contraction changes into expansion, and expansion changes into contraction; physicalization changes to spiritualization, and spiritualization to physicalization; movement changes to rest, and rest to movement; solidification changes to decomposition, and decomposition changes to solidification; prosperity ends in poverty, and poverty in prosperity; success changes into failure, and failure into success; joy changes into misery, and misery into joy; love becomes hate, and hate becomes love; pleasure changes to displeasure, and displeasure changes to pleasure. Day becomes night, night becomes day; winter turns into summer, summer turns into winter; darkness turns into light, light turns into darkness; health changes to sickness, and sickness changes to health. The rise of civilization brings about its decline. Difficulties produce strength and happiness. Tears lead to smiles. War results in peace; life turns into death; and death turns into life.

All spirals forming the various relative worlds appear and disappear constantly in the ocean of the infinite universe, throughout which the perpetual movement from yin ($\triangledown$) to yang ($\triangle$) and yang ($\triangle$) to yin ($\triangledown$) is operating everywhere, at all times. This motion between yin and yang is infinity itself, which we may call One Wholeness, God, or the order of the universe, which is eternal and universal. There are no natural phenomena which are not manifested within this order of the universe according to yin ($\triangledown$) and yang ($\triangle$), and there are no human affairs which do not represent this eternal and universal law of change. Whatever and whoever does not realize this infinite order sees his existence in this universe only in its relative worlds.

Examples of Yin and Yang

Attribute	YIN $\triangledown$ Centrifugal Force	YANG $\triangle$ Centripetal Force
Tendency	Expansion	Contraction
Function	Diffusion	Fusion
	Dispersion	Assimilation
	Separation	Gathering
	Decomposition	Organization
Movement	More inactive, slower	More active, faster
Vibration	Shorter wave and higher frequency	Longer wave and lower frequency
Direction	Ascent and vertical	Descent and horizontal
Position	More outward and peripheral	More inward and central
Weight	Lighter	Heavier
Temperature	Colder	Hotter
Light	Darker	Brighter
Humidity	More wet	More dry
Density	Thinner	Thicker
Size	Longer	Smaller
Shape	More expansive and fragile	More contractive and harder
Form	Longer	Shorter
Texture	Softer	Harder
Atomic particle	Electron	Proton
Elements	N, O, K, P, Ca, etc.	H, C, Na, As, Mg, etc.
Environment	Vibration ....Air......Water....	Earth
Climatic effects	Tropical climate	Colder climate
Biological	More vegetable quality	More animal quality
Sex	Female	Male
Organ structure	More hollow and expansive	More compacted and condensed
Nerves	More peripheral, orthosympathetic	More central, parasympathetic
Attitude, emotion	More gentle, negative, defensive	More active, positive, aggressive
Work	More psychological and mental	More physical and social
Consciousness	More universal	More specific
Mental function	Dealing more with the future	Dealing more with the past
Culture	More spiritually oriented	More materially oriented
Dimension	Space	Time

There are several fundamental laws in the movement of the universe, including all changes of natural phenomena in this relative world:

1. *The yin ($\triangledown$) centrifugal and expanding force and tendency attracts the yang ($\triangle$) centripetal and contracting force and tendency, and vice versa.*

In order to realize and maintain the harmony of one infinite universe, opposing forces and tendencies attract each other to achieve a harmonious state. The creation and dissolution of the universe, continually developing in almost infinite dimensions of time and space, constantly produces numerous varieties of phenomena. Among those phenomena, visible and invisible, small and large, physical and spiritual, movements to achieve harmony are continuously working. This movement of universal attraction among different forces and tendencies is called, in our human expression, "love." Love is therefore universal and permanent, arising everywhere and at all times, between man and woman, carbon and oxygen, electron and proton, low pressure and high pressure, cold and hot, slow and fast, plus $(+)$ and minus $(-)$ in electricity and magnetism, dark and bright, North and South, East and West, spirit and matter, short wave and long wave—whenever and wherever all relative phenomena of opposite tendencies attract each other to produce harmony.

2. *The yin ($\triangledown$) centrifugal and expanding force and tendency repels similar yin forces and tendencies, and the yang ($\triangle$) centripetal and contracting force and tendency repels similar yang forces and tendencies.*

In order to maintain universal harmony in this infinite ocean of the universe, while opposite tendencies attract each other, all similar forces and tendencies repel each other. In order to avoid possible disharmony, similar phenomena drive apart and remain apart from each other, avoiding excessive accumulation of the same forces and tendencies. No marriage takes place between the same sex; no melody is composed by the continuation of the same sound; no respiration occurs by either inhalation or exhalation alone; and no movement continues without rest.

Similar plus $(+)$ poles repel each other as do similar minus $(-)$ poles. Oil and water, which have like tendencies in a natural state, do not mix with each other; and among solid particles such as sand, condensation does not occur unless liquid acts as a binding agent. People of similar aggressive and outgoing character often create misunderstandings and arguments among themselves, as do people of similar gentle and withdrawn character.

This movement of repulsion between similar forces and tendencies is universally and permanently working throughout all relative phenomena. In more analytical terms, it may be called "separation;" and in more emotional terms, "hate." These, as well as love and harmony, are major principles of this endlessly changing universe.

3. *An excessive condition of the yin ($\triangledown$) centrifugal force and tendency, or the yang ($\triangle$) centripetal force and tendency, produces and changes into the opposite yang ($\triangle$) centripetal and contracting force and tendency, or yin ($\triangledown$) centrifugal and expanding force and tendency.*

Every relative phenomenon arising in the ocean of the infinite universe develops to its peak, and then turns to the opposite, declining course. All life has its beginning and end, passing through its most prosperous state. Any individual who continues to grow after his birth, starts to decay toward death after having his most active period during middle age. All civilizations rise and fall; all countries develop and decline; and all families prosper and perish. Higher pressures as well as lower temperatures usually produce a contraction of matter; but under their extreme conditions, expansion is produced instead.

Day changes into night and night into day; summer changes into winter and winter into summer; peace changes into war and war into peace; tranquility changes into excitement and excitement into tranquility; health changes into sickness and sickness into health; life changes into death and death into life; spirit changes into body and body into spirit; matter changes into energy and energy into matter.

In this infinite ocean of the universe there is nothing static. All phenomena are constantly changing from yin to yang and yang to yin, from the invisible to the visible, and from the visible to the invisible. Because of this universal and permanent order of change, everything in this universe is temporary and ephemeral. Because of this eternal cycle of movement from one to the other between the opposite tendencies, everything reincarnates endlessly.

These three major principles govern everywhere throughout the universe. Wherever, whenever, and whatever—everything changes according to these laws. The destiny of this Milky Way Galaxy and of our solar system, and the destiny of the earth upon which we are living are not excepted from this order. All our human destinies, personal and collective, are also changing according to these principles. Our physical, mental and spiritual manifestations as well as our social activities are also changing according to this order.

Those who know these orders working within and without us are able to attain health and peace. On the other hand, those who do not understand these orders suffer confusion and chaos, conflict and misery.

Those who know these orders and change themselves to adapt to the changing circumstances are able to achieve happiness; while those who do not know these orders are incapable of adapting themselves and suffer despair and disappointment, discontent and unhappiness.

Those who know these orders and actively take the initiative to lead the changing circumstances are able to attain freedom. On the other hand, those who do not know these orders and therefore unable to take the initiative in their surroundings, lose their freedom and enslave themselves, suffering endless struggles.

In order to live in health, happiness, peace and freedom, it is absolutely essential to understand these eternal and universal orders of the infinite movement of the universe.

2. Materialization and Spiritualization

In the infinite ocean of the universe, spirals arise, forming the entire phenomenal world. The formation of the relative world is promoted by the yang centripetal contracting force, which forms a spirallic movement from the periphery toward the center. This process of the creation of the relative world on the larger scale generally takes seven orbital stages:

The First Stage: One Infinity, beginningless and endless. God, the Whole and Absolute, which is omnipresent, omnipotent, and omniscient. The infinite ocean of endless movement which continually expands in all directions with infinite speed.

The Second Stage: The beginning of the poles, yin ($\triangledown$) and yang ($\triangle$). All antagonistic and complemental forces and tendencies result from the formation of spirallic movement which has come from the intersection of infinitely expanding forces. The beginning of time and space, directions and dimensions; the differentiation of speed, frequency, and forces. The beginning of all relative phenomena.

The Third Stage: Movement, energy, and vibration, waving between the poles which result from the differentiation of the second stage. Invisible, but phenomena. An infinitesimal part of this world is perceivable within the scale of human awareness as spiritual and mental phenomena, and a further smaller part is perceivable to the human senses. This world includes the infinite length of all vibrations, from the shortest waves to the longest waves.

The Fourth Stage: The world of preatomic movement, the beginning of the physical and material world. A condensed mass of the spirallic motion of energy, appearing as particles. A few of those numerous varieties of particles are known on this earth as electrons, neutrons and other preatomic particles.

The Fifth Stage: The world of elements, resulting from the spirallic molecular gathering of preatomic particles. Composing the world of nature—soil, water and air—the components of this stage include more than one hundred elements, from the lightest ones such as hydrogen and helium to the heavy and radioactive elements, insofar as this earth is concerned.

The Sixth Stage: The world of plant organisms—the vegetable kingdom. Molecules of elements charged electromagnetically develop into this world, especially when accelerated by the centrifugal expanding forces of the earth. Thousands of species have prevailed upon the planet, transformed from soil, water and air, and nourished by solar and other celestial radiation.

The Seventh Stage: The world of the animal kingdom, transformed and developed from the world of plant organisms, the vegetable kingdom. Their development has been influenced more by the centripetal contracting forces which the earth receives from heaven—outer space. There are a hundred thousand species, and each is highly charged electromagnetically, producing active independent movement. There are two major categories of species; water animals and land animals. Among them, seven major evolutionary developments have taken place: from the primitive cellular organism, passing through the stages of invertebrate, amphibian, reptile, bird, and mammal, toward man. The human being is the latest, most developed manifestation of this stage.

From the invisible ocean of the universe to the appearance of human beings upon the planet, seven orbital stages of creation have taken place. This is the course of physicalization and materialization, an inward course of the spirallic movement of creation which has arisen in the infinite ocean. There are no borderlines between these progressive stages: each preceding stage becomes the environment of the following stage. The seventh stage, the animal kingdom, is a manifestation transformed from a part of the sixth stage, the vegetable kingdom. The sixth stage, the vegetable kingdom, is a manifestation transformed from a part of the fifth stage, the world of elements. The fifth stage, the world of elements, is a manifestation transformed from a part of the fourth stage, the preatomic world. The fourth stage, the preatomic world, is a manifestation transformed from a part of the third stage, the world of vibration and energy. The third stage, the world of vibration and energy, is a manifestation transformed from a part of the second stage, the world of polarization. The second stage, the world of polarization, is a differentiated appearance of One Infinity.

Fig. 2 The Creation of the Universe

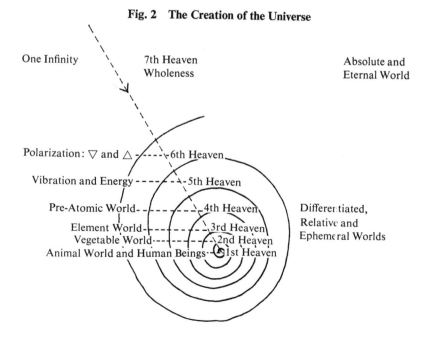

The infinite world of the first stage is the origin of all, yet it does not have manifestation in itself. The world of polarization is the principle of all movement, the whole phenomenal world, the order of the universe. The world of the third stage is the invisible spiritual world of which an infinitesimal part is perceivable as our sensory and mental experience. The worlds from the fourth to the seventh stages are the relative phenomenal worlds, some of which are increasingly perceivable through our daily experiences. Among them, the fourth and fifth worlds are the natural physical and chemical worlds, and the sixth and seventh stages are the worlds of organic life.

As this huge spiral of seven-orbited creation proceeds inward in its course of physicalization and materialization, the varieties of phenomena and manifestations in each stage become increasingly large in number. The first stage is the stage of oneness. The second stage is the stage of two—yin (∇) and yang ($\triangle$). Developing through the stages, the number of variations increases rapidly: in the world of elements, about one hundred; in the world of vegetables, thousands of species; in the world of animals, millions of species. In the last stage—human beings—in our present society and in this century, more than four billion different manifestations are currently acting independently.

This huge spirallic inward movement of creation, which has arisen in the ocean of the infinite universe, naturally has as its destiny to reverse its inward spirallic movement toward the direction of dissolving the entire spiral. In other words, the yang centripetal inward course of physicalization and materialization turns its direction at the center of the spiral toward the periphery, the infinite ocean, by the yin, centrifugal decomposing course. This yin, centrifugal decomposing course of dissolution by spirallic movement, returning to the endless ocean of the infinite universe, may be called dephysicalization or dematerialization, or the course of spiritualization. This course of dematerialization progresses in seven orbital stages, beginning from the center and moving toward the periphery of the spiral:

The First Stage: The world of organic life, the most condensed manifestation of vibration and energy, highly charged with electromagnetic activity, living actively and independently. The animal kingdom, especially the physical constitution of the human being, is the highest manifestation of this world.

The Second Stage: The world of physical vibrations and energy, discharged and radiated from the activity and decomposition of cellular organisms, namely, the body or physical constitution. Massive movements of caloric energy and heat vibrations together with massive evaporation of liquid molecules, and atmospheric motion between the body and the surroundings. Most of the moving phenomena in this level can be identified by our sensory and emotional perceptions.

The Third Stage: The world of vibrations and energy of shorter waves. The world of consciousness, vibrating and manifesting in various thoughts and ideas. A massive manifestation of thoughts and ideas in this world is often called the "astral body," and this world is called the earth's "astral world." The dimensions of this world are a thousand times larger than the world which is perceivable through our sensory and emotional experiences.

The Fourth Stage: The world of electromagnetic activity. All movements of high frequency forming currents between differentiated poles—plus-minus or yin-yang—throughout the dimensions of the universe. This world is a thousand times larger than the previous world from which all relative consciousness, thoughts, and ideas come, and in which all physical manifestations and phenomena of the previous stages result. The visible universe is a mere geometric point of this world.

The Fifth Stage: The world of radiation, streaming with high velocity throughout the infinite ocean of the universe. From this world, various spiritual manifestations and activities are born. The dimensions of this world are a thousand times bigger than the previous world.

The Sixth Stage: The world of centripetality and centrifugality, the primary forces of all spiritual, physical and material manifestations and phenomena; covering the entire scope of the infinite ocean of the universe, producing and diminishing all universes and all phenomena therein. This world is manifested throughout all movements, beyond time and space, as antagonistic and complementary tendencies whenever, wherever and in whatever is in this universe. This world may be called the Universal Spirit.

Fig. 3   Spiritualization of the Universe

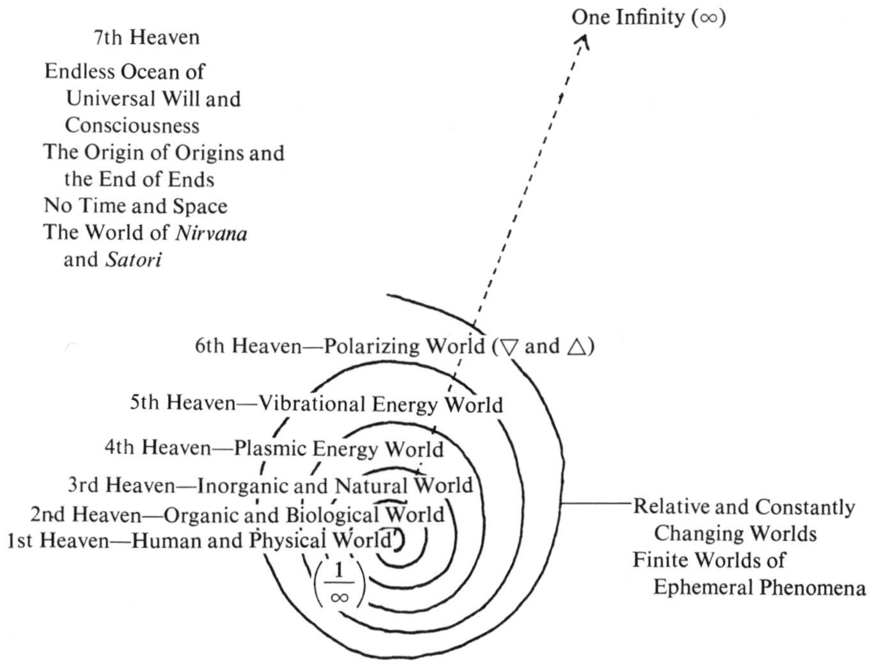

One Infinity (∞)

7th Heaven

Endless Ocean of
　Universal Will and
　Consciousness
The Origin of Origins and
　the End of Ends
No Time and Space
The World of *Nirvana*
　and *Satori*

6th Heaven—Polarizing World (∇ and $\triangle$)

5th Heaven—Vibrational Energy World

4th Heaven—Plasmic Energy World

3rd Heaven—Inorganic and Natural World

2nd Heaven—Organic and Biological World

1st Heaven—Human and Physical World

$\left(\dfrac{1}{\infty}\right)$

Relative and Constantly
　Changing Worlds
Finite Worlds of
　Ephemeral Phenomena

The Seventh Stage: One Infinity, endless and boundless. The world of constant expansion with infinite speed in all directions. The dimensions of this world are infinitely larger than all previous relative worlds. The everlasting origin of all, of every country of God and his manifestations in all beings. The home country for all lives and phenomena, forever. The past, the present, and the future of all relative worlds. The world of *Nirvana*—absolute freedom and absolute justice, absolute love and absolute peace. Everything has come out from this world and returns to this world, then comes out from this world again.

These stages of the yin, centrifugal returning course from the infinitesimal stage of life to the infinite ocean of life have no boundaries between them: there is continuous, progressive change in the decomposing process of the spirallic universe, which has arisen in the ocean of infinity. Each world becomes progressively larger in dimension in comparison with each previous world, in logarithmic progression.

Our human body, our massive physical manifestation, is the beginning of this returning course toward the infinite ocean of life. We have come from infinity; we are living within infinity; and we return to infinity. We are experiencing this journey of life of a hundred thousand million billion years, stage to stage, changing and adapting our constitution to the particular nature of each stage. The experience of human life is a mere blink of the eye in comparison with this long journey of life.

Human life is ephemeral, and whatever we do during this lifetime is in vain if we consider our human life as existing separately from this long journey of life. However, human life on this tiny planet, the earth, is a stage between the yang course of physicalization and materialization, and the yin course of dephysicalization, which takes place on the scale of the infinite universe, with an infinite length of time and with infinite dimensions of spiritual, mental, and physical phenomena. Human life is the result of a past journey of life of millions and billions of years. Human life is a result of all past experiences which have arisen in this universe, and it represents a burning wish, hope, and dream for the endless future, to become one with infinity, with absolute justice and freedom, with absolute peace and love. Our daily life is the process by which we are accumulating our physical, mental and spiritual development in preparation for the forthcoming stage in the journey of life. Whatever we do, whatever we think, will result in our life in the next stage, just as our present life has been influenced by whatever we did and whatever we thought in the previous life.

Those who understand the endless journey of life are wise to design and manage their human life, day to day, to develop their physical, mental and spiritual qualities, preparing themselves for the forthcoming stage of the journey. Those who do not understand this endless journey of life are unwise in the orientation of their daily life, wasting their life on this earth for trifling, invaluable matters, seeking ephemeral contentment and satisfaction.

3. The Eternal Journey of Life

In the long journey of life which has temporal dimensions of hundreds, thousands, millions and billions of years and spatial dimensions of almost infinite scope, human life is a stage which begins our returning course to the infinite ocean of life, the eternal home country of all lives and phenomena. Throughout our lives, day and night, we are all experiencing a part of this returning course.

Various stages of this returning course are experienced through our physical, mental and spiritual activities and remain in our memory. Practically speaking, we generally experience the various stages of the returning journey as follows:

The First Period of Life: The beginning of the returning journey occurs as our forms from the previous stages differentiate into two antagonistic and complementary reproductive cells—the mother's egg and the father's sperm. Both of these have come from the parents' blood cells, which have come from the vegetable kingdom. The reproductive cells which are active in the mother's womb are the result of a journey of life-transmutations of hundreds of billions of years, which began from the infinite ocean of the universe an almost unknown time ago. They have reached the stage of organic life as the primary constitution of animal life, highly charged electromagnetic vibration. When these antagonistic and complementary reproductive cells, the yang egg and the yin sperm, combine and fuse with each other, it is the beginning of the returning course of a hundred billion years toward the infinite ocean of life. Each of them carries its past memories and the vision of its future. When they fuse with each other—though their recent journeys separated them into different species of vegetables, different kinds of molecules and different blood cells of the father and mother—their memory that they have come from the same origin, one infinity, and their vision toward the future when they shall become one infinity, has never been forgotten. When they fuse with each other, memories and visions become manifested in one organism which succeeds them as an imperishable dream to accomplish the returning journey of life, in order to continue to realize absolute freedom, justice, love and peace.

Physically, the fertilized egg is a replica of the earth, which is rotating, therefore producing electromagnetic belts around itself and periodically undergoing axis shifts. Furthermore, the fertilized egg is nourished by electromagnetic currents which pass spirallically through the spiritual channel of the mother's body: the force of heaven, yang ($\triangle$), descending from heaven to the center of the earth; and another electromagnetic force coming from the earth, vertically passing through the mother's uterus —the force of earth, yin ($\triangledown$)—ascending centrifugally from the center of the earth toward heaven. By those two forces—one centripetal and the other centrifugal— the fertilized egg is continuously balanced between the heavenly motion of the constellations and the movement of the earth. The descending force of heaven passing through the mother's spiritual channel is also nourished by the mother's emotions, thoughts, ideas, and images. While it passes through the mother's brain, it is reoriented and reformed by her various thoughts and images into a new quality of energizing force.

The Second Period of Life: Life succeeding fertilization covers a period of about seven days. During this period the new life travels through the Fallopian tube in the mother's uterus, its cellular organisms multiplying rapidly through the movement of constant rotation and frequent axis shifts. This life period is a repetition of the primary growth of life toward multiple cellular organisms, in the ancient gaseous state of the primordial earth nearly four billion years ago. In this period, the life travels rapidly away from the ovarian region toward another pole which has been newly developed by the intensive charge of heaven and earth's forces at the innermost depths of the uterus where the placenta is to grow. Primary mechanical consciousness governs and directs this life. The memories and visions, which were carried by the parents' reproductive cells and fused into one by fertilization, are distributed to each of the rapidly-growing individual cells. Each cell carries the same memories and visions, and all cells comprehensively carry the same memory and the same vision as a whole. During this period, life is nourished by the flow of invisible electromagnetic charges which originate from the descending force of heaven and the ascending force of earth; and it is also nourished by the forces charging between the two poles, the ovary and the inner depths of the uterus—the region known as the *Hara*—as well as by the forces generated by its own rotation and axis shifts.

The Third Period of Life: The third stage of the returning process toward infinity begins with implantation at the inner depths of the mother's uterus and the growth of the placenta. This period continues until delivery, repeating the biological evolution of life in water. The amniotic sac, within which the embryo floats and receives nourishment from the placenta through the umbilical cord, represents the ancient sea which covered the entire surface of the earth until the formation of land. During this period the embryo develops its systems, organs, and glands, as well as all auxiliary parts of the body. Besides the nourishment received through the placenta and umbilical cord, primarily the filtered blood of the mother, the embryo continuously receives invisible vibrational energy passing through the mother's spiritual channel—the forces of heaven and earth together with the influence of energy passing through the meridians running along the wall of the uterus. The embryo rotates and repeats axis shifts, its memory and visions becoming further differentiated and distributed to the constantly increasing cells. In this period, the embryo develops nearly three billion times in weight compared with the original weight of the fertilized egg.

This life in water is the preparatory stage for the next stage, life in the air. During this embryonic period in water, cellular organisms are growing constantly, and the physical foundation for the following life in air is accomplished. In other words, the main purpose of this stage of life is the formation of the physical constitution, preparing a ground for mental-spiritual development in the next stage of life. Embryonic life in water proceeds by mechanical judgment, and almost no objective consciousness participates in the development until toward the last period of pregnancy. The constitution developed during this time is a foundation for the destiny of the next stage, and therefore it is of fundamental importance what quality of nourishment the embryo receives, what kind of energy it receives from the mother's activity, what kind of vibrations of consciousness it receives from the mother's thoughts and images. All of these things comprehensively accomplish the embryonic development and decide what kind of life in the forthcoming air world the new baby will experience.

The Fourth Period of Life: The returning course toward infinity further proceeds from life in the water to more expanded surroundings: life in the air. After an average of 280 days of water life in darkness, birth occurs with repeated contractions of the uterus, and a flood of water. The new life begins in an atmosphere which is half bright and half dark—day and night. The process of birth is a repetition of the occurrences on earth about 400 million years ago: repeated catastrophes in land formation, and large-scale flooding. In order to adapt to the new, expanded atmospheric environment, the newborn baby must experience contraction—yangization—by delivery through the narrow passage, by breathing out excessive substances, and by drinking yellow liquid through the mother's breast before starting to take normal milk. Loss of weight therefore arises within several days immediately after birth.

The life in air upon the earth is our human life, leaving behind the placenta and umbilical cord, and with all cellular organisms—the body—continuing further the returning journey toward infinity. The beginning period of approximately one year, however, repeats biological evolution on land, from the stage of amphibians, passing through the stages of reptiles, mammals and apes, reaching finally the stage of man. This process is accomplished by the time of erect posture—standing— together with the development of sensory and emotional consciousness, which has advanced along with the physical evolution from birth until the time of erectness.

With the ability to stand, real human life begins. Although physical growth continues during the first twenty years of this human life, succeeding the development made in the water life or embryonic period, most of our human life is used for the development of consciousness. The ratio between the period used for physical and mental development and the period used for mental and spiritual development is roughly one to five or one to seven.

The main objective of human life is the development of mental and spiritual consciousness upon the physical foundation. In other words, human life, physically speaking, aims to continuously refine its quality in order to secure the maximum capability for the maximum mental and spiritual development; and, spiritually speaking, to achieve, until the end of human life, the largest possible dimensions of universal understanding and consciousness.

The development of understanding and consciousness generally takes place during this human life in seven stages, which develop in a centrifugal, logarithmic spiral:

The First Level: Mechanical and Spontaneous Judgment. Most physical movement, especially that governed by the autonomic nervous activities, including all basic physical functions such as digestion, respiration, circulation, excretion, nervous reactions, and others.

The Second Level: Sensory Judgment. With the developing five senses—touch-ing, tasting, smelling, hearing, seeing—together with the sense of direction and sense of balance, this level of judgment grows during the time of infancy and early childhood. It continues to be refined through the improvement in quality of these sensory organs as well as through the widening of experiences through-out life.

The Third Level: Sentimental and Emotional Judgment. Soon after the sensory function begins to work, sentimental judgment starts to grow, recognizing joy and sadness, comfort and discomfort, like and dislike; and it continue to grow toward larger dimensions that we generally term emotional activity, including the recognition of love and hate, beauty and ugliness, excitement and tranquility, aggressiveness and passivity, and other mental phenomena. This sentimental and emotional judgment continues to grow with constant refinement until the end of human life.

The Fourth Level: Intellectual Judgment. At about the age of three, soon after sentimental judgment starts to work, a new judgment, intellectual, begins to grow. Identifying, counting, figuring, forming, numbering, organizing, analyz-ing, dividing, assimilating, synthesizing and other conceptual and mental acti-vities increase. Through experience and training this intellectual judgment grows, becoming able to use logic and form theories, evaluations, and assumptions. It continues to grow through experience and training until the end of human life.

The Fifth Level: Social Judgment. As intellectual judgment grows, observa-tion of the relations within the family, the society, the country, and eventually the world, starts to develop. The determination to maintain harmonious rela-tions with others, to improve social conditions and community living, to real-ize well-being, love and peace, begins to orient the way of life and the way of expression. This social consciousness is the sign of adulthood in human life, and includes respect for tradition, as well as planning for the future. This so-cial judgment also continues to develop, with constant improvement, until the end of human life.

The Sixth Level: Ideological Judgment. As social judgment develops with the experience of various conflicts that constantly arise among people and within society, philosophical and ideological questions begin to grow to reveal what man is, what life is, how the way of life should be conducted, how society is changing, why man is here, and for what purpose our life is to be directed. The understanding of these fundamental questions of human life ultimately inspires us to discover the endless order of the universe and its universal mechanism; and from this the following, ultimate level of judgment starts to grow.

The Seventh Level: Supreme and Cosmological Judgment. After all previous stages of judgment have been fully experienced, exercised and trained, an understanding of life, man, and the universe starts to develop. As it grows, all phenomena are understood as complementary manifestations of the one infinite ocean of the universe. We see that there is nothing antagonistic and that everything is moving and changing, according to the universal order, to achieve and maintain the endless harmony of infinity. In this level of consciousness all problems of health, war and peace, poverty and sickness, happiness and unhappiness, misery and prosperity, find their solution as varying manifestations of continuous change arising in the ocean of the universe.

Such development of understanding and consciousness which has continued during the period of human life, our life in air, is preparing the foundation for our forthcoming life. When death from the human life occurs, we discard the physical body, the cellular organism, which originated during the life in water—the embryonic age—and proceed to the next life with our vibrational mass of understanding and consciousness.

The Fifth Period of Life: The new life begins with the death from human life, which is the birth to the new environment. The environment of the pre-human life was water; the environment of human life was air; and the environment of the new life born out of the air is the world of vibration. While darkness was the environment for life in the water, and alternating brightness and darkness—day and night —was the environment for the human life in air, the new environment is full of constant brightness. Similarly, while space in the embryonic life was very limited, and space in the human life was hundreds of billions of times larger, covering the entire surface of the earth, the new life in the vibrational world experiences a far greater dimension—trillions of times larger than before, covering the entire scope of the solar system.

However, in this huge dimension, the newborn life of consciousness—you may call it the "soul"—experiences various levels according to its quality. Those that are a mass of delusional, heavy vibrations wander at the lower level of this new dimension of space, often attaching to the atmosphere surrounding a human being, and sometimes even becoming physically visible to people who have unusually sharp perception, under certain conditions. Those whose mass of vibrations is more refined, composed of shorter waves, travel and settle in the middle region of the huge vibrational world where their quality continues to develop further. From this level some proceed toward a higher dimension of the vibrational sphere and others descend to the atmospheric level, achieving rebirth through fusion with physical materials in the world of water and air. Those who have a highly refined vibrational mass gravitate to the higher level of the vibrational sphere, preparing for further refinement to advance to the next life by changing their vibrational mass toward waves and rays.

In this world all vibrational masses, commonly termed "souls," carry understanding and consciousness different from physical perception, but the same or similar to that experienced as mental and spiritual consciousness during human life. From this life, the previous life can be observed, just as during human life we can understand the previous embryonic life. Happiness and unhappiness in this vibrational life largely depend upon the degree of understanding and consciousness developed in the previous human life, just as our destiny in human life is largely owing to the period of embryonic development. Whether clear or unclear, higher or lower, all depends upon how our level of judgment and consciousness has developed during human life, as well as how its refinement continues in the vibrational life.

The Sixth Period of Life: Death from the vibrational life occurs with the dissolution of the vibrational mass, which is the birth to the next life as an entity of waves and rays moving with high velocity. The environment of this next stage of life is the world of radiation, which covers the entire galactic dimension of space. The living body is transferred at birth into this world of radiation, into sparkling light—you may say "spirit"—carrying thoughts and images, traveling within the scope of hundreds of thousands of light years.

From this world, some entities descend to the vibrational sphere of various solar systems and planets by transforming themselves into vibrational masses, and others advance further to dissolve themselves into movement of infinite speed. Among those who have descended to the vibrational sphere, some become further transformed into the atmospheric sphere and the spheres below it, taking the course of materialization toward physical manifestation upon the planet.

The Seventh Period of Life: Life is transformed and developed into movement of infinite speed, covering all dimensions beyond time and space. This stage of life is the terminal of the returning process to the home country, infinity. Life becomes one with the infinite ocean; it becomes absolute freedom—omnipresent, omnipotent, and omniscient. All relative nature which has characterized the previous lives completely disappears and, in this sense, life reaches the state of no phenomena, no appearances, and no manifestations. However, because it moves with infinite speed and constantly differentiates into the infinitely expanding stream, which eventually forms again the relative world through spirallic movement, you may say that this life has the Universal Will or Universal Consciousness, God.

From this infinite world, spirallic movement again arises here and there, and again the course of materialization and physicalization begins as forms appear and disappear on the wide ocean of the infinite universe. The universal Will produces and manifests as images and thoughts in the sphere of radiation, the spiritual world; further changing into various relative dreams and ideas in the vibrational world; and further forming physicalization in the spheres below it. Thus, reincarnation between each level takes place continually; and reincarnation on the universal scale, in the infinite dimensions of the universe, is also taking place endlessly. The memory of every previous level of life is carried, as well as the vision for the future. Eternal memory and endless dream covering the entire dimension of universal reincarnation is also carried through every stage of life, although it is often unrecognized, especially during the lower stages of life.

Fig. 4 The Eternal Cycle of Life

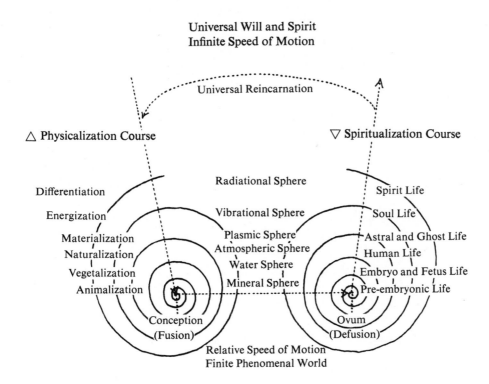

4. The Way of Eating

The macrobiotic way of life recommended by the ancient wise people and practiced widely for physical, mental and spiritual development consists of the following arts: the way of eating, the way of breathing, and the way of daily life.

Because a human being is part of his environment, and has evolved through biological development covering more than three billion years on this planet, his physical, mental, and spiritual conditions are based upon what he consumes from his natural environment and his food. The way of eating is the most essential factor for his development.

Macrobiotic dietary practice, recommended and traditionally followed for some thousands of years, consists of the following pattern of eating as long as we are living in a four-seasonal temperate climate or a semitropical climate.

a. Principal Food

At least one-half of our daily food consumption, or if possible, more than one-half —50% to 60%—is to be whole cereal grains or their products, including brown rice, whole wheat berries, barley, oats, rye, and millet. Corn and buckwheat may also be used as supplements to the cereal grains. Various cooking methods can be applied for each grain, including boiling, steaming, baking, and grinding into flour to make bread, chapati, noodles, and other products. According to the climate, various kinds of beans such as chickpeas, kidney beans, and lentils are also used as part of the pincipal food.

b. Supplemental Food

Supplemental foods consist of all other kinds of food in the vegetable and animal kingdoms, except the meat of the mammal species.

1. Land Vegetables. Among supplemental foods, the majority, or at least one-half, should be land vegetables growing in the same climatic region, in the same or similar natural environment. For this purpose, the selection of vegetables and other agricultural products was often made within a radius of approximately 500 miles, within the immediate and neighboring areas. Vegetables traditionally grown in each locale are more desirable than vegetables transported from distant regions.

Cooking methods for these vegetables are various, including boiling, steaming, baking, sautéing, frying, and pickling. However, the consumption of large volumes of raw vegetables, such as in the form of salad, is customarily avoided.

2. Legumes and Seeds. Beans, peas, and various seeds such as sesame seeds, pumpkin seeds, and sunflower seeds, as well as a small volume of nuts, are used as the secondary supplemental food. A larger volume of beans and peas are consumed, and a comparatively smaller volume of seeds.

These legumes and seeds are cooked in various ways, including boiling, steaming, baking, roasting, and grinding. Some of them, notably soybeans, are traditionally processed through natural fermentation with grains and sea salt, to make seasonings such as *miso* and soy sauce. Some seeds are pressed to yield oil, and some are used as condiments and snacks, lightly seasoned with sea salt.

3. Sea Plants (Seaweed and Sea Moss). Various kinds of sea vegetables are used as supplemental foods, including *kombu*, *wakame*, *arame*, *hiziki*, *nori*, agar-agar, dulse, irish moss, and many others, especially among people who live on islands or on the sea coast.

These sea vegetables are cooked alone or with land vegetables and beans. They are also toasted, roasted, and baked, and may be ground into powder after roasting. Often some of them are used as condiments, with or without the addition of seeds and sea salt.

4. Fruits. Among vegetable-quality foods, fruits are considered less important than land and sea vegetables, since cereal grains are the fruits that human beings should consume daily. However, fruits growing in the same climatic region are used as one of the supplemental foods, especially when they are in season.

The ways of preparing fruits are various. Fruits may be cooked, dried, or pickled, as well as eaten fresh. They are traditionally used as the last part of the meal, in a reasonably small volume, as dessert. People who do not consume a large volume of animal food have a natural tendency to take fruits infrequently.

5. Seafood. Seafood, including vertebrates and invertebrates, and both ocean and freshwater fish, are less frequently used as a supplemental food. Among fish, those with white meat are recommended for consumption. Red-meat fish, and blue-skinned fish—although they may have white meat—are traditionally avoided. Shellfish are also often avoided since they may spoil easily.

The preparation of these ocean and freshwater animals includes boiling, steaming, baking, drying, and smoking. When they are eaten, it is common traditional practice to accompany them with an equal or larger volume of vegetables, either slightly cooked or raw. It is also traditional practice to use a small amount of such vegetables as grated or sliced ginger, mustard, fresh green onions, and grated horseradish, in order to avoid the effects of toxication.

6. Land Animals. Some species of land animals are also used as one of the supplemental foods, and are consumed less frequently than all vegetable-quality food, and even less frequently than seafood. Among land animal species, more primitive species such as amphibians, reptiles, and birds are to be consumed, avoiding more biologically-evolved animals such as various members of the mammal species. Mammal species may be eaten when it is necessary, under special conditions: for example, in case of a scarcity of food when you are in the wilderness, or during very cold snowy weather. Mammals that eat vegetables are preferred over carnivorous species.

Preparations of these land animals are again various, including boiling, steaming, roasting, baking, drying, smoking and pickling. More deliberate caution has traditionally been exercised in their preparation than in preparing other kinds of food. For example, before cooking, meat was soaked in salt water for many hours, and the heavy fat portion was sliced off. The meat was cooked together with vegetables, and served with hot spices and raw vegetables in order to avoid harmful effects.

c. Beverages

Any additional intake of liquid other than the liquid naturally contained in foods or used in the process of cooking may be called a beverage. Good-quality water, hot water, traditional herb teas such as *bancha* twig tea, dandelion tea, and burdock tea, as well as many other teas, are recommended. The volume of beverages taken, however, should not exceed what we really need for physical, mental, and spiritual health. The barometer for finding how much liquid we should take as a standard or average is that we drink only when we feel thirsty, and urinate three to four times daily.

Fig. 5   Example of Standard Diet Oriented for Physical Development (Approximate Proportions)

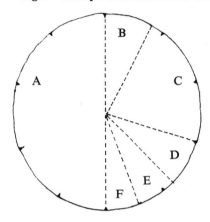

A— Whole cereal grains, cooked in various styles and forms.

B— Soup, mainly of vegetable quality and occasionally including animal quality food.

C— Vegetables, partly cooked and partly raw, locally and seasonally selected.

D— Animal quality foods including fish, seafood with occasional poultry, but not mammals' meat and fat.

E— Beans and sea vegetables, cooked together or separately.

F— Fresh, cooked or dried local and seasonal fruits, roasted seeds and nuts; pickles and other vegetable quality supplements, including dessert.

Fig. 6   Example of Standard Diet Oriented for Mental Development (Approximate Proportions)

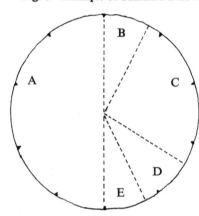

A— Whole cereal grains, cooked in various styles but more in grain form and less in flour form.

B— Vegetable quality soup including both land and sea vegetables.

C— Vegetables, partly cooked and partly raw, locally and seasonally selected.

D— Beans and sea vegetables, cooked together or separately, occasionally supplemented with whitemeat fish or seafood.

E— Fresh, cooked or dried fruits locally and seasonally grown; roasted seeds and nuts; pickles and other vegetable quality supplements, including occasional dessert.

Fig. 7   Example of Standard Diet Oriented for Spiritual Development (Approximate Proportions)

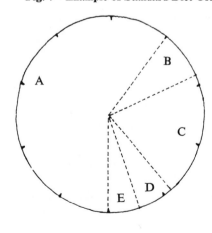

A— Whole cereal grains cooked more as grains and less as flour.

B— Vegetable quality soup, including both land and sea vegetables.

C— Locally grown vegetables partly cooked and partly raw.

D— Beans and sea vegetables cooked together or separately.

E— Fresh, cooked, or dried local and seasonal fruits, roasted seeds and nuts; pickles and other vegetable quality supplements, including dessert.

**Fig. 8   Example of Diet for Physical, Mental and Spiritual Development
for Persons Living Deep in the Mountains (Approximate Proportions)**

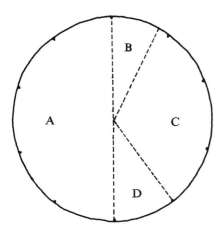

A.   Mountain millet, buckwheat and other grains. Various seeds and grain-type fruits of wild trees and grasses locally growing in the mountains, which are boiled, roasted or dried.

B.   Soup, containing mountain-growing grains, roots and grasses.

C.   Leaves, stems and roots of mountain-growing wild grasses and bushes, as well as edible barks of some trees, cooked, roasted, dried or pickled.

D.   Mountain-growing fruits of bushes and trees; occasional wild birds, and fish from mountain streams.

PRINCIPLES FOR DIETARY PRACTICE

The following principles are essential for our dietary practice:

1.   There is a clear distinction between principal and supplemental foods, and the principal food is always whole cereal grains.

2.   Because man and his environment are one, a human being is a natural product of his environment. The kinds of food he eats should be selected from among the vegetable and animal species growing and living in the same climatic region. Those people who live within the temperate region should avoid products growing in semitropical, tropical, or very cold polar regions, and vice versa.

3.   Because of the principle that soil is equal to blood, it is preferable that food be selected from the same geographical area in which we live: within about a 500-mile radius in America and other large countries, or within perhaps a 100-mile radius in such small countries as Japan and England, where the geographical and climatic conditions vary markedly from region to region.

4.   Human beings should depend primarily upon the vegetable kingdom for food as long as they are living in the temperate, semitropical, and tropical regions. Exceptions would occur under unusual circumstances, such as in the snowy winter season, or on a high mountaintop. In the cold polar region, it is possible to consume more animal-quality food than in the other climatic regions.

5.   Food should be primarily the whole food, which reserves its natural balance. We should avoid, as much as possible, consuming only a part of some organism.

6.   Food should be primarily cooked. As much as possible, raw food should be used only as a supplement to cooked food and eaten under special circumstances, such as during a period of unusually high consumption of animal

food, or under hot and dry climatic conditions.

7. Food should retain its life activity until cooking begins. All unrefined whole grains, beans, seeds, and vegetables keep their life activities if they are not processed with artificial methods such as milling, canning, and treatment with chemicals.

8. Seasoning should be used moderately, and should be as natural as possible in quality.

9. In the process of cooking, food should be comprehensively balanced between all antagonistic and complemental factors, such as minerals vs. carbohydrates, carbohydrates vs. water, fire vs. water, salt vs. oil, pressure vs. air, high temperature vs. low temperature, etc.

SERVING AND EATING

The way of serving and eating meals has the following principles:

1. The service of the meal should be gracefully and beautifully arranged to create a peaceful atmosphere.

2. Excessive noise should be avoided throughout the mealtime.

3. We should chew well, at least 50 times per mouthful—preferably toward 100 times—mixing the food well with saliva.

4. Gratitude should be expressed for the universe, nature, plants and animals, and to those who have produced, processed, cooked, and served the meal, before and after taking every meal.

5. Meals are to be taken usually two to three times a day, sometimes once a day, but preferably not for three hours before sleeping.

6. The principal food, grains, is to be consumed from the beginning of the meal to the end, while the supplemental foods are to be consumed along with the principal food, in the following order: soup; well-cooked land and sea vegetables and legumes; lightly-cooked land and sea vegetables and legumes; raw and fresh vegetables, if any; and, ending with a fruit dessert, if any.

7. In each meal, the volume of food eaten should be naturally limited to an amount not exceeding 70% of stomach capacity.

The pattern of eating described above varies naturally according to environmental condition, such as differences in climatic region, season, weather, sex, age, social conditions, type of work, as well as personal needs. In ancient times there were some people who trained themselves to develop their physical, mental, and spiritual conditions, staying in an isolated place in natural surroundings, often living alone deep in the mountains. In such cases it is unlikely that their dietary practice could have been the same as that of most people who usually live on the plains. Their eating would have included more wild plants, such as seeds, fruits, roots, and bark. Of course, their practice of eating these wild plants was conducted according to the principles of preparation and the way of eating. These wild plants often included wild buckwheat and millet, and these dietary practices were naturally macrobiotic, in their unique environmental circumstances. Among these people, those practices led to the development of cosmically universal consciousness, along with physical health and longevity, and they were often called *Sen-Nin* (仙人), or "free men." There is much evidence including records, documents, and legendary stories about their unusual abilities, which included:

1. Long life, over 100 years.
2. Extraordinary telepathic communication, beyond a distance of a thousand miles.
3. Transporting themselves with enormous speed, usually walking, but sometimes flying.
4. The ability to foresee future events clearly.
5. The power to heal various sicknesses.
6. The ability to convert vibrations and air into materials.
7. The ability to change weather, including the control of rainfall.
8. The ability to read people's minds and thoughts, and their spiritual past and future.
9. The ability to recover the dead.
10. The ability to walk on water.
11. The ability to know previous lives and the future in the spiritual world.

In the present world there are still some people who train in this ancient macrobiotic way, *Shin-Sen-Dō* (神仙道), especially in the oriental countries—Japan, China, India, and others. Their existence, and these practices, are not widely known among ordinary modern civilized societies. However, the principles of eating described above are the biological and psychological foundation for developing our physical, mental, and spiritual freedom. Through the daily practice of these dietary principles we experience almost immediately, generally in 10 days or thereafter, various positive changes in our physical, mental, and spiritual conditions, including the following:

1. Release from general fatigue.
2. Increasing clarity in thinking.
3. The gradual recovery of flexibility and endurance.
4. The beginning of release from various physical and mental disorders.
5. The gradual gaining of peacefulness and tranquility.
6. The gradual development of the spirit of loving other people.
7. The recovery of self-confidence, resulting in the development of honesty.
8. The steady development of adaptability to the changing environment.
9. Release from the nightmare of confusion, greed, and selfishness; and the dissolution of egocentric arrogance.
10. The gradual development of the spirit of adventure.
11. The gradual development of the spirit of appreciation.
12. The gradual development of orderliness in all aspects of living.

Unless there is the daily practice of proper diet according to macrobiotic principles, it is not possible for anyone to develop his spiritual, mental and physical conditions. There have been, however, here and there, some people who do not practice orderly eating and drinking, yet are able to reach fairly high levels of physical, mental, and spiritual development; but those people were nourished properly during their embryonic period through their mother's way of eating and drinking, and they were continuously nourished with reasonable orderliness during their period of infant and childhood eating. In other words, their native and early constitution is in good condition, and therefore, despite their ignorance of dietary influence, as well as their practice of a disorderly way of eating and drinking during their adulthood, they are still able to maintain their original sound constitution. To a certain extent they are able to keep their physical, mental, and spiritual condition, but of course they face rapid degeneration after they lose their original strength, probably after the age of 50 or 60.

All physical, mental, and spiritual exercises, traditional and modern, must be based upon the practice of the proper, macrobiotic way of eating. All ancient philosophers, thinkers, spiritual leaders, artists, political, economic and social leaders, as well as founders of other arts and techniques for the development of health, mind and spirit for total happiness, did actually observe the macrobiotic way of eating.

It is highly recommended that all modern people, especially those who wish to recover their physical and mental health and those who wish to develop their well-being and beauty as a whole together with unlimited understanding and consciousness, practice, before anything else, the proper way of eating according to macrobiotic principles.

5. The Principles of Breathing

Following the way of daily eating and drinking, the second important function between man and his environment is breathing. Food is a part of man's mineral, plant, and animal surroundings, his geographical and biological environment. The way of eating food is the way of harmoniously adapting ourselves to this environment as a part of these surroundings. Drinking is the way of adaptation by achieving oneness between ourselves and the liquid world, which is a part of our natural external environment. By exercising the way of drinking properly, we are able to harmonize ourselves with the liquid environment: oceans, rivers, rain, moisture in the soil, humidity in the atmosphere.

Similarly, breathing is the interchange between ourselves and the atmospheric environment—the air. The way of breathing aims to achieve, with the utmost effectiveness, our harmonious adaptation to the atmospheric environment as part of that environment, in the same way that the proper way of eating and drinking is essential for our physical, mental, and spiritual development. The proper way of breathing is also essential for our health and happiness, together with our universal understanding and consciousness.

Breathing is the manifestation of the yin ($\triangledown$) centrifugal expanding function and the yang ($\triangle$) centripetal contracting function, alternately exercised in harmonious movement, mainly through our respiratory organs. However, not only the respiratory organs such as the nasal and bronchial cavities and the lungs, but also the circulatory organs and their functions, are closely coordinated with breathing. The nervous system, including autonomic nervous reactions and brain functions, is also closely related to the function of breathing. Generally speaking, the active functioning of these systems and organs accelerates active breathing, and active breathing in turn accelerates the active functioning of these systems and organs. On the other hand, their slow and inactive functions bring forth slow and inactive breathing; and slow and inactive breathing results, in time, in their slow and inactive functions. Accordingly, our control of breathing, the volume of air in the inhalation and exhalation, the duration of the inhalation and exhalation, as well as the speed of breathing, have different effects upon all digestive, circulatory, nervous and excretory systems and functions. This also directly and indirectly influences our psychological and spiritual conditions, changing the kinds, volume, direction, and dimensions of image and thought.

Major examples of different ways of breathing and their effects on our physical, mental, and spiritual conditions are as follows:

a. Speed of Breathing

Slower Breathing (Giving More Yin ($\triangledown$) Effects)

1. Physical metabolism slows down, including heartbeat, blood circulation, and other body fluid circulation. Body temperature tends to become slightly lower.
2. Mentally, producing a more tranquil and peaceful state, more clear thinking and objective understanding, as well as a more sensitive response to the environment.
3. Spiritually, developing wider perception, deeper insight, and leading toward more universal consciousness.

Faster Breathing (Giving More Yang ($\triangle$) Effects)

1. Physically, resulting in the faster metabolism of various body functions. The heartbeat, as well as the circulation of blood and other body fluids, is accelerated. Body temperature tends to increase.
2. Mentally, producing a more unstable and excitable condition, paralleling emotional changes. The attitude tends to become either more offensive or more defensive.
3. Spiritually, developing more subjective and egocentric observation and evaluation of surrounding conditions, with more attachment to fragmented and partial affairs, rather than broad and universal awareness.

b. Depth of Breathing

Shallow Breathing (Giving More Yin (∇) Effects)

1. Physically, resulting in more inactive metabolism as well as incoordination and disharmony among various physical functions. Body temperature tends to change irregularly.
2. Mentally, producing a tendency to be more anxious, unstable, frustrated and discontented, often resulting in the development of fear.
3. Spiritually, developing a tendency toward shallow perception, frequent changes in evaluation, loss of confidence, lack of courage, as well as loss of memory and vision of the future.

Deeper Breathing (Giving More Yang ($\triangle$) Effects)

1. Physically, resulting in more profound and active metabolism, and harmony among the systems and organs. Body temperature tends to be stable.
2. Mentally, producing deeper satisfaction, emotional stability, stronger confidence, and maintaining steady and even expression.
3. Spiritually, developing more thoughtfulness and unchangeable faith as well as the tendency to become all-embracing, together with a more loving personality.

c. Length of Breathing

Longer Breathing (Giving More Yin (∇) Effects)

1. Physically, resulting in better coordination among the metabolism of various functions. Body temperature tends to be stable and, in general, the activities of all organs and glands tend to slow down.
2. Mentally, producing a more peaceful and satisfied feeling. More endurance, patience and quietness also result, as well as less emotional excitement and irritability.
3. Spiritually, developing more objective and wider perception, as well as deeper understanding. Past memories and visions of the future tend to become more extended.

Shorter Breathing (Giving More Yang ($\triangle$) Effects)

1. Physically, resulting in a tendency to create faster and irregular metabolism in various body functions. Body temperature tends to slightly increase.
2. Mentally, producing more frequent changes of image and thought, as well as more frequent changes of mind. The tendencies to become more impatient, to have less endurance, and a shorter temper are all accelerated.
3. Spiritually, developing more disharmony with the environment. More con-

flicting and antagonistic feelings are developed, together with the increase of short-sightedness and a more subjective view.

According to the above differences in the effectiveness of various kinds of breathing, it is advisable that we maintain a breathing pattern that is slower, deeper, and longer, rather than faster, shallower and shorter. Physical, mental, and spiritual development parallel the degree of breathing by the adjustment of these variables. However, any conscious adjustment of the speed, depth, and length of breathing should be developed toward more natural breathing, which works without any artificial intention or special effort. Slow, deep, and long breathing can in fact be developed automatically by the practice of the macrobiotic way of eating and the consumption of more vegetable quality food—centered around whole cereal grains and supplemented by vegetables growing on the land and in the sea, locally and seasonally, with a minimum consumption of animal food, avoiding various kinds of meat and dairy food. Drinking a larger volume of liquid as well as eating sugar products also tends to make breathing faster, shallower and shorter. Eating and drinking a larger volume, in general, also tends to increase the speed of breathing, making it shallower and shorter. Therefore, in order to develop physical, mental and spiritual harmony and peace, the daily intake of a reasonably lower volume of food and liquid is more advisable.

FIVE STANDARD WAYS OF BREATHING

As a standard practice for physical, mental, and spiritual development, breathing can be used in five different ways according to the degree of strength:

1. *Very Slow, Quiet, and Long Breathing: The Breathing of Selflessness:* This breathing is done through the nose for both inhaling and exhaling, very quietly, to the extent that a piece of rice paper hanging in front of the nose does not move. The duration of the out-breath should be two to three times longer than the duration of the in-breath. The effect of this breathing is to calm down all physical, mental, and spiritual activities, so that we enter into deep meditation to develop inner sight by achieving the maximum degree of adaptation to the environment. This breathing also produces the effect of minimizing egocentric delusion.

2. *Normal Slow and Quiet Breathing: The Breathing of Harmony:* This breathing is also done through the nose, but it is slightly stronger than the breathing described above (No. 1). This is the usual quiet breathing of a time of stillness. Again, the duration of the out-breath should be two to three times longer than the duration of the in-breath. The effect of this breathing is to maintain peaceful, harmonious relations with the actively-moving surroundings, keeping the self in the central position, which increases our awareness of our surroundings.

3. *Slow and Quiet but Stronger Breathing: The Breathing of Confidence:* This breath is inhaled through the nose and exhaled through the slightly opened mouth.

The exhalation is three to five times longer than the inhalation. This breathing is stronger than the two ways of breathing described above. Its effect is to accelerate active harmony among all physical, mental, and spiritual functions by developing inner confidence, preparing for any active movement which may be necessary, at any time, to adapt to rapidly-changing environmental conditions.

4. *Long, Deep, and Strong Breathing: The Breathing of Action:* This breathing is done through the slightly opened mouth for both inhaling and exhaling. The duration of exhaling should be three to five times longer than the duration of inhaling. The effect of this breathing is to activate all physical, mental, and spiritual powers in order to initiate any necessary motion upon environmental conditions without losing objective observation. This breathing can be used also to release physical and mental stagnation, producing relaxation.

5. *Long, Deep, Strong and Powerful Breathing, with Sound: The Breathing of Spiritualization:* This breathing is done through the mouth for both inhaling and exhaling. The exhalation should be three to five times longer than the inhalation. When breathing in, the sharp sound "HI" occurs naturally, because of the intense inhalation made between slightly opened teeth, with the tongue lightly tensed. During exhalation, a long, natural sound of "FU" is made continuously. The effect of this breathing is to actively energize the physical and mental metabolism, and to spiritualize the entire personality. The sound "HI" has the meaning of "spirit," "fire," and "sun," in a prehistoric pronunciation universally and intuitively used throughout the ancient world. The sound "FU" has the meaning of "wind," "differentiation," and "expansion," in the ancient pronunciation. At that time, HI and FU also had the respective meanings "one" and "two."

FIVE SPECIAL METHODS OF BREATHING

As special breathing practices for physical, mental, and spiritual development, the following five methods can be used, each for its special purpose.

1. *Breathing with the Tan-Den (Hara, the Center of the Abdomen): The Breathing of Physicalization:* This breathing is done deeply and slowly with the natural movement of the *Hara* region (the central region of the abdomen). Another word for *Hara* is *Tan-Den* (丹田), the most inner depths of the abdominal region. At the time of slow but deep inhalation, the *Tan-Den* is filled with energy and the lower abdomen naturally expands toward the front. At the time of slow and longer exhalation, the same region naturally contracts.

Between inhaling and exhaling, the breath should be held for several seconds. The exhalation should be generally two or more times longer than the inhalation. The effectiveness of this breathing is to generate physical energy, mental stability and spiritual confidence. It results in the firm establishment of the self upon this earth, and the ability to avoid being influenced by changing surroundings. It produces an increase in body temperature. This breathing also accelerates active digestive and circulatory functions throughout the body, which results in the development of total health and longevity.

2. *Breathing with the Center of the Stomach Region: The Breathing of Power:* This breathing is done with the natural movement of the region of the stomach. At the time of inhaling, the stomach region, the area of *Chū-Kan* (中脘), naturally expands toward the outside, and at the time of exhalation, it contracts. Between inhaling and exhaling, the breath should be held for several seconds. The duration of exhaling is slightly longer than the duration of inhaling.

The effect of this breathing is the development of endurance, patience, and tolerance, and when the breath is held for longer time between inhaling and exhaling, it intensifies internal energization throughout the whole body, so that the body is filled with what we may call spiritual power—electromagnetic energy. As it is repeatedly exercised, this breathing results in the development of various physical and mental abilities.

3. *Breathing with the Heart Region, or the Center of the Upper Chest: The Breathing of Love:* In this breathing, both the inhalation and the exhalation are slow and long, concentrating in the heart region, or the central region of the upper chest. The duration of inhaling is almost equal to the duration of exhaling, and the breath is not held between inhaling and exhaling—both naturally and smoothly continue in slow, long movements.

The effect of this breathing is to harmonize the beating of the heart and to generate smooth circulation of the blood and other body fluids. Mentally, it generates a feeling of harmony and love with all aspects of the environment as well as with the surrounding people. It also develops sensitivity, sympathy, understanding, and compassion.

4. *Breathing with the Region of the Throat and the Root of the Tongue: The Breathing of Intelligence:* This breathing is done at the region of the throat and the root of the tongue, with stronger inhaling and weaker exhaling. At the time of inhaling, the breath is concentrated and held at the region of the throat and root of the tongue for several seconds, and then is released.

The effect of this breathing is to develop keen senses, for physical and mental concentration toward a certain objective. It further develops clear observation and penetrating insight into the problem being faced. Spiritual concentration is accelerated and intellectual comprehension is stimulated.

5. *Breathing with the Region of the Midbrain: The Breathing of Spiritualization:* This breathing is done at the region of the midbrain, the inner center of the head. The inhalation is made slowly but sharply, as if breathing up toward the zenith of the head, with the feeling of lifting the body upward. This inhalation should be made smoothly and continuously, as long as possible, and at its extreme point, the breath is suddenly but gently released. The exhalation should be made downward toward the mouth.

The effect of this breathing is to spiritualize our relative consciousness toward a more universal scope, and it further serves to release our perception into boundless dimensions, including the understanding of events taking place at a distance. The entire physical metabolism rapidly slows down as this breathing is repeatedly exercised, and body temperature decreases as if approaching toward death.

The above five standard ways of breathing for the general development of our physical, mental and spiritual condition, and the five special ways of breathing for specific purposes in physical, mental, and spiritual development can be used freely during our daily life: while sitting, working, and acting, as well as while meeting and working together with other people. There are many other variations of breathing to maintain general health and well-being as well as to develop special physical, mental and spiritual abilities, but these ten kinds of breathing introduced above are the fundamental methods for all other ways of breathing.

In order to perform these ways of breathing effectively, however, it is essential we maintain our dietary practice in moderation.*

6. The Daily Way of Life

In order to develop physical, mental, and spiritual happiness, it is important that we harmoniously order our daily life in the following ways:

1. *We Should Rise Before Dawn:* The year's schedule begins on the first day of the first month, and the day's activity begins at the rising of the sun. Leaving our bed before sunrise and preparing ourselves to meet the rising sun with a simple Dō-In exercise is essential for our physical, mental and spiritual orientation for the day's activity. When the rising of the sun is near, the atmosphere surrounding us begins to be charged more actively, stimulating our physical and mental conditions. In ancient times in Far Eastern countries like Japan and China, governmental deci-

---

* "*Respiratory Quotient (RQ):* This is the ratio of the volume of CO_2 produced and oxygen (O_2) consumed, expressed as follows:

$$\frac{\text{Volume of } CO_2 \text{ expired}}{\text{Volume of } O_2 \text{ inspired}} = \text{Respiratory Quotient}$$

In the oxidation of a carbohydrate, the following reaction takes place:

$$C_6H_{12}O_2 + 6O_2 \rightarrow 6CO_2 + 6H_2O \text{ plus energy}$$

Then,

$$\frac{6 \text{ volumes of } CO_2}{6 \text{ volumes of } O_2} = 1.0 \text{ (RQ of a carbohydrate)}$$

Similarly, The RQ for a fat is 0.71; for a protein, it is 0.80. For a person on an average mixed diet, it is 0.85. For a person who has fasted for 12 hours, the RQ is 0.82." (From *Anatomy and Physiology*, Vol. 1 by Steen and Montagu, Harper & Row, 1959, p. 195.) RQ indicates that if we eat animal food in large volume, which consists of much protein and fat, more rapid and rough breathing is required, which influences our mind, disturbing us from normal quietness. Accordingly, those who practice meditation and other spiritual exercises should avoid the consumption of large amounts of animal food.

sions on public affairs were made before dawn. From this ancient practice, the center of the government was called *Chō-Tei* (朝廷), "The Morning Court." The atmosphere of early morning is beneficial for our clear vision in making future plans.

2. *We Should Clean Ourselves and Our Surroundings Soon After We Rise in the Morning:* We should clean our face and body, preferably with cold water, and brush our teeth with sea salt or other traditional natural tooth powders, making our physical and mental conditions keenly alert to meet the activities to follow in the day's work. At the same time, we should clean our surroundings, beginning with our immediate room, moving toward the periphery of the home, and including the yard outside.

3. *We Perform Dō-In or Other Physical, Mental and Spiritual Exercises:* Any morning exercise we perform should serve as an activation of harmonious energy flow, including the circulation of blood and other body fluids as well as electromagnetic current throughout the entire body. Such exercises should include breathing and the frequent use of proper voice or chanting to achieve an active interchange between ourselves and the natural environment.

4. *We Dedicate Our Prayer to People and Phenomena:* After we inspire our well-being through cleaning and exercise, we dedicate our prayer to all ancestors, people, living beings, and all phenomena with the order of the infinite universe—the Universal Spirit, God. This prayer extends our whole-hearted gratitude to them, asking their guidance and encouragement for our performance during the day. At that time, it is often important to offer them a meal prepared with grains and vegetables.

5. *We Express Gratitude and Respect for What We Eat:* At the time of breakfast, lunch and dinner, when we consume meals, we should consider that our food has come from nature, creating us as beings in harmony with the whole natural environment and enabling us to develop our physical, mental, and spiritual quality toward our well-being and happiness. When everyone and every family expresses gratitude and respect for each meal, for nature, and for those who produced and prepared the food, it is the beginning of peace in society. We should:

    a. Reflect whether we deserve this meal.
    b. Think of the immeasurable elaboration of natural order, and of those who produced and prepared the meal.
    c. Consider that the meal changes into ourselves, creating our destiny of the following day.
    d. Think of the people on this earth who may not be able to afford this meal.
    e. Think of our ancestors, who have eaten food, and of those who have descended from them through the succession of eating.
    f. Think of our offspring who will continue to eat as we are doing and spread our spirit upon the earth.

During the meal, we should practice the following manners:

a. Chew each mouthful at least 50 times.
b. While chewing, it is preferable to place the eating utensils down on the table.
c. Maintain straight posture from the beginning to the end of the meal.
d. The conversation exchanged among the family and friends who are eating together at the same table should be merry but peaceful.
e. Let the serving of the meal be graceful and orderly.
f. Do not leave food on your dish when you are finished eating.
g. Always keep the dishes, utensils, pots and pans, as well as the cooking and eating areas, clean and orderly.

6. *We Begin Our Daily Work with Enjoyment and Enthusiasm:* We handle any sort of activity in a positive, creative and energetic manner. We should relax completely in order to maintain accurate and speedy work. We should not calculate our work or the amount of compensation; we should enjoy our work as a means of achieving physical, mental and spiritual satisfaction, with compensation naturally following such enjoyment.

We extend help to our working colleagues in a spirit of brotherhood, considering all colleagues as our brothers and sisters, and sharing with them their happiness and their sorrow. We maintain our working environment as a peaceful, happy place, as we make our home a peaceful and happy place. The working place is an externally extended home for us and for all other colleagues who are working together with us.

7. *We Take Responsibility for Any Social Condition:* We all are members of human society. When there is confusion and chaos in the social order, it is our own responsibility. When there is misery and suffering somewhere in our community and in our human society, it is our responsibility. When there is war and hunger somewhere in the world, it is our responsibility. All people are related organically, and we all influence one another in our living conditions.

a. Do not complain about others, but consider our own inability to improve situations.
b. Do not accuse others, but consider our own errors.
c. Do not criticize others, but consider our own inadequacy.
d. Do not depend upon others, but consider our own independability.
e. Do not ignore others, but consider our own ignorance.

8. *We Dedicate Our Appreciation for the Day:* After we complete our daily work, either before or after the evening meal, we dedicate our appreciation to nature and the universe, as well as to society and the friends who have been cooperating with us throughout our day's activity. We make our own evaluation of what we have done during the day's activity, as to:

a. Whether we made errors or mistakes.
b. Whether we gave displeasure to others.
c. Whether we worked inefficiently.
d. Whether we did not overlook any problem.
e. Whether we have enjoyed what we were doing.

This self-evaluation guides us for the better performance of the coming day's work, helping us to avoid repeating the same mistakes in the various aspects of our activities.

9. *We Study the Way of Life:* After the day's active life, we spend at least a few hours quietly to develop our aesthetic, theoretical, and spiritual understanding of the way of life. By either reading, writing, performing, or thinking and meditating, we should continuously refine our personality and deepen our understanding of art, literature, science, philosophy, religion, and various other arts.

Our life should be well-balanced with both yang ($\triangle$) physical activity and yin ($\triangledown$) mental activity. We need to develop both physically and mentally as oriental tradition has taught for many centuries, as expressed in the term *Bun-Bu Ryō-Dō* (文武両道). A valiant *samurai* was required to refine his personality by the learning of poetry, arts, music, and literature, even including the tea ceremony; and a gentle woman who was mainly engaged in housekeeping was also required to become proficient in some martial arts in order to cope with any emergency.

10. *We Complete the Day with Self-Reflection:* Before we enter into the night's rest, we finalize the day's activity by reflecting on our own conduct of that day:

a. Biological Self-Reflection: Did I eat properly?
b. Spiritual Self-Reflection: Did I think of my parents, and have gratitude for our ancestors?
c. Social Self-Reflection: Did I extend greetings happily to any person whom I encountered?
d. Natural Self-Reflection: Do I marvel about nature and the universe: their beauty, their grace, and their magnificence?
e. Comprehensive Self-Reflection: Can I say that this life is wonderful, extending unlimited thankfulness to all beings and to the infinite universe?

Together with these reflections, we purify ourselves by washing our face, hands, feet, and body, as well as cleaning our teeth. We change our clothing and enter into complete rest—sleep—with a simple Dō-In exercise if necessary.

Chapter 2

The Physical and Spiritual Constitution of Man

1. Stages of Spiritual Transformation

The relationship between spiritual phenomena and physical entities is simply a difference of degree: whether they are yin, expanded, invisible phenomena, including various manifestations of vibration, waves, rays, and other invisible forces; or yang, contracted, visible phenomena, including bodily movement and sensory perception as well as material experience.

The term "spirit," as used in our daily conversation, generally has three different meanings:

a. Physicalized Spirit

We express "spirit" in terms such as "our human spirit," "the spirit of my country," "the spirit of our family," "the spirit of man or woman," "the spirit of Christianity or Buddhism," and the like. "Spirit" in this sense expresses tradition, heritage, ideals, discipline, and other similar concepts which we manifest in our physical life within the external society. This expression of spirit may be called the "Physicalized Spirit."

b. Vibrational Spirit

We also use the term "spirit" when we talk about a dead person or about past events which are no longer physicalized in the present world. We often say "my dead father's spirit," "the spirit of the unknown soldier," "the spirit of a late great personality like Jesus, Buddha," etc., as well as "the spirit of lovers who have passed away." In this sense, we often revere or enshrine these spirits, and we dedicate our consolation or prayer for them. We mean by these expressions that such a spirit is similar to the "soul," astral manifestation, or waves and vibrations which can be perceived and interpreted as the image of those personalities that is in our memory. This kind of spirit may be called the "Vibrational Spirit."

c. Universal Spirit

We further express "spirit" in the universal and permanent sense, such as in the meaning of God, eternity, universality, immortality, and absoluteness, bearing the nature of omnipresence, omnipotence, and omniscience. It is used in expressing absolute justice, unconditional love, all-embracing wisdom, and universal principles. This meaning of "spirit" does not refer to any phenomenon in the relative world; it indicates something beyond all relative concepts like life and death, time and space. This may be called the "Universal Spirit."

These three categories expressing the different meanings of "spirit" actually make one continuity, manifesting differently in each stage of development in the spirallic movement of this physical universe, which arises in the infinite ocean of the Universal Spirit. Physicalized spirits are a finite part of the vibrational spirit, and vibrational spirits are a finite part of the Universal Spirit. The boundless area of the Universal Spirit can be recognized as God, the whole, oneness, *Nirvana*, *Yahweh*, which is omnipresent, omnipotent, and omniscient. It is beginningless and endless. It does not manifest itself as any relative phenomenon, and is beyond any relative relation with any existence. It is eternal as well as universal, and therefore it is unidentifiable—impossible to name. It is the Will of all phenomena arising within itself. It is the origin of origins of all appearances, and it is the end of ends of all beings.

The stage of vibrational spirit is a transitory process, both in time and space, between the infinite Universal Spirit and finite physical manifestations. A part of this transitoy area can be perceived as radiations, waves, and vibrations as well as all manifestations of energy. These are more condensed than the infinite Universal Spirit, but they are far more expanded than physicalized beings. This is the world of dreams, images, and thoughts, which is transferred to and realized in the physical world. At the same time, when the physical world is dissolved, it is transferred into this world of dreams, images, and thoughts. This world of vibrational spirit is the original constitution of physicalized phenomena. We human beings also have physicalized from this world.

When man is physicalized upon the earth as one of the biological species, the world of dream, image, and thought precedes the biochemicalization of all energies—such as radiation, waves, and vibrations, as well as the movement of preatomic particles —into the human constitution, along which the cellular organism is formed. These complex forces in the world of energy may be summarized as the force of electromagnetic current, which is constantly moving between opposite poles: yin ($\triangledown$) and yang ($\triangle$), centrifugal and centripetal, plus and minus, alpha and omega, space and time, slow and fast, high and low, front and back, outside and inside, up and down, and all other antagonistic and complemental relativities.

All physicalized phenomena are ephemeral. They are changing without pause—endless change from yin to yang, expansion to contraction, birth to death, rise to fall—this is the universal principle governing the physical world. In this world of inconsistency, man aspires to the eternal consistency of the Universal Spirit, which is lying deep in his memory, because he has come out from the Universal Spirit into this physical world, passing through the stage of vibrational spirit. His aspiration is evidence that he has known the Universal Spirit and that he was the Universal Spirit himself.

In order to return to the Universal Spirit—God, Infinity, or Will—mankind wishes to realize perfect harmony with his environment, to achieve oneness. This process of harmonizing himself with the environment is exercised as the realization of physical health, beauty, mental peace, and spiritual universality. It is inevitable that everyone seeks health and happiness, for everyone is a manifestation of the Universal Will to achieve oneness with Infinity, the origin of origins. The Universal Will to be One Infinity is equal to the personal will to seek and realize health and happiness through physical, mental, and spiritual development during our time on this earth as human beings.

2. The Spirallic Constitution of Man

All phenomena which appear and disappear in this infinite ocean of the Universal Spirit form, without exception, spirallic constitutions. The constitutions of galaxies and atoms, the movements of wind and water, the growth of plants and animals all follow this universal pattern—the spiral.

Man also appears and disappears in this spirallic pattern, with his physical, mental, and spiritual constitutions which are spirallically formed. The formation of the spiral for the development of the human constitution as well as for our physical, mental, and spiritual development generally proceeds in a multifold pattern of spirallic movement as outlined below:

a. The Environmental Period

We transform ourselves from One Infinity of the endless ocean of oneness through the stage of polarization—yin ($\triangledown$) and yang ($\triangle$), antagonistic and complemental forces—forming all relative worlds in the spirallic pattern structured in logarithmic development. The world of vibration and energy produces preatomic phenomena, including various particles, with the spirallic movement of energetic forces. Atoms are constructed in manifold complex spirals, and molecules are also formed in a spirallic chain linking various atoms, such as in the case of DNA. The world of nature, which is composed of soil, water, and air, is manifested in the spirallic movement of these molecules, as we are able to observe easily in the apparent motion of galaxies, water currents, wind movements, and patterns of air pressure. All biological lives including all plant and animal species also develop in a spirallic pattern, as we can observe in the growth processes of roots, stems, vines, leaves and flowers, as well as in the formation of cellular organisms, including muscles, bones, organs, glands, as well as the digestive, respiratory, circulatory, excretory, and nervous functions in animal bodies.

b. The Preconception Period

As food is absorbed in the digestive system, it is distributed throughout our body in the form of the various constituents of blood, lymph, and other body fluids, which are actually circulating in spirallic patterns, which we can notice if we observe our body from either above or below. This food in the form of blood and body fluids is further transformed into various body cells as well as reproductive cells, which are simply gathering spirals compacted tightly and forming organs, tissues, and muscles together. In the reproductive organs, such as the testicles and ovaries, reproductive cells—follicles—form sperm by a centrifugal spiral in the case of the male organs, and form ova by a centripetal spiral in the case of the female organs. When both the sperm and the ova are radiating vibrations toward the surrounding environment in the form of spirallic patterns as they are attracted to each other in the woman's uterus, their own movement also follows the form of spirallic patterns, augmented by their own rotation.

c. The Embryonic and Fetal Period

From the time of conception to the time of birth the fertilized ovum grows in four major periods. Each period develops toward the next in a logarithmic pattern of duration, by the ratio of one to three.

1. *The first period: seven days, from the time of fertilization to the time of implantation,* which takes place in the most inner depths of the uterus. During this period, the fertilized ovum increases cell division in a logarithmic pattern: 1 to 2, 2 to 4, 4 to 8, 8 to 16; and this movement of cell increase occurs in a spirallic pattern, together with rotational movement of the egg as well as the motions of its axis shift.

2. *The second period: 21 days, from the time of implantation to the time of general system formation.*   During this period, the inner system which will later develop into the digestive and respiratory functions, the peripheral system which will develop into the nervous system, and the central system which will develop into the circulatory and excretory functions, are formed. The inner digestive and respiratory systems grow in spirallic patterns which expand centrifugally, and the peripheral nervous system grows in a spirallic pattern which is governed more by the centripetal, contracting force. The central circulatory and excretory systems are further formed by spirallic movement, between the first two major systems. Not only is each system formed spirallically, but also, these three major systems—inner, peripheral, and central—are composed as a whole in spirallic layers during this period, connecting with each other at both ends.

3. *The third period: 63 days, the period of formation of organs, glands, and other major structures.*   During this period, future organs, glands, and other major body structures are formed along the three systems. All of these structures grow in spirallic patterns, either by centrifugal force or centripetal force. The former result in more hollow and movable structures such as the large intestines, small intestines, stomach, gall bladder, and bladder, and the latter result in more compacted structures such as the lungs, heart, spleen, liver, and

kidneys. Because they are formed respectively by the spirallic movement of energy, they are constructed in several layers.

4. *The fourth period: 189 days, the period of general development up to the time of delivery.* During this period, systems, organs, glands, major body structures, and all other auxiliary instruments and functions continue to grow and become complete toward the end of the entire 280 days of the embryonic period. Throughout this period, the embryo alternates between active motion and slow motion. Further, it moves spirallically, by a combination of rotation and axis shifts. Throughout these orderly spirallic movements, the embryo accomplishes its balance between head and body, left and right, front and back, inner and outer, as well as among systems, organs, glands, and the circulation of various body fluids. Antagonistic yet complementary tendencies, yin ($\triangledown$) and yang ($\triangle$), are well balanced, preparing as a whole for birth. For example, the region of the head becomes more compact, while the region of the body becomes more expanded. The front of the body becomes softer while the back becomes harder. The areas of muscles and tissues gather more protein and fat, while the bones gather more minerals.

d. The Period of Infancy

This period extends from the time of birth to the time of the accomplishment of erect posture as a human child. During this period, we repeat the experiences of the ancient evolution of the animal species that took place on land after the formation of continents, up to recent times when the human race began to appear. In this period of repeating approximately 400 million biological years, we develop mechanical, sensory, and sentimental perception, again in a logarithmic pattern. During the first four weeks after birth, our functions are almost all mechanical; during the second 12 weeks, growing sensory perceptions develop together with the mechanical functions; and during the third 36 weeks, approximately, our sensory consciousness continues to grow. During this time, together with the preceding mechanical and sensory reactions, we enlarge the dimensions of our surrounding space logarithmically, while our posture proceeds toward erection through the stages of amphibian, reptile, mammal, and ape. The movements our growing body makes also reflect spirallic motion: when we bend our body forward, we contract our body spiral; and when we extend our body, we dissolve our body spiral. Similarly, when we contract our arms we form spirals, and when we extend them we dissolve the spirals. In our breathing, inhaling and exhaling form opposite spirallic motions of air as it passes through the nasal cavities. When we swallow food and liquid, their motion going down forms a spiral that is opposite to that of the movement of discharging urine and feces.

e. Childhood

During the period of childhood, from the time of postural erection to the time of puberty, our physical movement becomes more active, following a spirallic pattern between expansion and contraction. When we stand, during the daytime, we tend to fully extend our body spirals, keeping our body generally straight; and while we sleep, during the night, we tend to contract our body spiral, with the head and legs bent inward. When we move rapidly, as in running, we tend to form our spiral in a more bending form; when we rest, we tend to extend our spiral with the legs, arms, and whole body stretched in a relaxed condition. When we utter sounds, air circulates out, forming an expanding spirallic pattern; when we breathe in, air circulates inward, forming a more contracting spiral. Our sensory functions such as tasting, smelling, hearing and seeing are also accomplished with spirallic motion of the head to identify the intensity, direction, and distance of sensory impulses.

At the same time, psychological functions as well as the course of various thoughts, develop in a spirallic pattern. Following the earlier period of infancy in which we develop sensory and sentimental consciousness, we further continue to develop intellectual consciousness during this fifth period. It grows and functions spirallically toward the larger dimensions of the external environment in the form of imagination, speculation, calculation, assumption, and other functions we generally know as "understanding." As we use the right side of the brain, which deals more with basic mechanical conceptualization, we form vibrations of thought around the right brain in a spirallic form; when we use our left brain, which produces more aesthetic, complex thinking, we form thought vibrations around our left brain in another spirallic pattern.

Each of our various physical movements as well as our various psychological activities forms a specific spirallic pattern—either expanding centrifugally or contracting centripetally, either in a clockwise direction or in a counterclockwise direction—spirallic motions of energy and vibration.

f. The Adult Age

The period from puberty to approximately the age of 50, when menopause generally occurs in women, can be called the adult age. During this period, physical growth does not continue but psychological and spiritual development does. This development takes place, again, in a logarithmic spiral, succeeding the psychological development accomplished in the previous stage. Our mechanical, sensory, sentimental and intellectual consciousness continue to grow and, in addition, social concepts continually develop through our experiences in human relations. This social awareness produces more advanced consciousness, ideological and philosophical—the understanding of society, life, and the universe as a whole; and this continues to develop, again in a logarithmic spiral, enlarging our dimensions of time and space.

Our interest in personal affairs enlarges to family and group affairs, and further enlarges to include the affairs of the community and society and, ultimately, the whole world. Ideological and philosophical understanding begins from our personal experience with other people and the surrounding conditions. It continues to grow into our concern for the destiny of all mankind, which further develops toward the understanding of the universe, including the visible and invisible, material and spiritual, physical and mental, finite and infinite worlds—why are we here, from where have we come, and where are we going? What is the purpose of life? What is love, peace, justice, and freedom? Has this universe some specific direction in its movement? Is there a universal order governing all phenomena arising in this universe?—and so forth.

Because these aspects of our mental development grow spirallically in a yin (∇) expanding direction, our physical activities, which produce our human contact with other people and natural beings, also tend to enlarge in a yin expanding pattern. In the beginning of this period, our contacts are limited to our immediate families and friends; as we grow, our contacts increase in the number of people, affairs, and events we experience in both society and nature. Further, we reflect more upon the past, and plan more for the future. As a general tendency in family formation, a single person becomes a couple, and a couple produces several children, who respectively create more children. Material accumulation during this period generally tends toward a similar expanding pattern. As a general tendency, it appears that the speed of material accumulation is slower than the speed of human contacts, and that the increase in human contacts is slower than the development of consciousness. These three phases of development form the inner, middle, and peripheral orbits of a logarithmic spiral which represent the whole development of our human life during this period. In this growing pattern, in the event that the speed of material accumulation is unreasonably high, the development of the other two aspects—human contacts and consciousness—tends to slow down.

g. The Age of Maturity

The period from approximately 50 years of age until the time of death may be called the age of maturity, the accomplishment of human life. In this period, our consciousness further grows rapidly in a logarithmic pattern, expanding our social awareness and our ideological and philosophical understanding. These are followed by the development of spiritual and cosmological awareness, which leads us to recognize our life as a mere transitory process in the long journey which began in the infinite ocean of the universe and which ends by returning to this ocean. This further leads us to the understanding that this long journey of life cycles endlessly between One Infinity and the countless finite manifestations. In this endless cycle of life, all physical manifestations are the compacted yang ($\triangle$) form of non-physical vibrational and spiritual being, and all spiritual beings are nothing but the expanded yin (∇) form, covering all dimensions of this universe and even far beyond the universe—being as the infinite omnipresence.

During this stage of life, true happiness is realized as our consciousness develops cosmologically and spiritually. Our material life, as well as our relations with other people and other beings, becomes naturally adjusted by the supreme cosmological and spiritual awareness of eternal life. Toward the end of life, physical and material development generally tend to slow down or decline, while social and human contacts continue to grow steadily, and the development of consciousness grows with increasing speed.

h. The Post-Human Life Period

Together with death from the human life on this earth, the yin growing pattern of life is further accelerated by active decomposition of the human constitution. Some parts such as cellular organisms return to their original world of elements, differentiated and distributed into the soil, water, and air; and other parts of the human constitution such as vibrations, waves, and radiations, which have been manifested as physical and mental energy, are also returned and distributed to their original worlds. Furthermore, what we call our consciousness remains as a massive vibration, continuing to exist in the form of "souls" or "spirits," which are transferred into various wave lengths and can influence the memory, images, and thoughts of our still-living human fellows.

These vibrational existences continue to dissolve and expand to larger dimensions, and eventually return to the infinite dimension, covering the entire universe.

These eight stages of development of the physical, mental, and spiritual constitution of man, although they change in the pattern of a logarithmic spiral as a whole, vary according to the following factors:

1. The traditional and hereditary quality received from our parents and ancestors, biologically and psychologically.
2. Environmental influences, including climatic and weather conditions, geographical differences, and atmospheric conditions, as well as celestial influences.
3. The volume and quality of food and drink consumed throughout our life, day by day, which determines our physical, mental, and spiritual qualities and tendencies.
4. The social environment, including various relations with other people, and the nature of the civilization and culture surrounding us.

Whether these influences are positive or negative, however, everyone of us has the freedom to manage these influences through our initiative in our own daily life. Hence, in order to have health and happiness it becomes necessary to regulate our daily life in an orderly way, according to macrobiotic principles, including our dietary practice and physical, mental, and spiritual exercises such as Dō-In.

3. The Human Constitution of Ki — Electromagnetic Energy

During the period of embryonic development which proceeds with spirallic movement, the embryo continuously receives heaven's force going downward through the spiritual channel of the mother, entering the mother spirallically through the upper magnetic pole, the center of the hair spiral on the head. The embryo also receives, from the rotating earth, forces generated in an expanding direction, going upward through the lower magnetic pole, the mother's genital organs. Both forces charge the embryo from above and below, generating vital forces of electromagnetic energy. We call this charged state of the embryo "being alive."

These two charging forces, together with the rotational movement of the embryo, produce expanding energy radiating out from the inside of the embryo toward the surrounding space, forming an invisible electromagnetic layer of energy around the embryo. This layer is charged vertically in 12 sections due to the influence of the 12 major electromagnetic meridians running vertically along the inner wall of the uterus.

Each of these 12 inner meridians running in the uterus corresponds respectively to each of the mother's surface meridians, and these surface meridians further correspond to the earth's atmospheric charges, influenced by the 12 constellations which are revolving far away in space along the earths' ecliptic.

These surface meridians and the constellations to which they correspond are as follows:

Meridian	*Constellation*
Lung Meridian	Aries
Large Intestine Meridian	Taurus
Stomach Meridian	Gemini
Spleen Meridian	Cancer
Heart Meridian	Leo
Small Intestine Meridian	Virgo
Bladder Meridian	Libra
Kidney Meridian	Scorpio
Heart Governor Meridian	Sagittarius
Triple Heater Meridian	Capricorn
Gall Bladder Meridian	Aquarius
Liver Meridian	Pisces

Between the electromagnetic layer around the embryo and the center of the embryo, an electromagnetic charge is exchanged in the form of invisible currents which spiral in from the layer toward the inner part of the embryo as it rotates in 12 different ways. When these invisible currents reach the central part of the embryo, they each form a spiral. Some form inward-moving spirals due to their slow speed, and others form outward-moving spirals due to their faster speed. These spirals, inward and outward, grow continuously during the embryonic period, developing into various major organs and functions. The inward spirals form more compacted organs which are slower in movement, and the outward spirals create more expanded organs which are faster in movement. Among these organs, those having yang ($\triangle$) compacted structure and yin ($\triangledown$) slow movement balance with those having yin ($\triangledown$) expanded structure and yang ($\triangle$) active movement, as if forming pairs. These pairs of balancing organs and functions are as follows:

Compacted Orgvns ($\triangle$)	*Expanded Organs* ($\triangledown$)
Slow Movement ($\triangledown$)	*Active Movement* ($\triangle$)
Lungs	Large Intestine
Spleen and Pancreas	Stomach
Heart	Small Intestine
Kidneys	Bladder
Heart Governor	Triple Heater
Liver	Gall Bladder

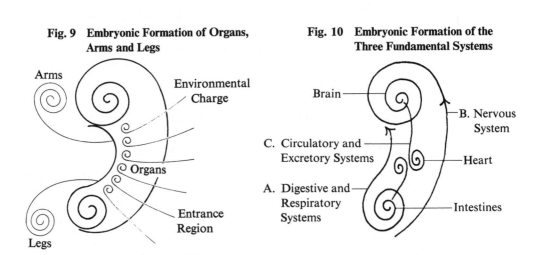

Fig. 9 Embryonic Formation of Organs, Arms and Legs

Fig. 10 Embryonic Formation of the Three Fundamental Systems

After forming these spirals which later develop into the major organs and functions, electromagnetic energy begins to discharge in both upward and downward directions. Energy discharged upward is energy which has been charged more at the peripheral parts of both sides of the embryo, and energy discharged downward is energy charged more at the central part of the embryo. These discharged energies also form outer spirals, upper spirals and lower spirals, and these spirals later develop as arms and legs. Accordingly, electromagnetic currents running through the arms and legs in the form of meridians develop as follows:

Arms	*Legs*
Lung Meridian	Spleen Meridian
Large Intestine Meridian	Liver Meridian
Heart Governor Meridian	Stomach Meridian
Triple Heater Meridian	Gall Bladder Meridian
Heart Meridian	Bladder Meridian
Small Intestine Meridian	Kidney Meridian

They respectively form the fingers and toes at the terminals of the meridians, forming as a whole spirals of seven logarithmic orbits such as in the following example:

Stage 1: The part of the collarbone and shoulder blade which is the root of the arm.

Stage 2: The upper arm.

Stage 3: The forearm.

Stage 4: The back of the hand, up to the fingers.

Stage 5: The back of the upper part of the fingers, from the point where it joins the hand to the first finger joint.

Stage 6: The back of the middle part of the fingers, between the two finger joints.

Stage 7: The back of the fingertips.

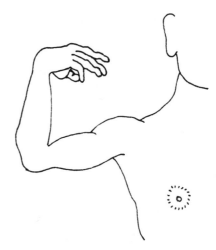

Fig. 11. Spirallic Formation of the Arm

Because the arms and legs are structures formed by electromagnetic flow discharged from the organ spirals produced in the body, the arms and legs as well as the fingers and toes have complemental relationships with the organs or the inner part of the body. The peripheral parts of the arms and legs, including the fingers and toes, correspond to the more inner parts of the related organs: and the more inner root or joint parts of the arms and legs, near the body, correspond to the outer layers of the related organs. Accordingly, stimulations and impulses given to the peripheral parts of the arms and legs, including the hands and fingers, feet and toes, produce an immediate reaction in the inner part of the respective organs; while those given to the more root parts of the arms and legs produce immediate reactions in the surface layers of the organs.

Because the embryonic body receives energy from the surrounding electromagnetic layer which is formed around the embryo, the entering points are on the peripheral surface of the embryo. This peripheral surface of the embryo, as electromagnetic currents are discharged toward the future arms and legs, gradually changes into what we know as the back part of the body. In the fully-developed human body, therefore, along the spine on the back part of the body, there are major entering points of electromagnetic charges, which are called in oriental medicine *Yu-Ketsu* (俞穴), "*Yu* Points," or "Entering Points." The meaning of *Yu* is "pouring in." Through these entering points, atmospheric charges enter the inner part of the body, charging various organs, activating their functions. Each of these *Yu* Points is therefore specifically related to the particular organ and its function, and these points traditionally bear the name of the related organ, such as *Hai-Yu* (肺俞), "Lung Entering Point," *Kan-Yu* (肝俞), "Liver Entering Point"; *Shō-Chō-Yu* (小腸俞), "Small Intestine Entering Point"; and so forth.

After the electromagnetic currents which have entered from the *Yu* Entering Points charge the respective organs, then, as mentioned before, they stream out from the surface of the front of the body, gathering into certain points which are traditionally called *Bo-Ketsu* (募穴), "Gathering Points," in oriental medicine. Therefore, in the front part of the body there are Gathering Points for each electromagnetic current which has charged each organ. In other words, these Gathering Points also represent particular organs and their functions. These Gathering Points are in complementary relationship with the Entering Points. These pairs of complementary points are as follows:

Fig. 12

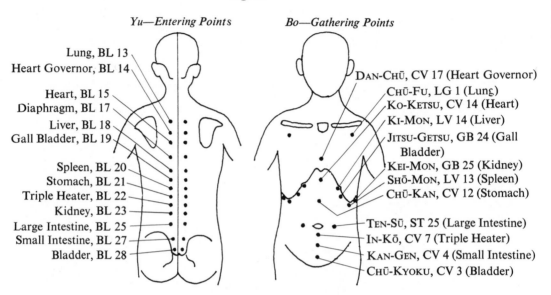

Yu—Entering Points

- Lung, BL 13
- Heart Governor, BL 14
- Heart, BL 15
- Diaphragm, BL 17
- Liver, BL 18
- Gall Bladder, BL 19
- Spleen, BL 20
- Stomach, BL 21
- Triple Heater, BL 22
- Kidney, BL 23
- Large Intestine, BL 25
- Small Intestine, BL 27
- Bladder, BL 28

Bo—Gathering Points

- DAN-CHŪ, CV 17 (Heart Governor)
- CHŪ-FU, LG 1 (Lung)
- KO-KETSU, CV 14 (Heart)
- KI-MON, LV 14 (Liver)
- JITSU-GETSU, GB 24 (Gall Bladder)
- KEI-MON, GB 25 (Kidney)
- SHŌ-MON, LV 13 (Spleen)
- CHŪ-KAN, CV 12 (Stomach)
- TEN-SŪ, ST 25 (Large Intestine)
- IN-KŌ, CV 7 (Triple Heater)
- KAN-GEN, CV 4 (Small Intestine)
- CHŪ-KYOKU, CV 3 (Bladder)

The electromagnetic current which has gathered in the Gathering Points in the front part of the body starts to be discharged toward the arms and legs, forming meridians for each current, ending at the tips of the fingers and toes. The terminal points of these meridians are called *Sei-Ketsu* (井穴), "Well Points." The name "Well" indicates that the electromagnetic flow is bubbling out like water coming from an underground well. Each Well Point of each meridian is located, therefore, at the end of each finger and toe, with the exception of the Well Point of the Kidney Meridian, which is located in the central front part of the sole of the foot. These *Sei*—Well Points are therefore in complemental relationship with the *Bo*— Gathering Points, as far as the meridians are concerned, and are also in complemental relationship with the *Yu*—Entering Points in regard to the flow of electromagnetic current as a whole.

Between the *Bo*—Gathering Points and the *Sei*—Well Points, each meridian generally forms seven logarithmic parts. Accordingly, electromagnetic current flowing through the meridian balances in the area of the fourth section, counting from both ends of the meridian. Because the length of each section composing the arms and legs becomes increasingly shorter as we move toward the periphery, these balancing points are generally located around the wrist in the case of meridians on the arm, and around the ankle and heel in the case of meridians on the leg. These points are traditionally called *Gen-Ketsu* (原穴), "Source Points" or "Balancing Points." These Balancing Points are one of the most important groups of points, together with the *Yu*—Entering Points, *Bo*—Gathering Points, and *Sei*—Well Points, in balancing the elctromagnetic charge throughout the meridians and organs and the organ functions as well.

The *Sei*—Well Points and *Gen*—Balancing Points of each meridian are listed below:

Fig. 13   Gen—Source Points on the Hands and Feet

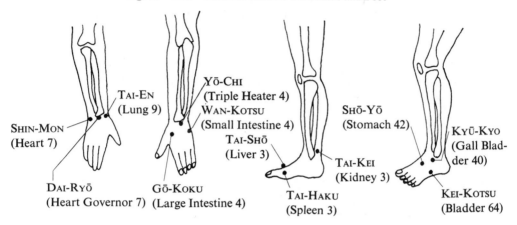

Fig. 14   Sei Points of Each Meridian

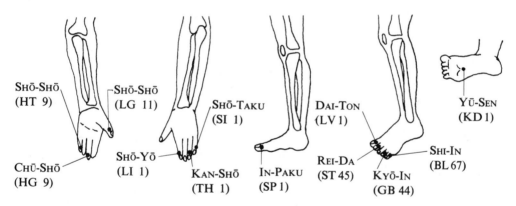

The meridians running throughout our body are something like the meridians running on the surface of the earth. Electromagnetic currents running on the surface layer of the earth form mountain ranges, aligned mainly in a North-South direction. Some mountain ranges running East-West or Northeast-Southwest have arisen in the past, before or during axis shifts of the earth, which have changed the magnetic poles. On the mountain ranges there are springs, waterfalls, and streams, as well as volcanoes, valleys, forests, and plains. Each of these places has certain characteristics, produced by atmospheric pressure and other surface conditions, together with underground forces and movement. Similarly, along the body meridians there are various points which are characterized as if they were various natural phenomena arising on mountain ranges. Some points on the meridians are more watery in nature—the electromagnetic current is streaming, pooling, falling, and bubbling up. Other points are characterized more by the fire nature, metal nature, wood nature, and soil nature, as well as other characteristics. These points are therefore traditionally named according to their character, although in the modern orientation of oriental medicine a series of numbers has been fixed to identify them. These points mainly exist along the meridians, particularly around the joints of the arms and legs; and between these points, balancing points are further produced. In this way, throughout our body along the 12 major meridians, more than 360 points are produced; and throughout the surface of our body, more than 2,000 points.

Major electromagnetic currents appear as meridians running throughout the body, with varying degrees of speed and intensity of current among the 12 major meridians. Among these meridians, six currents are running with more active energy, while six other currents are running with less active energy. The active currents may be easily identified as yang ($\triangle$) meridians, because they are coming from the more active organs, which have a generally more yin ($\triangledown$) expanded structure. The less active currents can be called yin ($\triangledown$) meridians, coming from the less active yang ($\triangle$) compacted organs. The yang meridians are running on the inner part of the arms and legs while the yin meridians are running more on the outer part. Their varying degrees of activity, yin and yang, are as follows:

Varying Degrees of Activity in the Meridians

Lung Meridian—Great Yin	Gall Bladder Meridian—Small Yang
Spleen Meridian—Great Yin	Triple Heater Meridian—Small Yang
Kidney Meridian—Small Yin	Large Intestine Meridian—Middle Yang
Heart Meridian—Small Yin	Stomach Meridian—Middle Yang
Heart Governor Meridian—Very Small Yin	Bladder Meridian—Great Yang
Liver Meridian—Very Small Yin	Small Intestine Meridian—Great Yang

Among these 12 meridians, two meridians, the yang Heart Governor Meridian and the yin Triple Heater Meridian, complement each other in their functions. These meridians have no specific organs to and from which energy enters and leaves; rather, they are more comprehensive electromagnetic currents. For example, in the case of the Heart Governor Meridian, energy generated by the movement of the heart region is administering the circulation of blood and body fluids throughout the body. In the case of the Tiple Heater·Meridian, vibrations discharged from the metabolic movement of the upper heart region, middle stomach region and lower abdominal region are constantly adjusting and controlling heat metabolism throughout the body. Accordingly, the conditions of the other ten meridians influence these two meridians, and the conditions of these two meridians are influencing all the other ten meridians. In other words, both the Heart Governor and Triple Heater Meridians are comprehensive functions representing all other ten meridians, which respectively represent the functions of the major organs.

Besides the aforementioned 12 meridians, the embryo forms two other fundamental meridians. These are traditionally called *Nin-Myaku* (任脈), the "Conception Vessel," and *Toku-Myaku* (督脈), the "Governing Vessel." Electromagnetic energy functioning as the Conception Vessel is flowing upward along the front of the body, beginning from the point between the anus and genital area and ending at the mouth. During the embryonic period, the Conception Vessel is the most inner layer of the body, and the Governing Vessel is the most peripheral layer of the body.

Furthermore, these two functions are actually connected as one circulatory flow of electromagnetic energy. From the end of the Conception Vessel at the mouth region, energy enters into the digestive system, moving toward the most inner part of the body, the lower abdomen, coming out at the end of the coccyx area. From there it flow upward along the spinal cord, reaching the head and ending at the mouth. From the mouth region it further enters into the inside of the body along the digestive system, again toward the lower abdomen, and comes out the area between the anus and genital region, and then changes into energy flow moving upward along the Conception Vessel.

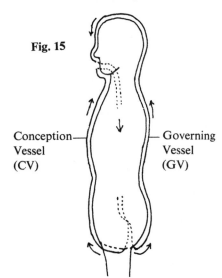

Fig. 15

Conception Vessel (CV)

Governing Vessel (GV)

These two meridians, the Conception and Governing Vessels, which are actually one energy flow, correspond to and overlap the energy flowing along both the Heart Governor and Triple Heater Meridians. These four meridians, accordingly, have a comprehensive influence upon all of our physical, mental and spiritual activities, while the other ten meridians respectively have partial influences.

Electromagnetic energies functioning as the 12 meridians, including the Heart Governor and Triple Heater Meridians, are not totally independent currents operating separately from each other. These currents of all of the meridians are connected at both ends: at the peripheral parts of the body—the hands and fingers, feet and toes, especially at the *Sei*—Well Points—and at the central points of the upper, middle and lower areas of the Triple Heater Meridian.

Therefore, electromagnetic energy flows from one meridian to another as a continuous current, which is constantly receiving charges from the external atmosphere through various points, and constantly discharging through various other points, while the current is circulating throughout all the meridians. The following chart shows the order of current flow from one meridian to another, alternating between yin meridians and yang meridians:

Yin (∇) Meridians	*Yang ($\triangle$) Meridians*
Lungs	Large Intestine
Spleen and Pancreas	Stomach
Heart	Small Intestine
Kidney	Bladder
Heart Governor	Triple Heater
Liver	Gall Bladder

Accordingly, stimulation of any sort, including pressure, given on certain meridians or some points of certain meridians, eventually influences all of the meridians as well as the electromagnetic activity of various points—not only on that particular meridian but also on the other meridians. These influences, creating responses of activity and interactivity in the electromagnetic flow among meridians, can be generally understood through the experiences which have been formulated in the traditional theory of the *Five Stages of Transformation.*

The Five Stages of Transformation universally occur in all phenomena in this relative world, in any domain such as chemistry, physics, biology, and astronomy, as well as in physical, psychological, and social phenomena. These transformations are the movements from yin (∇) centrifugal expansion to yang ($\triangle$) centripetal contraction, and from yang ($\triangle$) centripetal contraction to yin (∇) centrifugal expansion, repeated endlessly.

In nature, matter changes from its solid state into a liquid state by applying centrifugal factors, such as through the use of higher temperature. It further changes into the stage of evaporation, and continues to change into the stage of plasma. This continuous yin (∇) expanding course would change into the yang ($\triangle$) contracting course through the application of lower temperature, from the stage of plasma through the process of solidification, returning to the stage of solid. This latter yang ($\triangle$) contracting course again changes to the yin (∇) expanding course, repeating similar processes.

These Five Stages of Transformation have been explained in simple terms which are understandable to anyone, using examples of relative objects commonly available around us:

The Stage of Evaporation . . . . Wood
The Stage of Plasma . . . . Fire
The Stage of Solidification . . . . Soil
The Stage of Solid . . . . Metal
The Stage of Liquid . . . . Water

This universal pattern of change between the yin (∇) expanding course and the yang ($\triangle$) contracting course, which is cycling endlessly, also explains the reincarnation arising universally in all phenomena. Electromagnetic energy flowing along the meridians throughout the body, feeling to and discharging from various organs and their functions, is also not excepted from this universal law of change. Electromagnetic currents running along the ten meridians and the two comprehensive meridians create reactions to each other as indicated in Fig. 16.

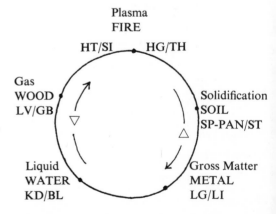

Fig. 16 Five Transformations in Phenomenal Change and Correlated Functions of Organs and Meridians

In other words, excessive energy given to one meridian gives energy to the next meridian as a natural progression, and reduces energy in the preceding meridian. For example, excessive energy given to the Liver Meridian naturally passes to the Heart Meridian, and results in a reduction of energy in the Kidney Meridian. This relation may be called a "complemental relation," or "the relation of parent and child," as it has been called traditionally in oriental medicine.

Furthermore, meridians listed on opposite sides of the chart are governed by opposite tendencies: some with more expanding energy, and others with more contracting energy. Accordingly, among these five groups of meridians, there are antagonistic relations as indicated in Fig. 17.

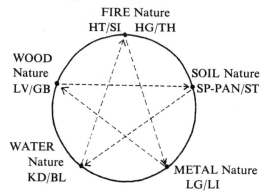

Fig. 17 Conflicting Tendencies in the Functions of Organs and Meridians

In other words, a stimulus given to generate the active functioning of the Liver Meridian would inhibit the active functioning of the Spleen-Pancreas Meridian, and a stimulus given to reduce activity, for example in the Kidney Meridian, would accelerate the activity of the Heart Meridian. This reaction arising among the meridians may be called an "antagonistic relation" or a "conflicting relation," as it was traditionally called.

These Five Stages of Transformation also arise on each meridian at its peripheral part. Among the points from the tips of the fingers to the elbow on the arm and from the tips of the toes to the knees on the legs, there are five points on each meridian that represent respectively the natures of Wood, Fire, Soil, Metal, and Water. These points are used in various ways in the treatment of electromagnetic energy, either to supply or reduce energy. For example, stimulation applied to the Water Point of the Liver Meridian gives an influence not only to the Liver Meridian, but also to the Kidney Meridian. Similarly, stimulation given to the Fire Point of the Stomach Meridian gives an influence not only to the Stomach Meridian, but also to the Small Intestine Meridian. These points are listed in Fig. 18.

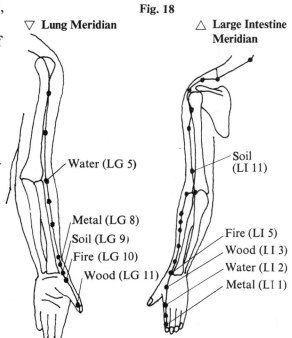

Fig. 18

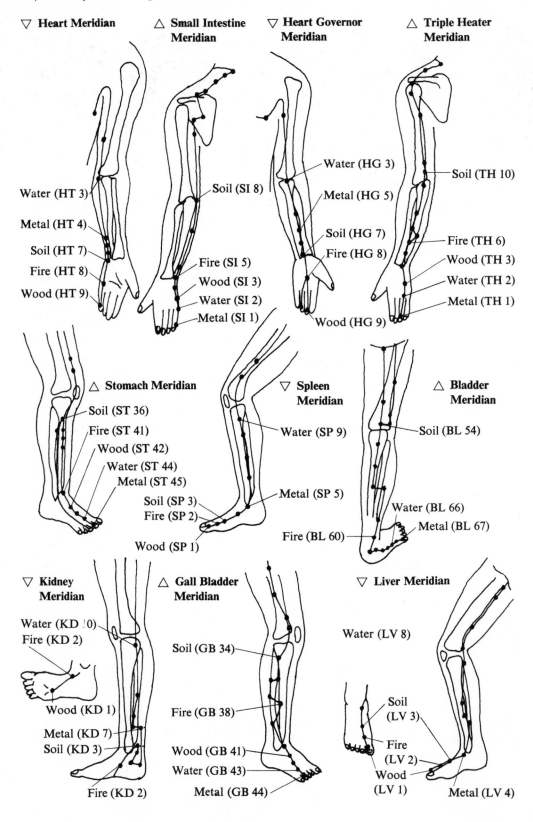

▽ **Heart Meridian**

△ **Small Intestine Meridian**

▽ **Heart Governor Meridian**

△ **Triple Heater Meridian**

Water (HT 3)
Metal (HT 4)
Soil (HT 7)
Fire (HT 8)
Wood (HT 9)

Soil (SI 8)
Fire (SI 5)
Wood (SI 3)
Water (SI 2)
Metal (SI 1)

Water (HG 3)
Metal (HG 5)
Soil (HG 7)
Fire (HG 8)
Wood (HG 9)

Soil (TH 10)
Fire (TH 6)
Wood (TH 3)
Water (TH 2)
Metal (TH 1)

△ **Stomach Meridian**

Soil (ST 36)
Fire (ST 41)
Wood (ST 42)
Water (ST 44)
Metal (ST 45)
Soil (SP 3)
Fire (SP 2)
Wood (SP 1)

▽ **Spleen Meridian**

Water (SP 9)
Metal (SP 5)

△ **Bladder Meridian**

Soil (BL 54)
Water (BL 66)
Metal (BL 67)
Fire (BL 60)

▽ **Kidney Meridian**

Water (KD 10)
Fire (KD 2)
Wood (KD 1)
Metal (KD 7)
Soil (KD 3)
Fire (KD 2)

△ **Gall Bladder Meridian**

Soil (GB 34)
Fire (GB 38)
Wood (GB 41)
Water (GB 43)
Metal (GB 44)

▽ **Liver Meridian**

Water (LV 8)
Soil (LV 3)
Fire (LV 2)
Wood (LV 1)
Metal (LV 4)

4. Treatments

Treatments using these meridians and the points along the meridians are mainly aiming to harmonize electromagnetic currents throughout the body. When the energy flow along certain meridians is less than normal, stimulation is applied in order to supply energy or activate energy flow. When some meridians have excessive energy, stimulation is applied to reduce energy in order to achieve a harmonious relation among the meridians.

The arts for supplying or reducing energy have been developed, mainly in the oriental countries, for more than 5,000 years. Among these arts of harmonizing energy, there are the following:

a. Acupuncture

The art of acupuncture mainly uses needles, traditionally made of gold and silver, and recently of stainless steel. In treatment, one or several needles are used on the proper meridian in the proper points, sometimes inserting them and taking them out immediately, and at other times inserting and leaving them in for some duration. By the varying use of needles, energy is supplied or reduced in various degrees. You may consider these needles as antennae which receive and discharge electromagnetic current between the atmosphere and the body.

b. Moxibustion

Stimulation using the active vibration of fire can also release the stagnated flow of energy along meridians or certain areas around points. Usually, the substance burned has been *moxa*, which was traditionally processed out of mugwort, though other sorts of fire stimulation can produce similar effects: rice grain moxa, paper moxa, and cigarette moxa may also be used in various circumstances.

c. Shiatsu or Meridian Massage

Unlike western massage, oriental massage has used the meridians and the major points along the meridians to harmonize electromagnetic currents throughout the body. Since the hands and fingers as well as the feet and toes are electromagnetically charged, applying them on stagnated meridians or hardened points can activate the smooth circulation of energy through the meridians, and applying them in an area where energy flow is less than normal can activate the current. Using the fingers in a certain way, excessive energy in certain areas can also be reduced. This *shiatsu* or meridian massage has been widely practiced in oriental countries, even among ordinary people at home.

d. Palm Healing

Because the palms, and all other areas of the hand including the tips of the fingers, receive and discharge energy, a certain way of using the palms and fingers, applying them gently upon a part of a meridian or upon points in an area of sickness, can reduce various disorders. In some cases, two or more fingers can be used to reinforce energy, or both palms may be used together. In other cases, the fingers can be used in antagonistic ways; and sometimes two fingers may be used, one for supplying energy, the other to reduce energy.

e. Yoga and Other Physical Exercises

Many exercises that call for bending or stretching the body, neck, head, arms, and legs in certain ways give various effects to the energy flow along the meridians, releasing stagnation arising in some areas. These exercises, though it is not well understood at the present time, were originally designed in ancient times to harmonize the electromagnetic currents of the meridians, which naturally results in the harmonious development of our physical, mental, and spiritual condition.

All of the arts mentioned above have originated from *Shin-Sen-Dō*, the art of longevity and rejuvenation for physical, mental, and spiritual development practiced thousands of years ago. Among the various arts of *Shin-Sen-Dō*, Dō-In is the most simplified exercise in comparison with other arts of healing: it can be practiced alone, using any spare time. Dō-In does not require the expert knowledge and technique which is required in the practice of acupuncture. Dō-In does not require any instruments, as in the case of acupuncture and moxibustion, however simple they may be. Dō-In does not require a person who performs as a healer as in shiatsu massage and palm healing, as well as acupuncture and moxibustion. And, Dō-In does not require any vigorous or unusual activity which may be required from time to time in the exercise of yoga and other physical training.

Dō-In, in its various exercises, uses the electromagnetic flow or energy currents running throughout the body, with more simple, normal movements, including the use of meridians and points, but it also uses other principal functions of the body, such as breathing, chanting, thinking, and meditating.

5. The Chakras and the Spiritual Channel

During the embryonic period as well as the growing period, like all other organic and inorganic existence upon the surface of the earth, including soil, water, and air, our constitution—both physical and mental—is fundamentally oriented by the forces of heaven and earth. The force of heaven is coming from infinite outer space toward the center of the earth, and the force of earth is radiating from the center of the earth toward peripheral space. The former is the yang ($\triangle$) centripetal contracting force, and the latter is the yin (∇) centrifugal expanding force. Without these forces, no phenomenon would arise upon the earth. These forces are all moving toward the surface of the earth, from external space and from the internal center of the earth; but they also manifest in the formation and existence of all beings, of whatever kind, that appear upon the earth.

The earth is discharging more yin (∇) centrifugal expanding force at the region along the equator, where the continuous movement of rotation has the highest speed due to the long distance of the earth's circumference there. The earth rotates in a counterclockwise direction, as we can see if we look down from the direction of the North Pole toward the center of the earth. Accordingly, this yin centrifugal expanding force forms a clockwise spiral when it is discharged. Conversely, the force of heaven, descending toward the polar regions, forms a counterclockwise spiral as it comes in toward the center of the earth. The earth's yin (∇) expanding force thus forms a clockwise centrifugal spiral, and heaven's yang ($\triangle$) contracting force forms a counterclockwise, contracting spiral.

Yang, heaven's centripetal contracting force, when it enters most intensively at the polar region, produces a highly-charged atmosphere which appears as the aurora borealis. Then it enters toward the center of the earth, colliding with another contracting force of heaven, coming in a counterclockwise direction from the southern polar region, producing a curving orbit (Fig. 19). Furthermore, they produce another layer of electromagnetic currents which form the region of the mantle. In a similar way they produce the crust, and several layers of electromagnetic currents encircling the earth, some of which are known as the Van Allen Belt.

Similar constitutions appear in everything which has a generally round form upon this earth. For example, in the case of fruit, the core area is the nuclear region where seeds are usually produced, and the mantle area is the region of the fruit's pulp. The crust of the earth corresponds to the skin of the fruit. Heaven's force comes into the fruit through the top stem, and another force comes in from the bottom. In the same way, our human constitution is formed between two forces, each of which is coming in spirallically from heaven—outer space—and from the earth, the force radiated spirallically from the ground.

Formation of the Apple and Fruits in General

Fig. 19

Formation of the Earth

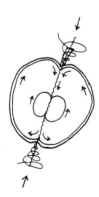

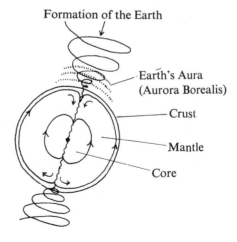

Earth's Aura (Aurora Borealis)

Crust

Mantle

Core

Fig. 20 The Aura

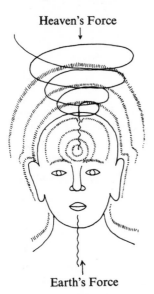

Heaven's Force

Earth's Force

In the case of the human body, heaven's force enters into the head region, forming the counterclockwise hair arrangement and producing the aura, which corresponds to the aurora borealis of the northern sky of the earth. After entering the head, heaven's force intensively charges the most inner region of the brain—the area of the midbrain—from which charges are distributed to all other parts of the brain, sending electromagnetic influences to millions of cells. Because of these charges distributed to all parts of the brain, these cells, organized in each region of the brain, operate as highly-communicative instruments and receive various sorts of vibrations as well as electromagnetic impulses, producing images. Television, as a very primitive mechanism, performs a similar operation. Our brain is able to function as the major organ of consciousness and the controlling center of many physical and mental activities as a result of being constantly charged by heaven's force.

Heaven's force continuously descends, forming the uvula at the deep inner region of the mouth cavity, which is the opposite pole to the spirallic center of the head. Around the uvula, therefore, electromagnetic forces intensively charge the liquid gathering inside the mouth cavity. As an example, saliva can melt various substances and decompose chemical compounds such as carbohydrates because of its electromagnetic nature.

The force is transmitted from the uvula to the root of the tongue and the throat region, including the vocal cords. For this reason, the tongue is movable, and the vocal cords as well. The thyroid and parathyroid glands which are charged by this force produce the hormones, as the pituitary gland in the brain also produces various hormones, due to the electromagnetic charge distributed from the midbrain.

Heaven's force further descends to the heart region. Electromagnetic forces activate the external muscles of the heart, and the charge is distributed from there throughout the circulatory system within the blood and the lymph system in the same way that the charges are distributed from the midbrain to all brain cells. For example, due to these distributed charges, blood plasma as well as some organic compounds and some organic chemicals are ionized. Because of their ionization, they are also able to rapidly transform their chemical nature, including transmutation which may arise in the blood. Charges carried through the circulatory system are further distributed to all the trillions of cells throughout the body.

Heaven's force continues to descend, charging the stomach region, from which it is distributed to other surrounding organs such as the pancreas and spleen, the liver and gall bladder, and the kidneys. Accordingly, these organs produce various liquids which are charged electromagnetically, including gastric acid, pancreatic juice, liver and gall bladder biles, as well as the pancreatic and duodenal hormones.

Heaven's force continues to descend, and intensively charges the lower part of the small intestine. This region is the center of the abdominal area, called *Ki-Kai*

(気海), the "Ocean of Electromagnetic Force." This region is also called *Tan-Den* (丹田), the "Central Field" or *Hara* (肚), the "Abdominal Center." Because of this charge, distributed throughout the small and large intestines in the form of waves, these organs move by contracting and expanding. Intestinal digestion, decomposition, and absorption of food molecules, as well as the movement of food and bowels, become possible due to these distributed forces.

This force further descends, charging the lower part of the body, including the bladder and genital area. The functions of the bladder, collecting and eliminating urine, and the functions of the genital area, producing and eliminating reproductive cells, result from the charge of these electromagnetic forces. Heaven's force, descending from the head, then creates another "uvula," the penis in the case of man, and the clitoris in the case of woman, as it produced the uvula in the mouth cavity of the head region.

Fig. 21

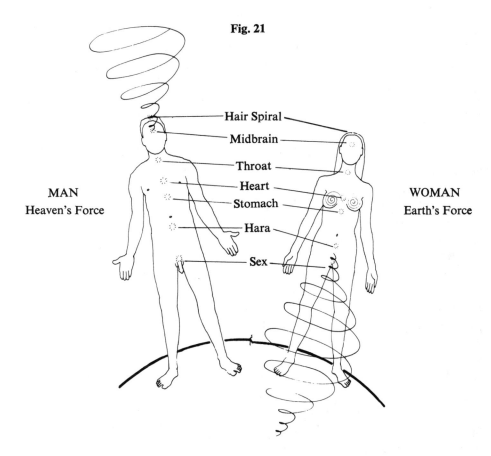

MAN
Heaven's Force

WOMAN
Earth's Force

Hair Spiral
Midbrain
Throat
Heart
Stomach
Hara
Sex

On the other hand, the force from the earth ascends from the ground toward heaven, passing through the same channel through which heaven's force descends. The force of the earth enters into the body through both feet, going up toward the area of the *Tan-Den*. It also enters through the lowest part of the body, including the genital area, creating a unique form or indentation—the prostate gland in the case of man, and the uterus and ovaries in the case of woman.

Earth's force continues to ascend and intensify its charge, colliding at the abdominal area with heaven's descending force. This accelerates various intestinal activities, including the secretion of intestinal juice and the gonad hormones. In the case of woman, the place of the *Tan-Den*, which is known as the "Ocean of Electromagnetic Force," is the most inner part of the uterus, where implantation and the formation of the placenta occur. These charges are intensified in this area, especially in the case of woman, to the extent that it is possible to generate embryonic development in the uterus.

Earth's force continues to ascend and charges the middle region of the body, including various organs such as the stomach, pancreas and spleen, liver and gall bladder, as well as the kidneys. These areas are charged in coordination with heaven's force. For example, the liver is influenced more by heaven's force, while the spleen is more influenced by earth's force; and insulin secreted by the pancreas is charged more by heaven's force, while the secretion of anti-insulin is accelerated more by earth's force.

This force continues to ascend and charges the heart region, coordinating with heaven's force. Cardiac movement is governed by these two forces—contraction by heaven's force, and expansion by earth's force. The force of the earth is also distributed throughout the circulatory system into all parts of the body, as heaven's force is distributed, sending nourishing electromagnetic forces to all muscles, tissues, and cells.

Further ascending, the force of the earth vibrates the vocal cords, reinforcing the breathing function and accelerating tongue activity as well as releasing charges into the mouth cavity. Because of this charge, high-pitched sound can be created and inhalation can be made, and faster motion of the tongue is facilitated.

Across the space between the root of the tongue and the uvula, earth's force is transmitted toward the brain region and charges its center, the midbrain, from which the charge is distributed to all parts of the brain as well as to all cells. While the distribution of heaven's force from the midbrain tends to charge more the inner and back part of the brain, the distribution of earth's force tends to charge more the peripheral and front regions of the brain. The former also tends to charge more the right side of the brain, while the latter tends to charge more the left side of the brain. These differences naturally result in various different psychological effects.

These two forces, heaven's yang centripetal contracting force and earth's yin centrifugal expanding force, form one vibrating stream passing vertically through our body, between the spirallic center of the head and the lowest part of the body. This stream may be called the "spiritual channel," or the "primary life energy channel."

The parts of the body where the forces from heaven and earth collide and charge have been traditionally called *chakras*, especially in the ancient medicine of India. These places are each generating electromagnetic flow toward the outside and, at the same time, they are receiving invisible force from the surrounding atmosphere to charge the internal functions. The locations of the chakras are shown in Fig. 22.

The functions of the chakras are as follows:

Fig. 22 The Seven Chakras and Four Hand and Foot Chakras

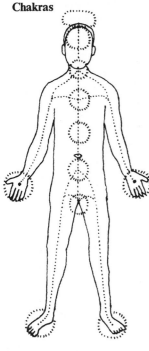

A. The Crown or Seventh Chakra: Governing the brain cortex and various kinds of consciousness, including the unified administration of spiritual, mental, and physical activities.

B. The Aina or Sixth Chakra: Governing control of consciousness and physical reactions. Most nervous stimulations are assimilated in this place and distributed to all parts of the brain.

C. The Throat or Fifth Chakra: Governing the functions of respiration and vocalization as well as the motion of the tongue. The quality and volume of saliva and bronchial functions are also influenced.

D. The Heart or Fourth Chakra: Governing the heart and circulatory activities and charging electromagnetically the blood and body fluids, including the lymph. It also indirectly controls the respiratory and digestive functions.

E. The Solar Plexus or Third Chakra: Governing the activities of the stomach, the spleen and pancreas, the liver and gall bladder, and the kidneys. The secretion of hormones and digestive liquid in this area are also controlled.

F. The Sacral or Second Chakra: Governing intestinal digestion and absorption in the small and large intestines, where the secretion of digestive liquid is also influenced. Reproductive functions, including ovarian activities, pregnancy, and the secretion of gonad hormones, are also controlled.

G. The Base or First Chakra: Governing the functions of the bladder and rectum, as well as the reproductive function; and also controlling part of the nervous and circulatory functions.

Excessive charge arising in any of these chakras stimulates these above-mentioned functions, and a decrease of charge results in the slowing down of these functions. Among these seven chakras, the Sixth Chakra is the central administrator of various functions controlling consciousness in the head region, and the Second Chakra is the central administrator for the body region. The Sixth Chakra is the area known as the midbrain, and the Second Chakra is the area called the *Tan-Den*. Between these two chakras is another important chakra—the Fourth Chakra, at the region of the heart. It balances all of the other chakras and physical and mental functions because of its control of the circulatory system. You may say the Sixth Chakra is the center of the nervous system, the Fourth Chakra is the center of the circulatory system, and the Second Chakra is the center of the digestive system.

Stimulation given to these chakras also produces different mental and spiritual conditions. Stimulation can be given to these chakras by self-exercise such as the practice of Dō-In, using various forms of posture, breathing, and chanting.

The qualities produced by the various chakras are as follows:

The Seventh, Crown Chakra: Consciousness expansion toward the development of universal understanding, diminishing egocentric thinking.

The Sixth, Ajna Chakra: Control of consciousness, including the purification of various thoughts into more concentrated forms of thinking, with the gradual diminishing of sensory perception.

The Fifth, Throat Chakra: Developing the ability of intellectual, logical expression, as well as artistic expression.

The Fourth, Heart Chakra: Generating emotional feelings, including love and sympathy toward others. Sensitive perception in the relationship with the external world can be developed.

The Third, Solar Plexus Chakra: Generating various physical and mental powers, including an extraordinary ability to control physical movement, and the performance of unusual powers which require balance among all physical movements.

The Second, Sacral Chakra: Generating physical stability as well as mental confidence. Unmovable strength, physical and mental, can also be developed.

The First, Base Chakra: Generating physical and mental harmony with the earth, including its atmospheric conditions. It also strengthens sexual vitality as well as the ability to adapt to surroundings.

Besides these seven chakras, there are four additional chakras, one on each hand and foot. The center of the hand chakra is the center of each palm: *Rō-Kyū* (労宮) —Heart Governor No. 8; and the center of the foot chakra is the central part of the sole of the foot, which is usually called *Soku-Shin* (足心), the "Heart of the Foot." The hand chakras are extended centers of the Fourth, Heart Chakra, and the foot chakras are extended centers of the Second, Sacral Chakra.

The Right-Hand Chakra: Governing the discharge of electromagnetic charges toward the periphery. These charges have been generated internally by various body chakras, especially the Second, Sacral; Third, Solar Plexus; and Fourth, Heart Chakras.

The Left-Hand Chakra: Governing the active reception of invisible electromagnetic flow from the surrounding atmosphere. These in-flowing energies are feeding various internal chakras, especially the Second, Sacral; Third, Solar Plexus; and Fourth, Heart Chakras.

The Right-Foot Chakra: Governing the discharge of electromagnetic energy toward the earth—energy which has been received from various body chakras, especially the Seventh, Crown; Sixth, Ajna; and Fifth, Throat Chakras.

The Left-Foot Chakra: Governing the reception of energy from the earth and generating various body chakras, especially the First, Base and Second, Sacral as well as the Fifth, Sixth, and Seventh Chakras.

Stimulations given on the fingers and palms as well as on the toes and soles of the feet directly and indirectly influence various activities of the chakras, which in turn control various functions of the organs and glands. Also, using the hands and feet in various ways—including holding the palms together—and various combinations of the fingers, gives different effects to our physical, mental, and spiritual conditions. The use of various forms and combinations of the feet and toes also gives similar effects.

These stimulations are given through various treatments, including acupuncture, moxibustion, shiatsu massage, yoga and other physical exercises. In the case of Dō-In, we give proper stimulation in the form of self-massage and pressure applied in various parts of these areas by our fingers.

6. The Antagonistic, Complemental Structure of Man

All relative phenomena which arise within the universe are structured between two antagonistic and complemental forces, namely the yin ($\triangledown$) centrifugal expanding force and the yang ($\triangle$) centripetal contracting force. In the case of human beings, these two forces are represented by the yang centripetal contracting force of heaven and the yin centrifugal expanding force of the earth, as mentioned before. Accordingly, our human constitution as well as all plants and animals are structured in an antagonistic, complemental way among various systems, organs, glands, and all other parts and their functions.

These antagonistic and complemental structures and functions among various parts of the body can be observed in all levels, and even in infinitesimal, minute functions. Such antagonistic and complemental relations can be observed, for example, in red blood cells vs. white blood cells, insulin vs. anti-insulin, sympathetic nerves vs. parasympathetic nerves, male vs. female hormones, positively-ionized mineral compounds vs. negatively-ionized mineral compounds, alkalinity vs. acidity, Vitamin C vs. Vitamins D, K, E or B-12, and so forth.

However, the comprehensive relations which we need to understand for the practical conduct of our daily life, including physical, mental, and spiritual exercises, can be more generally categorized into several groups of antagonistic, complemental relationships. These are the relationships of (1) front and back; (2) upper and lower areas; (3) left and right; (4) periphery and center; (5) organ and meridian function; and (6) the part and the whole.

a. The Relationship of Front and Back

The front part of our body is softer, while the back part is harder. In the embryonic period, the front was the more yang ($\triangle$), inside part of the embryo, while the back was the more yin ($\triangledown$), peripheral part. Taking in nourishment, the embryo distributed more yin protein and fat toward the inside, and more yang minerals toward the periphery. As a result, the front digestive system develops a more yin, long and hollow structure, while the back nervous system is structured in a tight, solid form, including the vertebrae.

Early in the embryonic stage, the digestive system is formed by a yin expanding spiral, and the nervous system is formed by a yang contracting spiral. According to this difference, as the animal species evolves from more simple structures toward more complex structures, the digestive system grows longer while the nervous system tends to become shorter in comparison. The back nervous system receives electromagnetic vibrational stimulae from the surroundings, carried upward toward the brain, while the front digestive and respiratory systems receive the physical environment such as solids, liquids, and gas by way of eating, drinking and breathing. These two systems have an antagonistic and complemental relationship. Each front organ is related to a part of the spinal cord, and stimuli applied to the vertebrae respectively influence the corresponding front organs and glands.

Similarly, as mentioned previously (page 62), surrounding energies enter the body through the *Yu*—Entering Points along the bladder meridians, which run parallel with the spinal cord. After these energies form and activate the various organs, they are gathered in the front surface of the body, namely at the *Bo*—Gathering Points. Stimuli given either the *Yu*—Entering Points or the *Bo*—Gathering Points influence the respective complemental points as well as their related organs.

In the same way, marks and spots appearing on the surface of the back indicate that an abnormal condition is present or has previously existed in the front part of the body, including the internal organs. The back system, namely the nervous system, is resistant to and adaptable to colder temperatures, while the front systems, namely the digestive and respiratory systems, are more active under warmer atmospheric temperatures.

b. The Relationship between Upper and Lower Areas

The human body has two spheres: the head region and the body region. These two spheres are antagonistic and complementary. The head region is structured in a more yang compacted form, and the body region is structured in a more yin expanded form. If these two areas were structured with exactly the same form and size, whatever is present in one region would be repeated in the other sphere like a mirror image. Due to the difference between the two regions, however, whatever is present in the upper region, the head, exists in the lower region, the body, in an expanded form; and whatever is present in the body region exists in the head region in a compacted form. For example, the small and large intestines are the expanded form of the brain, which in turn is the contracted form of the intestines. Accordingly, both organs, the intestines and the brain, are taking in the environment, but in different qualities—the physical environment for the intestines, and the non-physical, vibrational environment for the brain.

According to this understanding of the antagonistic and complemental relationship between the two spheres, the head and body, it is easy to correlate the various parts of the body with the various parts of the head and face, beginning from the points connecting these two regions—the area of the mouth cavity and vocal cords in front, and the area of the *medulla oblongata* in back. The lower part of the face corresponds to the upper part of the body. For example, the cheeks correspond to the lungs; the tip of the nose to the heart; the nostrils to the bronchi.

Similarly, the middle area of the face corresponds to the middle part of the body. For example, the bridge of the nose corresponds to the stomach and pancreas; the area around the eyes, to the kidneys; the area between the eyebrows, the "root" of the nose, to the liver and gall bladder; the temple area to the spleen and lymph system.

Both ears respectively correspond to both kidneys: the ears are centrally located in the head, and the kidneys are located in the middle region of the body. The kidneys comprehensively represent the condition of our body functions. Accordingly, the ears also represent the whole constitution of our physical and mental condition.

Furthermore, the upper part of the head generally corresponds to the lower part of the body. For example, the forehead corresponds to the intestinal area; the upper forehead near the hairline to the bladder; and both sides of the upper forehead to the reproductive function.

The mouth corresponds to the digestive organs, as we can see since the mouth is the entrance to this system. As far as the area around the mouth is concerned, it corresponds to the area around the anus—the exit of the digestive system—and the genital organs. Therefore, the upper lip shows the stomach condition while the lower lip indicates the condition of the intestines; and in the area around the mouth, the conditions of the prostate, ovaries, and uterus are clearly discernible.

Similar antagonistic and complemental relationships exist between the 32 teeth and the 34 sections of the vertebrae. This kind of relation also exists between the upper part of the body, the shoulder region, and the lower part of the body, the intestinal region.

Abnormal swelling, unusual color, hardening, stiffness, tumors, freckles, pimples, and black and red spots which appear in certain areas indicate abnormal conditions in the corresponding parts of the body, including disorders in organ functions. Accordingly, stimuli given by the palm or fingers to these areas directly and indirectly produce reactions in the corresponding internal areas of the body. Exercises such as Dō-In applied in any region of the head and body bring forth beneficial results, not only for that particular region, but also for the corresponding parts of the body and their related functions.

c. The Relationship of Left and Right

Fig. 23 **Alternating Balance of the Yin (∇) and Yang ($\triangle$) Natures**

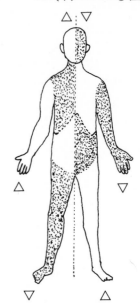

The shaded areas indicate yin nature and the white areas indicate yang nature in the alternating areas of the body.

The left side of the body is antagonistic and complementary to the right side of the body, as we can usually observe in the movement of the body. We use left and right arms and legs alternately while we are in motion, such as during walking or running. In our body structure, the left lung has asymmetric balance with the right lung. A similar asymmetrical balance maintains coordination between the liver for processing blood, and the spleen for processing lymph. It also exists between the two kidneys, the two ovaries, the two testicles, the left and right auricles of the heart, and the ascending and descending colons. It exists between the left and right shoulders, the arms, and the hands, as well as the waist, legs, and feet.

In the head and face region, the right sphere of the brain deals with more basic mechanical mental activity, while the left sphere deals with more complex aesthetic thinking. The left brain relates to the physical movement of the right side of the body, while the right brain relates to the left side of the body. In seeing, everyone uses either the right or left eye to focus visual attention upon a particular object, and the other eye to give dimension. In hearing, everyone uses either the left or right ear to distinguish the nature of a sound, while the other is used to determine distance. When we breathe through the nose, we use either the left or right nostril primarily for inhalation, and the other more for exhalation. In taste, we mainly use either side of the tongue, and in chewing, either side of the teeth.

On the face, in general, the left side represents the inheritance of the father's physical and mental constitution, while the right side represents the mother's constitution. No one has perfectly symmetrical balance between left and right. In the abilities of thinking, seeing, smelling, hearing, breathing, talking, and all other activities and expressions appearing in our face, asymmetrical balance is always maintained.

If the left side of the face is more active than the right, it indicates that the biological inheritance from the father through his reproductive cells is more influential than that of the mother.

These antagonistic and complemental relationships also exist in the hands, fingers, feet, and toes. For example, the electromagnetic currents entering and leaving the fingers and toes are precisely opposite in the left and right thumbs, left and right index fingers, and all other paired fingers and toes. Due to such complemental relationships, when we hold our palms together with the opposite fingers lightly attached, as in a praying or meditating position, physical and mental balance between the right and left parts of the brain and body is in a state of peaceful harmony.

Various spiritual exercises, including prayer, meditation, and self-reflection, seek to realize harmony between the antagonistic and complemental constitutions and functions of left and right, in order to achieve togetherness or oneness. The practice of acupuncture, moxibustion, and various physical adjustments also aims to achieve a balance between left and right. Dō-In exercise uses these antagonistic and complemental balances in its various postures and movements, and helps to bring about their unification into a harmonious oneness.

d. The Relationship of Periphery and Center

All relative phenomena which appear in this universe have an antagonistic and complemental relationship between the periphery and the center. Without the surface, there is no inside, and without the inside, there is no surface. The condition of the surface, therefore, reflects the condition of the interior, and the internal condition is either causing or caused by the external condition. As for our human structure, the relations between external conditions and internal conditions are generally seen in the following ways:

1. Skin Color. In oriental medicine as in western medicine, skin color is one of the important ways of diagnosing the condition of the internal organs and their functions.

Skin Color	*Internal Condition*
Yellow	Disorders in the function of the liver and gall bladder, such as in the case of jaundice.
Red	Disorders in the heart and circulatory system, as in capillary expansion on the cheeks, or abnormal blood pressure.
Pale	Disorders in the lungs and respiratory function, as in pulmonary tuberculosis. It also often indicates disorders in the spleen and lymph system.
Dark	Disorders in the kidney and urinary functions, as in the case of kidney infection and stones.
Purple	Disorders in the respiratory and circulatory systems, as in the case of purpura, and some cases of low blood pressure.

Skin Color	*Internal Condition*
Blue-grey	Disorders in the liver and pancreatic functions, as in hardening of the liver.
Light green	Disorders in the cellular organism, as in the progressive stages of cancer.
Translucent	Advanced disorders in the respiratory and circulatory systems, as in advanced tuberculosis, leukemia, and leprosy.
Milky white	Disorders in the lymph system, and mucus accumulations in various parts of the body, as in the early stages of various degenerative diseases.

2. Marks and Spots on the Skin. Various marks appearing on the surface of the body result from an abnormal condition which either occurred in the past, or which is currently progressing. These marks are a form of discharge from the internal organs, glands, tissues and muscles, and are a manifestation of the energies which are working in the internal part of our body. They often appear along muscles, meridians, and at the location of the organs. The following are some examples:

Marks	*Condition*
Freckles	Discharge of excessive sugar, including fruit sugars. Disorders in the liver, kidneys, and their functions.
Moles	Discharge of excessive protein, especially caused by animal food such as meat, poultry and eggs. Disorders in the digestive system.
Warts	Discharge of excessive protein and fat, especially caused by meat, eggs, dairy food, and sugar. Disorders in the intestinal and pancreatic conditions.
Dry skin	Lack of metabolism due to fat layers under the skin, caused by excessive consumption of fat and oil, including meat, dairy food, sugar, and fruits.

Marks	*Condition*
Red spots	Discharge of excessive minerals, especially caused by animal food and salt. Disorders in the liver and gall bladder and their functions.
Black marks	The so-called "beauty mark"; these appear along the meridians. Discharge of excessive carbon and other minerals after an infectious disease. Indication of disorders in particular organs and their functions, according to the meridian.
White patches	Discharge of excessive fat, mainly caused by the consumption of dairy food. Disorders in the spleen and lymph system as well as the respiratory organs.

3. Body and Head Hair. Hair is one form of elimination from the inside of the body through the circulatory and endocrine functions. The condition of the hair on either the head or the body indicates the internal conditions of the organs, glands, and their functions. Some examples are as follows:

Hair Condition	*Internal Condition*
Baldness on the peripheral region of the head	Excessive intake of liquid, including fruits, juice, soft drinks, milk, and alcohol, as well as sugar. Disorders in intestinal digestion and the kidney and excretory systems.
Baldness on the central region of the head	Excessive intake of animal food, including meat, poultry and eggs; as well as alcohol. Disorders in the functioning of the intestines, liver, kidneys, and excretory system.
Grey hair	Excessive intake of minerals, or lack of protein in comparison with carbohydrates, as in the case of excessive intake of salt. Disorders in the kidney and excretory systems, and in the liver and nervous systems.
Split hair ends	Excessive volume of food; excessive volume of fruits, juice, soft drinks, and spices. Disorders in the intestinal digestion and reproductive functions.

Hair Condition	*Internal Condition*
Moustache and beard appearing in women	Excessive volume of food, especially animal protein and fat, including dairy food. Disorders in the reproductive organs and their functions, as well as in the endocrine system.
Lack of moustache and beard in men	Excessive intake of sugar, fruits, animal fat and dairy food. Disorders in the reproductive organs and functions, and in the endocrine system.
Short and thin eyebrows	Excessive animal food, including meat, poultry and eggs. Disorders in the respiratory, digestive, and reproductive functions.
Excessive body hair	Excessive intake of animal protein and fat; overconsumption of all food. General disorders in the digestive system.

4. *Hands and Fingers, Feet and Toes.* The hands and fingers are peripheral manifestations of the internal organs and their functions, as well as the energies working among these organs. Each finger carries particular meridians related to the functions of certain organs. Any excess is discharged through the hands and fingers toward the surrounding atmosphere, being carried from the internal part of the body toward the periphery through the circulation of blood and body fluid as well as through the electromagnetic flow along the meridians. Accordingly, the conditions of the hands, fingers, and nails show present and past internal conditions. The following are some examples:

Peripheral Condition	*Internal Condition*
Redness of the tips of the fingers	Active discharge of excessive energy caused by the intake of sugar, fruits, juice, soft drinks, spices, and other similar foods. Disorders in the nervous, respiratory, and reproductive functions.
Splitting of the nails and tips of the fingers	Excessive discharge of liquid, sugar, fruits, juice and soft drinks. Disorders in the reproductive organs and functions.
Irregular depressions on the surface of the nails	Imbalance of nourishment, especially caused by worms. Disorders in the digestive system.

Peripheral Condition	*Internal Condition*
Ridges on the nails	Excessive intake of salt and minerals, or, lack of protein and fat. Disorders in the liver and gall bladder or kidney and excretory systems.
Curved fingers	Disharmonious energy flow, particularly in the meridians appearing on that finger. Disorders in those related organs and their functions.
Rigidity of the fingers	Stagnated flow of energy through the meridians related to that finger, caused mainly by the intake of excessive salt and animal protein. Disorders in the corresponding organ and its function.
Wet hands and feet	Excessive intake of liquid, including fruits and juices. Disorders in the digestive, circulatory and excretory systems.
Warm hands	Excessive consumption of food and drink, including animal food. Disorders in the digestive and circulatory systems.
Cold hands and feet	Excessive sugar, fruits, and cold drinks. Disorders in the digestive and excretory systems, and in the nervous functions.
General swelling of the hands and feet	Excessive liquid and fat intake, especially caused by fruits, juices and dairy food. Disorders in the circulatory and reproductive systems.

The examples given above are only a few of the easily-noticeable conditions appearing at the peripheral part of the body in connection with disorders in the internal organs and functions. These peripheral areas can be used for the purpose of diagnosis and, at the same time, for the purpose of treatment. The acceleration or reduction of energy at the periphery can immediately influence the energy flow in the corresponding organs and other internal parts of the body. Stimulation given to these peripheral areas, such as through the use of pressure and temperature, can change the internal condition. Like many other medical treatments and physical exercises, Dō-In actively uses these peripheral areas to improve the internal condition.

e. The Relationship of Organ and Meridian Functions

Meridians, as mentioned before (on page 59)—14 major meridians, including the Conception and Governing Vessels, plus some additional auxiliary meridians—are electromagnetic currents appearing on the surface of the body, correlating with certain internal organs and functions. You may consider these meridians as energy flow extended from the compacted internal energy flow which is the organ and its activity. Accordingly, conditions appearing on these surface meridians reflect the conditions of the corresponding organs and functions. These appearances on the meridians are of numerous variety, indicating different conditions of the internal functions. The following are merely some examples of the relationships between the meridians and the internal conditions:

a. When a certain organ and its function becomes increasingly active due to excessive electromagnetic energy, a corresponding meridian running on either the arms or the legs produces more active vibrations, and points located on the fingers or toes along that meridian produce more active energy discharge.

b. When the metabolism of an organ is slowing down, the corresponding meridian decreases its energy flow and produces less vibration.

c. If there is any stagnation which appears as hardening, stiffness, or swelling at some part of a meridian, it indicates that a corresponding organ or function is stagnated.

d. If there is pain, soreness, or a tight muscle on some spot along a meridian, it shows that a certain area of the corresponding organ or its function is affected.

e. If a callus forms on a finger or toe, or on the sole of the foot, a corresponding organ is discharging accumulated mucus, fat and excessive energy.

f. If unusual skin color appears along a meridian, a corresponding organ is suffering with a degenerative condition.

These relationships between the meridians and the organs as well as their functions reveal that any stimulation given on a part of a meridian produces an immediate reaction in a corresponding organ and its function. Like all other forms of treatment and exercise, Dō-In actively uses the relationships between the meridians and the internal organs and functions: by giving pressure upon certain points, dissolving stagnation along a meridian, applying the palms to give heat and vibrations, or giving massage in order to accelerate the energy current flowing in the meridian.

f. The Relationship between the Part and the Whole

Every existence within the universe reflects all conditions of the entire universe within its constitution, structure, form, nature, and functions. The human being is a miniature of the universe. Within man, all factors composing the entire universe are practically manifested—space and time, radiations and waves, vibrations and currents, electromagnetic phenomena, as well as the motion of preatomic particles, elements and molecules, inorganic and organic substances, plasma and gas, liquid and solid; material and spiritual, physical and mental. Microorganisms are a living reflection of the macro-universe. A part represents the whole. The whole manifests into a part.

Similarly, a part of the body reflects the whole constitution of the entire body, physical and mental, and the entire body appears in a part of the body. There are numerous examples throughout our body, including organs, glands, tissues, and cells. The following are some examples which serve as common knowledge for our physical, mental, and spiritual development through the daily practice of exercises:

1. The Condition of the Eyeball

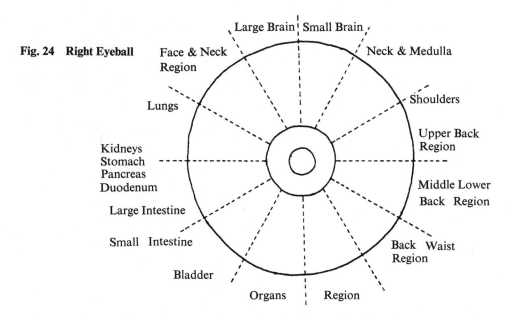

Fig. 24 Right Eyeball

The inner areas of the white of the eye represent the more compacted organs or areas in each region of the body, and the peripheral areas represent the more expanded organs or areas of the body.

In the science of iridology, the condition of the iris is examined for the purpose of diagnosing the internal condition; but the eyeball as a whole also indicates the whole physical and mental condition. As shown in the diagram, each section of the eyeball represents a different part of the body and its functions. Some of the major examples for diagnosis are as follows:

1. The Color of the Eyeball. In adults, the eyeball is normally white, while in the case of infants, it is slightly blue. If a part or all of the eyeball changes color, it indicates disorders in certain organs and functions.

2. A Bloodshot Condition, showing the expansion of capillaries, indicates the overflow of energy and the excessive circulation of blood in the corresponding region of the body. It also indicates emotional instability and nervousness as well as general physical and mental fatigue.

3. *Dark Brownish Spots* appearing in a certain region on the white of the eye represent hardening of stagnated mucus and accumulated fat, including the formation of stones. They also represent the formation of cysts if they appear in the region corresponding to the breasts or ovaries.

4. *White and Yellow Patches* appearing on the white of the eye often indicate heavy fat accumulation which is progressing toward the formation of cysts, tumors, and eventually cancer, in that particular region.

5. *Yellow and White Mucus Accumulation* on the lower part of the eyeball shows a heavy accumulation of fat and mucus in the lower part of the body, such as around the prostate gland, or around the ovaries and in the uterus. This indicates that a vaginal discharge is present in the case of women, and deterioration of sexual ability in the case of men.

6. *Red Spots* appearing in certain regions are probably at the end of expanded blood capillaries, and indicate stagnation of the blood or formation of blood clots in the circulatory system and organs in that particular area.

7. *Excessive Liquid* pooled around the eyeball generally indicates disorders in the circulatory and excretory systems, together with enlargement of the heart, expansion of the intestines, and frequent urination.

Fig. 25

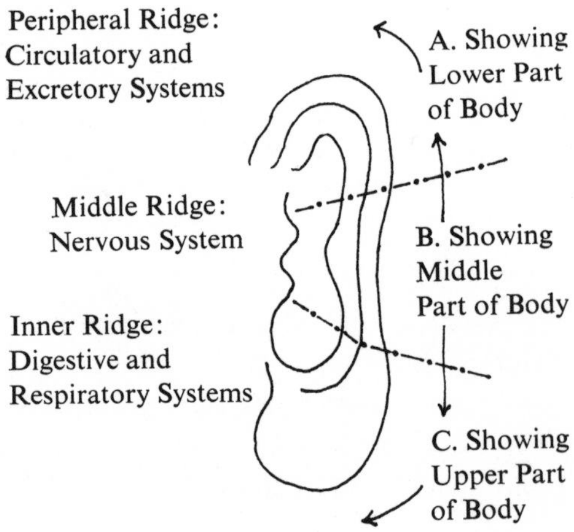

2. *The Condition of the Ear*

The ear represents the whole physical and mental constitution by its size, thickness, angle, position, and structure. Some major indications are as follows:

1. *Size:* Bigger ears indicate a stronger constitution developed during the embryonic period, while smaller ears show a weaker constitution. Especially wellformed ears with good, long earlobes represent a well-oriented constitution together with a balanced mentality. On the other hand, an ear with the upper portion more developed, and lacking an earlobe, indicates that nourishment during the embryonic period was more by animal food, resulting in an unbalanced physical and mental constitution.

Region "A" is nourished and developed more by protein; region "B" is nourished and developed more by carbohydrates; and region "C" is nourished and developed more by balanced minerals. (See Fig. 25)

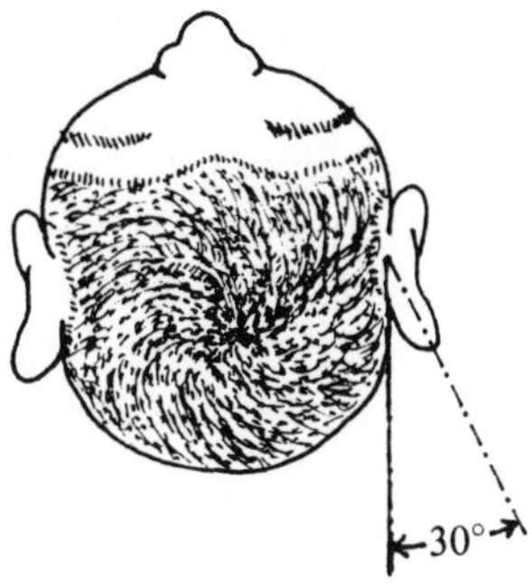

2. Thickness: Thick ears indicate a healthier digestive condition as well as a stronger bone structure, while thin ears indicate a weaker constitution which tends toward mental nervousness.

Fig. 26   Angle of the Ears

3. Angle: The angle between the ear and the head should be less than 30 degrees in the case of a normal ear, showing a harmonious balance between the physical and mental status. In the event the angle of the ear is more than 30 degrees, the physical constitution tends to be unbalanced, and also the mental condition.

4. Position: A normal ear is positioned so that the upper portion of the ear begins from the head at about the level of the eyes, and the lowest part of the ear-lobe ends at the level of the mouth. However, in the modern age, many ears begin their upper portion far above eye level, and the lower part ends far above the line of the mouth. The former condition represents a stronger constitution and a large mental capacity, while the latter indicates the opposite tendencies.

Fig. 27   Position and Shape of the Ears

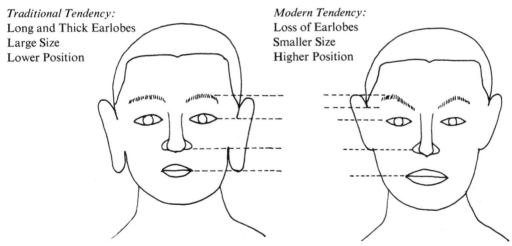

Traditional Tendency:
Long and Thick Earlobes
Large Size
Lower Position

Modern Tendency:
Loss of Earlobes
Smaller Size
Higher Position

5. Structure: The ear is structured in three vertical layers which respectively reflect the conditions of the interior to the periphery. In Fig. 25, the inner ridge shows the digestive and respiratory systems; the middle ridge, the nervous system; and the peripheral ridge, the circulatory and excretory systems. The lower portion of these three layers corresponds to the higher part of the body—for example, the area of the earlobe corresponds to the head and face; and the upper portion of the ear corresponds to the lower part of the body—for example, the area enclosed by the dotted line in Fig. 25 corresponds to the reproductive and genital organs. Along these three layers, approximately 200 points are located, each of which corresponds to a part of these systems, including the organs and glands, joints and muscles.

Accordingly, pressure, massage, and other stimulation given to these layers and points immediately influence the corresponding areas of the body.

3. The Condition of the Palm

The palm is another part of the body which represents the whole constitution and condition, physical, mental, and spiritual. It has been well known in oriental medicine as well as in ancient and medieval occidental medicine that the palm, including the fingers, represents personal physical and mental tendencies. With this knowledge, palmistry or palm reading has been developed, from an unknown ancient time. Palmistry is able to reveal personal tendencies and destiny, since each part of the palm correlates to part of the physical constitution. The following are some examples:

There are three major lines on the palm which represent the three fundamental systems of our body:

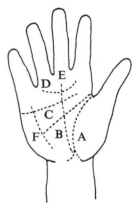

Fig. 28 Major Lines on the Palm

Line A, running from the indentation between the thumb and index finger down around the base of the thumb. This line represents the digestive and respiratory systems. The upper portion of this line shows the lower part of the digestive and respiratory systems, and the lower portion shows the upper part of the digestive and respiratory systems. In normal health, this line should be clear, deep, and the longest among all the lines on the palm. The reason this line is called the "Life Line" in palmistry is that physical vitality and longevity largely depend upon the condition of the digestive and respiratory functions. If this line ends before reaching the wrist, or if it is weak and shallow, it shows an inferior ability in the digestive and respiratory functions.

Line B, beginning at the inside edge of the hand near the beginning of Line A, crossing the palm toward the outside edge of the hand. This line represents the nervous system as well as the thinking capacity of the brain. It can be shorter than Line A, but should be clear and powerful in normal health. In palmistry, this line is called the "Line of Intellect." It shows a tendency toward determination if the line is shorter and deeper, although it also indicates a tendency toward rigidity. On the other hand, it shows broad comprehension if the line is long and flowing downward, although it also shows a tendency toward indecisiveness.

Line C runs from the outside edge of the hand below the little finger toward the inner edge of the base of the index finger. This line represents the circulatory and excretory systems, and it is desirable for it to be clear and powerful. This line could be shorter than Line A, the "Life Line," but the same or a little longer than Line B, the "Line of Intellect." If this line is weak and shows irregularities, it means the circulatory and excretory functions are not operating effectively at present. If this line is long, reaching almost to the root of the index finger, physical vitality and emotional aspiration are stronger than average. Due to the nature of the circulatory and excretory functions in influencing emotional change, this line is called the "Line of Emotion" or the "Heart Line" in palmistry.

Line D begins between the index and middle fingers, and curves toward the root area of the ring finger. This line is called the "Line of Love," indicating deep affection for other people or other beings. At the same time, it indicates possible complications in emotional affairs as well as human relations. This line does not necessarily appear on everyone's palm.

Line E, running from the center of the base of the palm, ascending vertically toward the middle finger, is called the "Line of Success" in palmistry. It does not appear on everyone's palm. When the mother was a hard worker during the time she carried the baby in her womb, or if a person has been working hard himself, especially in physical and social activities, this line often appears. Because this line has been created through physical and social activity, it has been considered as an indication of possible future success.

Line F, beginning near the center of the base of the palm, ascending toward the area between the little finger and ring finger, is called the "Line of Health," and appears only in some people. Like Line E, the "Line of Success," this line is created by good physical activity, either by the mother during the time of embryonic development or by the person himself during his growing period. If this line appears, his physical constitution has good resistance to environmental difficulties.

Other Lines.   There are many other minor lines running here and there throughout the palm. The more minor lines appear, the more changes in physical, emotional and social life tend to take place, and the more variety of foods have been consumed. Generally, it is more desirable that the lines on the palm be more simple and clear, showing that the person's growing conditions as well as his environment have been more simple and straight. It shows also that his consumption of foods has been simpler, but more well-balanced than average. All of the various minor lines have their respective correspondences to our physical, mental and spiritual conditions but, in general, lines going toward the fingers in a vertical direction are more desirable indications than lines running horizontally.

Because of the nature of the lines on the palms, as explained above, the palms can be used for diagnosis and treatment through the application of pressure, massage, and other stimulation. A stimulation given on a certain area or point of the palm immediately influences the corresponding system, organ, or area of the body.

4. The Condition of the Feet

In our usual daily posture, including most normal body movements, the relation of the feet to the body is complementary. For example, in the standing posture, while the whole body is vertical, the foot has a horizontal position; and in the sleeping posture, the resting body has a horizontal posture while the feet tend to be held nearly vertically. Accordingly, it has been known for the past several thousand years that the feet represent and correspond to the rest of the whole body. From this understanding, a modern physiotherapy called *reflexology* has been developed. Not only do each of the toes represent the functions of different organs, through the meridians connecting the toes with the inner organs, but also each area of the foot, especially on the sole, indicates each part of the body.

Such corresponding relations between the feet and the parts of the body are generally indicated in Fig. 29 below:

Fig. 29   Reflex Areas on the Feet

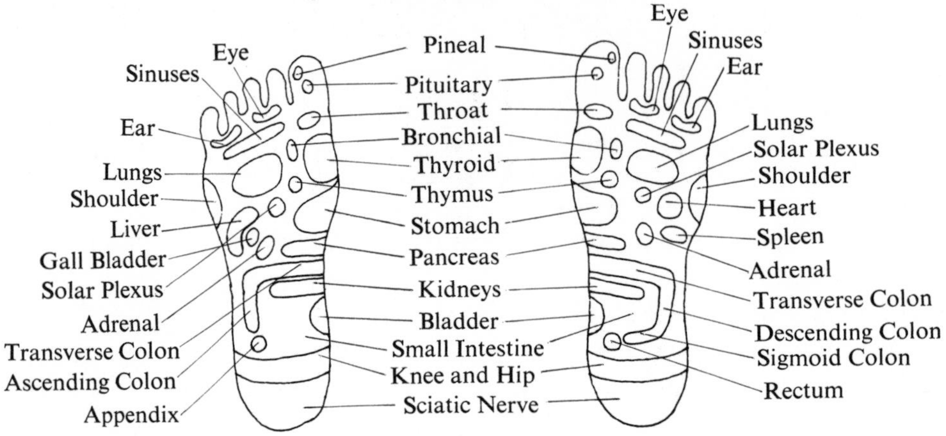

The area of the Achilles tendon, the top of the foot, and the area around the anklebones also have corresponding relations to various functions of the body.

Accordingly, pressure and stimulation which is given to a certain area by the application of a needle, moxibustion, finger pressure, or massage, can influence a corresponding organ, gland, or area of the body. When these stimulations are applied properly, with the appropriate kind of vibration and degree of intensity, they serve for the effective relief of disorderly conditions existing in the inner areas of the body.

These foot-organ correspondences also suggest that it is more advisable for the activation of physical and mental metabolism to walk or exercise with bare feet on the grass or earth from time to time, when circumstances permit. It is also advisable that we keep the feet and toes clean by washing them with hot or cold water once or twice a day, serving for the maintenance of general health.

In accordance with the physical and spiritual constitution of man, which is composed, as generally explained above, with antagonistic and complementary relations among the various parts of the body as well as physical and mental phenomena, any stimulation given to any part of the body, regardless of the nature of such stimulation—either material or spiritual, physical or vibrational—is able to alter the conditions and functions of various physical and mental phenomena. Dō-In exercises, like all other physical, mental and spiritual exercises, use such stimulations actively. But in the case of Dō-In, such stimulation is given in more peaceful and natural ways, in the form of self-adjustment. Dō-In aims not only for the healing and improvement of disorderly conditions, but also for the comprehensive development of our physical, mental and spiritual conditions in a harmonious daily life.

Part Two

The Exercises of Dō-In

Introduction to Dō-In Exercises

There are many exercises and treatments to improve our physical, mental and spiritual conditions, including western and oriental medicine, psycho- and physiotherapies, psychiatric and physical treatments, and the use of chemical and herbal medicines, as well as various technological branches of oriental medicine such as acupuncture, moxibustion, palm healing, and many others. However, Dō-In has unique characteristics in comparison with these other ways of physical, mental and spiritual development:

1. Dō-In has been developed from an unknown ancient time through intuitive responses which arise without special elaboration or theories, as everyone's natural reactions of self-adjustment.
2. Dō-In is completely self-exercise, unlike many medical treatments, martial arts, and other therapies which require the participation of other people.
3. Dō-In exercises do not require the use of any instruments, unlike acupuncture, moxibustion, and many other physiotherapies. They require only our own physical and mental functions, properly applied through self-adjustment.
4. Dō-In exercises aim toward our physical betterment and well-being, but they also aim far beyond the physical dimension toward the development of our mental and spiritual abilities for the achievement of true human nature as a whole, in all dimensions.
5. Dō-In exercises can be practiced by anyone, in any place, using only a short period of time; and therefore, they can easily be a part of our daily life, not requiring any special effort or placing a burden upon our daily activities.
6. Dō-In does not regard human beings as physical and material existences, but rather as manifestations of vibrational and spiritual movement, arising in the infinite dimension of vibration and energy in the ocean of the infinite universe.
7. Dō-In exercises are done in harmonious relationship with the natural environment, using the most advantageous time, place, and posture, as well as natural phenomena such as the motions of the sun and the wind.

There are several series of Dō-In exercises, which are introduced in the following order:

1. Special Exercises: These exercises are not presented as a series of movements, but are introduced independently as basic physical, mental and spiritual exercises. Any of them may be practiced at any time for their specific purposes.

[95]

2. Spiritual Exercises: This series is especially designed for mental and spiritual development in the form of daily exercises. When this series is practiced, it can effectively achieve mental and spiritual development in harmony with nature and the universe, resulting naturally in physical well-being.

3. Daily Exercises: These Daily Exercises encourage the smooth and orderly functioning of our daily way of life as well as the harmonization of our condition as a whole. They include Morning Exercises, Evening Exercises, Meridian Extensions, and Additional Exercises.

The series of Morning Exercises aims to generate our physical, mental and spiritual vitality, actively but in peaceful harmony with the surrounding conditions. The Evening Exercises are to bring about a state of physical and mental peace and relaxation at the close of the day. The series of Meridian Extensions aims to generate active and harmonious energy flow through the meridians, in order to relieve any fatigue caused either by stagnation or by lack of energy flow throughout the body after unnatural activities. The Additional Exercises include exercises to induce sound, peaceful sleep by complete relaxation in a reclining posture, and the method of keeping the nasal cavities clean in order to maintain smooth breathing.

4. General Exercises: This series of exercises aims to activate energy flow in each area of the body together with the recovery of the harmonious functions of various organs, glands and systems. These exercises cover the whole body, using various applications of pressure, massage, rubbing, and other stimulation which can be done easily.

Chapter 1

Special Exercises (SP)

Introduction

The Special Exercises introduced here are some representative exercises, each of which has a special purpose. These Special Exercises can be practiced any time and any place, not as a series, but as independent exercises. All of these exercises, however, require the proper biological and psychological conditions as a preparatory ground, realized through the daily practice of the macrobiotic way of life.

These Special Exercises are mainly oriented toward our mental and spiritual development, but they naturally include physical improvement as well. Some of them have been practiced in Zen and other types of meditation. Some of them have been used in yoga training, and others in prehistoric Shinto and other religious practices. Many of them are here recovered and modified into simple, practical form, with the addition of new understanding.

Using the exercises introduced here, an almost limitless variety of exercises can be developed in order to reach the same goal—that is, the unlimited development of the whole personality. Spiritually developed personalities known throughout our history practiced one or more of these exercises, through which they could begin to master their physical and mental freedom.

I have named each of these exercises according to its traditional meaning and purpose, and have specially refined and modified some of them in order to introduce the general scope of the various exercises. Through any of them you may begin to enter into the larger domain of the mental and spiritual world.

The exercises introduced are as follows:

SP 1 (天台) Ten-Dai: Heavenly Foundation: In this exercise, we study several sitting postures which are essential to practice physical, mental and spiritual exercises. In the beginning and at the end of each Dō-In exercise, we should return to one of these postures. These sitting postures are all centered at the lower abdomen—the Second Chakra, the physical center—to stabilize ourselves firmly upon the earth.

SP 2 (愛和) Ai-Wa: Love and Harmony: This exercise is centered at the Fourth Chakra, the heart and emotional center, to develop our devotion together with love and harmony. This exercise generates harmonious relations with all surrounding people and environmental conditions.

SP 3 (昇天) Shō-Ten: Ascending to Heaven: This exercise is centered at the

[97]

Sixth Chakra, the midbrain area, in order to expand our consciousness beyond the relative world, freeing us toward the unlimited sphere beyond time and space. It is also an experience of the gradual process toward our physical death and the birth of unlimited awareness.

SP 4 (霊能) *Rei-Nō: Development of Spiritual Power:* This is an exercise to develop our extraordinary power—physical, mental and spiritual. It is centered at the Third Chakra, the stomach region, to keep energy fully within our body, producing unusual physical and mental abilities when it is released. Through the daily practice of this exercise, many people may be able to develop almost miraculous powers.

SP 5 (和順) *Wa-Jun: Development of Gentle Harmony:* This exercise is for the purpose of producing harmony among our own physical, mental and spiritual functions. Through this exercise, a well-rounded, peaceful personality can be developed. This exercise is very useful for harmonious human relations.

SP 6 (内観) *Nai-Kan: Inner Reflection:* Whenever we encounter difficulties, this exercise can be practiced in order to recover our real self and regain personal confidence within the universe. The discovery of our own defects and mistakes, as well as the solution for our problems, can be achieved through this practice.

SP 7 (外観) *Gai-Kan: Outer Reflection:* This exercise is complementary to the above internal reflection. Its purpose is to release our self-centered consciousness toward the infinite dimension, developing selflessness. It is essential to realize in all aspects of our life that life is eternal and universal.

SP 8 (神拝) *Shin-Pai: Spiritual Worship:* This exercise automatically results from the state of selflessness; it is the action of the humble person who surrenders his ego to the environment, as well as to nature and the universe. The daily practice of this exercise develops the spirit of endless gratitude toward everything, through which daily happiness is experienced.

SP 9 (天舞) *Ten-Bu: Heavenly Dance:* The practice of this exercise enables us to remember our infinite life from which all creation has developed. The frequent performance of this dance establishes our unshakeable faith as one with the infinite universe.

SP 10 (霊視) *Rei-Shi: Spiritual Sight:* This exercise encourages our potential power to see the vibrational world: the aura, mind, thoughts, waves, and various spiritual phenomena arising around us. It includes the development of the ability to see the energies and radiations nourishing us and discharging from us, as well as the forms of energy known as ghosts, souls, and spirits appearing and disappearing around us.

SP 11 (靈動) *Rei-Dō: Spiritual Movement:*   This exercise allows us to experience the natural movement arising at the time of complete selflessness, as we become the subject of environmental·forces, especially the powerful influences from heaven and earth. These "spiritual movements" are the ultimate expression of the individual person, utilizing various forces of the environment without the participation of our consciousness. The daily practice of this exercise can develop our ability to submit ourselves to such natural forces, sometimes resulting in the production of miraculous performances.

SP 12 (地行) *Chi-Kō: Walking on the Ground:*   This exercise is further divided into (A) Ordinary Walking, and (B) Faster Walking, which also represent various other methods of walking. Through the exercise of these ways of walking we are able to develop the most natural, tireless, and effective physical movement. This exercise also enables us to understand our physical relationship with the environment, especially the atmosphere.

SP 13 (降魔) *Gō-Ma: Cutting through Delusions:*   When we are suffering with heavy delusions in the form of confusion, unpleasant memories, and various other mental disturbances, this exercise greatly helps to clarify these circumstances. This exercise can also help to awaken us from any obsession by gathering our physical, mental and spiritual conditions into one force.

SP 14 (言靈) *Koto-Dama: The Spirit of Words:*   Words represent all environmental vibrations, together with our physical and mental conditions. The practice of the proper pronunciation of certain sounds can alter our physical, mental and spiritual conditions. Several examples are introduced for daily practice to strengthen our physical conditions as well as our mental and spiritual powers. The use of the Spirit of Words can develop our experiences of unlimited vibrational words, through which we are able to direct our destiny toward a certain orientation.

SP. 1 （天台） Ten-Dai: Heavenly Foundation

Select any of the following sitting postures in order to stabilize the physical, mental, and spiritual condition toward the center of the earth, using the force of heaven which passes straight through our body vertically.

Fig. 30

Fig. 31

a. （正座） Sei-Za: Right Sitting Posture

Sit on either the ground or the floor with natural straight posture, the muscles relaxed, including the shoulders and elbows. Leave a distance the size of one fist between the knees (Figs. 30 and 31).

b. （中座） Chū-Za: Right Sitting Posture on a Chair

Sit deeply in the chair with natural straight posture, the knees bent at a ninety-degree angle. There should be a distance the size of one fist between the knees, as in the *Sei-Za* posture (Figs. 32 and 33).

c. （蓮華座） Ren-Ge-Za: Lotus Flower Posture

Sit on either the ground or the floor, the legs crossed with each foot on the opposite thigh. Hold the spine naturally straight by putting a cushion about four inches in height under the buttocks (Fig. 34).

Fig. 32

Fig. 33

Fig. 34

Fig. 35

Fig. 36

d. (半蓮華座) Han-Ren-Ge-Za: Half-Lotus Flower Posture

Sit on the ground or floor, the legs crossed, with one foot resting on the opposite thigh and the other on the floor (Fig. 35). In order to keep naturally straight posture, a cushion approximately four inches in height may be placed under the buttocks.

e. (胡座) Ko-Za: Rounded Sitting

Sit with naturally straight posture, the legs open more than ninety degrees, the soles of the feet flat against each other (Fig. 36). In order to keep the spine naturally straight, a cushion may be placed under the buttocks.

After selecting one of the above postures, rest the left hand on the right, palms up, thumbs touching one another so that the spirals at the tips of the thumbs meet. Keep the eyes either half-open or lightly closed. Relax the eyes, looking forward to the ground approximately ten to fifteen feet away, without focussing upon any particular object.

Begin long, deep breathing through the nose. Breathe in deeply, downward toward the lower abdomen, the region of the *Tan-Den* (丹田). Hold the breath for several seconds, allowing the abdomen to remain expanded toward the front. Then exhale with a slow, long breath. Repeat this breathing for about three to

Fig. 37 Heavenly Foundation: Inhaling

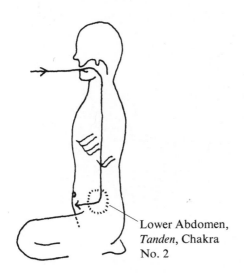

Lower Abdomen, *Tanden*, Chakra No. 2

five minutes.

During this period, have the image that we are stabilizing ourselves firmly upon the earth, as if we were immovable regardless of any circumstance.

The purpose of this exercise is to develop oneness in our physical, mental and spiritual constitutions as a part of the natural environment, and to establish inner confidence, invincible and unshakeable in universal faith. It also actively harmonizes the entire metabolism of the body.

SP. 2 (愛和) Ai-Wa: Love and Harmony

The purpose of this exercise is to develop our feeling of love and harmony either toward a certain person or many people, or toward a certain idea or thought. It is also to dissolve our emotional conflicts and obstacles which may exist in our relation with some other person or unfamiliar thought.

Although there may be no particular person to whom we wish to dedicate our love, and no particular thought with which we wish to realize our harmony, if we practice this exercise every so often, dedicated to all people and beings, we are able to achieve a spirit of universal love and harmony.

This exercise can be practiced alone or with any other person. Especially for two persons between whom mutual love and harmony are to be achieved, the practice of this exercise, performed by looking gently into each other's eyes, can heighten the inspiration of love and harmony to realize the feeling of oneness.

This exercise generates the active flow of the electromagnetic force running through our spiritual channel, and especially illuminates the region of the heart, accelerating the circulation of blood. It produces active vibrations which are spirallically radiated from the center of the chest area—the emotional chakra— which results in the rapid elevation of the feeling of love and harmony.

We make our back naturally straight in Natural Right Sitting Posture on a chair, the ground, or the floor so that our spiritual channel may smoothly carry the forces of heaven and earth.

We keep our eyes half-open, looking toward the infinite distance without focussing on any particular point.

We open both our arms wide, as if ready to accept and embrace all things. Both hands are naturally opened toward the front, with no tension. (See Figs. 38 and 39.)

Fig. 38 **Fig. 39**

We start to breathe with our chest, especially at the area of our heart, with a long, gentle inhalation slightly longer than the exhalation. Both inhaling and exhaling should be done through our slightly opened mouth. At the time of inhaling, we slightly move our chest area forward, as if our body is beginning to glide toward flying in space. As we gently exhale, our body naturally returns to the original straight position.

Fig. 40   Meditation of Love: Inhaling

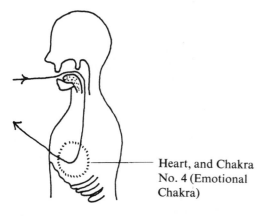

Heart, and Chakra No. 4 (Emotional Chakra)

While we are repeating this breathing and motion of our body, we have an intensive clear image in our mind of the person or persons to whom our love is to be dedicated, or of the thought or idea with which harmony is to be realized. During this exercise, we silently repeat the words "love" and "harmony" in our mind.

We continue this exercise for three to five minutes, and then return to the normal meditating posture and gradually diminish the image and words.

SP. 3   (昇天) Shō-Ten: Ascending to Heaven

This exercise emphasizes the inner brain chakra—the region of the midbrain, where most stimuli gather from all peripheral regions of the body, and from which they are distributed to various parts of the brain. The region of the midbrain is also the center for generating consciousness. The opposite of SP 1, which strengthens the area of *Tan-Den* (丹田), the abdominal center or physical center, this exercise inspires the mental center, *Ten-Dai* (天台). Accordingly, SP 1, Heavenly Foundation, may be called a yang ($\triangle$) exercise or yang meditation, while this exercise, Ascending to Heaven, may be called a yin ($\triangledown$) exercise or yin meditation.

The practice of this exercise produces the gradual slowing of all physical metabolism, including slowing of the heart beat, decrease of body temperature, and gradual loss of sensory perception. Together with the decline in physical metabolism, mental function becomes more intensified toward a pure state, overcoming various illusional thoughts, and our consciousness as a whole tends to experience separation from physical bounds. So-called "consciousness travel" or, more simply expressed, "seeing distant events," can be experienced. In this sense, this exercise may be called the "Meditation of Death," while SP-1 may be called the "Meditation of Life."

In the midst of a quiet environment, we sit with Natural Right Sitting Posture (DSE 1, page 131), making ourselves completely relaxed.

Fig. 41   Fig. 42

We open both arms in complete relaxation and keep our eyes either lightly closed or half-opened, looking up at least forty-five degrees or higher and, if possible, toward the center of our forehead—the place of the "Third Eye." All muscles of the face are to be relaxed.

We breathe through the mouth, with a long intensive inhalation, and a short relaxed exhalation which occurs as a natural reaction to the release of the long breath. The inhalation should be made toward the midbrain, as if the breath is passing out toward heaven through the center of the brain. The longer we breathe in, the more profound the effect becomes; and the higher our breath goes up, the deeper the result becomes.

Fig. 43 Meditation of Spiritualization (▽ Meditation): Inhaling

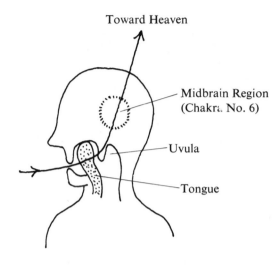

Toward Heaven

Midbrain Region (Chakra No. 6)

Uvula

Tongue

We repeat this special breathing for three to five minutes. During this period, we increasingly experience our physical metabolism slowing down, our body temperature becoming lower, and our mouth and hands becoming drier. Together with these changes, we experience our relative senses gradually diminishing and our consciousness starting expand.

After some duration of these experiences, we gradually return to normal breathing and return both eyes to normal condition. In the event we feel unbearably cold, we practice, for only a few minutes, the Breathing of Physicalization (page 44) in order to vitalize our physical energy.

SP. 4 (霊能) Rei-Nō: Development of Spiritual Power

This exercise is to develop our potential ability for extraordinary physical, mental and spiritual power. Among the seven chakras, this exercise is centered upon the Third Chakra, at the stomach region, which is centrally located among the five chakras of the body area. Concentration of our consciousness on the region of this chakra brings forth the intensive unification of various physical functions which, in turn, influence the unity of our mental and spiritual functions in other aspects, including our brain and nervous activities.

The continuous practice of this exercise thus produces the intensive unification of our physical, mental and spiritual capacities.

In the exercise, the region of the Third Chakra is fully energized, and all activities of the various organs in the middle region of the body, such as the stomach, pancreas and spleen, liver and gall bladder, and the kidneys, together with the orthosympathetic nervous actions, are intensively and harmoniously united. This active unity of the various functions of the middle region of the body can release free activity of energy and electromagnetic charge in all other regions, including the brain and nervous system, lungs and respiratory system, intestines and digestive system, as well as the arms and hands, legs and feet. Thus, consciousness which functions freely becomes able to govern our physical activities freely, resulting in the development of extraordinary physical, mental and spiritual powers.

It is preferable to do this exercise in natural surroundings outdoors, where the forces from heaven and earth are actively charging our body, rather than inside the

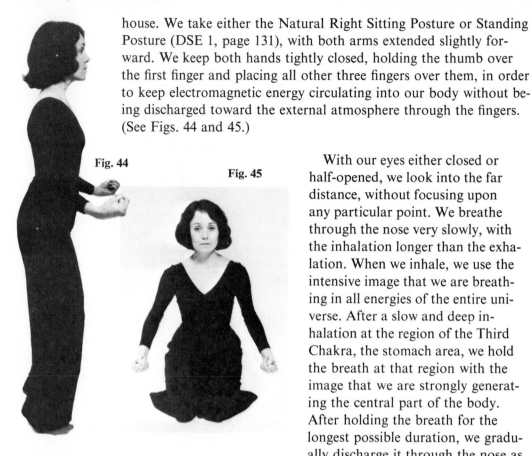

Fig. 44

Fig. 45

house. We take either the Natural Right Sitting Posture or Standing Posture (DSE 1, page 131), with both arms extended slightly forward. We keep both hands tightly closed, holding the thumb over the first finger and placing all other three fingers over them, in order to keep electromagnetic energy circulating into our body without being discharged toward the external atmosphere through the fingers. (See Figs. 44 and 45.)

With our eyes either closed or half-opened, we look into the far distance, without focusing upon any particular point. We breathe through the nose very slowly, with the inhalation longer than the exhalation. When we inhale, we use the intensive image that we are breathing in all energies of the entire universe. After a slow and deep inhalation at the region of the Third Chakra, the stomach area, we hold the breath at that region with the image that we are strongly generating the central part of the body. After holding the breath for the longest possible duration, we gradually discharge it through the nose as slowly as possible with the image that we are returning our energy to the universe.

During this exercise, we pay no attention to other parts of the body, making all other regions including the head and neck, chest and abdomen, arms and hands, legs and feet, completely relaxed. If we have taken the standing posture, our body naturally bends forward slightly as if the whole body is floating in the air.

We practice this exercise for fifteen to thirty minutes. We practice it every day, as often as possible—at least once a day. If we practice it during the daytime, we face toward the sun; and if we practice it at night, we face toward the South, in order to produce the maximum effect.

SP. 5　(和順)　Wa-Jun: Development of Gentle

Using the vibrational flow that circulates vertically around the peripheral sphere of the body, this exercise is to achieve peaceful stability in our physical and mental conditions. The Conception Vessel flows in the frontal periphery of the body, and electromagnetically generates the Heart Governor and Triple Heater functions. It also internally coordinates the respiratory and digestive functions, together with the circulation of blood and other body fluids. The Governing Vessel runs along the

Fig. 46   Fig. 47

spinal column and vertebrae, parallel with the Bladder Meridian, in the posterior region of the body. These energies flowing in both regions, front and back, coordinate together to maintain harmonious functions among the body and mind, digestive and nervous actions, as well as among various organs and glands.

In order to achieve peaceful and harmonious relations among our physical, mental and spiritual functions throughout the whole body, three major functions are to be in harmony: (1) eating and drinking, (2) breathing, and (3) thinking. The way of eating food and drinking liquid is to be practiced daily according to macrobiotic principles. In this exercise, therefore, the control of breathing and thinking are the major factors to be emphasized. If we practice this exercise regularly and often, we develop a peaceful personality with clear gentle expression and attitude.

We take the Natural Right Sitting Posture for meditation, as illustrated in Figs. 46 and 47, with both hands placed near the body on the thighs, the left hand on the right hand in the case of right-handed persons, and the right hand on the left in the case of left-handed persons. In the beginning we maintain natural and quiet breathing—the Breathing of Harmony (see page 43), with the eyes lightly closed or gently half-open, without focussing upon any particular point. We make our various thoughts quiet down gradually to reach the state of no-thinking.

Then, we begin to breathe deeply and slowly. During the inhalation, we draw our image clearly that the energy of the earth enters into the lowest end of the spine, going up along the vertebrae, and circulates around the surface of the head from the neck to the forehead, passing through the nose and ending by reaching the mouth. During the exhalation, our image guides the force of heaven coming down from the mouth toward the throat and chest, then the stomach to the abdomen, ending by reaching the region between the anus and the genital area. In other words, through the guidance of our conscious image, smooth circulation of the energies of both heaven and earth envelop our body along the Governing and Conception Vessels, the nervous system and the respiratory-digestive systems.

We repeat this special breathing deeply and slowly in smooth, circular rhythmic movement, for about five to ten minutes. Then we return to meditation, keeping silence and peace in our mind, where we stay for another two to three minutes.

SP. 6 (内観) Nai-Kan: Inner Reflection

This exercise can be used anywhere in quiet surroundings, whenever we wish to reflect within ourselves by recovering the clear consciousness that we are physically ephemeral but spiritually eternal. The major purpose of this exercise is to harmoniously charge our body with the forces of heaven and earth, realizing oneness between our physical and mental existence and our surroundings, especially the infinite universe. In this exercise, the use of any compulsory force should be avoided; rather, we should achieve complete relaxation within the stable posture. Thinking should go on naturally, like the wind whispering; breathing should be natural, like water streaming down. Whatever motive prompted us to perform this meditating exercise, it is important not to attach to that motive, but to try to make ourselves a pure existence as part of the universe.

Fig. 48

Facing to the South, we take the sitting posture as illustrated in Fig. 48, the head slightly bowed with no tension in the neck and shoulders, in order to receive from the infinite distance of the northern sky the heavenly force penetrating and charging our body through the center of the hair spiral, which meets with the earthly force in the spiritual channel. The fingers are interlaced and the thumbs touch at the tips. The elbows, wrists, and all joints of the fingers should be relaxed to facilitate the harmonious flow of energy.

We begin to breathe naturally and peacefully, with long duration. The exhalation should be three to five times longer than the inhalation. However, in the performance our consciousness of breathing should soon be eliminated. We keep both eyes half closed, focussing slightly downward at no particular point, toward a distance of ten to fifteen feet. Our mouth should be closed naturally, in a completely relaxed state.

With this posture and breathing, we begin to diminish our various thoughts and delusions. If we have been suffering with unsettling images and confusion, we try to gradually change them into more peaceful images, which are much easier to diminish, When our consciousness reaches a state of peaceful silence and deep tranquility we develop the image that we are nothing but one with the infinite universe, with no boundary or limitation between ourselves and the universe. There is only endless and universal being, with no individual and personal manifestation: seeing, but not seeing; hearing, but not hearing; feeling, but not feeling; imagining, but not imagining.

We maintain ourselves in this selfless state for a duration of five to ten minutes. During this time, we are immovable and unshakeable by any external force: even if fire, earthquake or other catastrophes arise nearby, we remain undisturbed.

After this exercise, we gradually open our eyes, lift our head, and return to normal breathing. From that moment, we are able to conduct our physical, mental and spiritual activities as a newborn person, as if our life is fresh.

SP. 7 (外観) Gai-Kan: Outer Reflection

The human constitution is composed of the internal environment—the body and its components—and the external environment, nature and the universe. Humanity lives and works in harmonious balance between these internal and external environments. However, the internal environment has come from the external environment in the form of food and drink, which are inorganic and organic minerals, vegetables, animal life, and natural water. It has also come from the air—the gaseous environment—through our breathing; and from the world of vibrations, radiations, waves, and rays through our nervous system, together with their electromagnetic reinforcement.

Therefore, our human origin is the infinite universe, and our future is the infinite universe. Our present human status is nothing but a reflection of the endless and boundless external environment which ultimately expands beyond all relative worlds, space and time.

The meditation of Outer Reflection aims to discover our origin and source, our present and future, in the largest possible dimension in regard to the outer world, and to achieve our complete adaptation to the boundless outer world as its infinitesimal part. In this meditation, the ephemeral ego should be dissolved into the imagination of infinte space by the experience of a selfless state.

Fig. 49

We take the Natural Right Sitting Posture (as described in DSE 1, page 131), keeping the spiritual channel straight, with natural relaxation of all other parts of the body (Fig. 49). We take this posture with the sun at our back. As the position of the sun moves in the heavens, depending on the time of day, the direction we face may change. At night, we face toward the South if we are living in the Northern Hemisphere, and toward the North if we are in the Southern Hemisphere.

We place our hands on the thighs, holding them upward, touching the tips of the thumbs to the tips of the index and middle fingers, as illustrated. The shoulders, elbows and wrists as well as all joints of the fingers should be relaxed. We keep our face slightly upward, with the eyes half-closed, looking far into the distance toward infinite space, or lightly closed with the imagination that we are looking far into the distance. We breathe slowly and naturally through the slightly-opened mouth, the inhalation longer than the exhalation. The inhalation should be done toward the midbrain, as if air is being gathered in the inner depths of our brain. The exhalation should be done as if the gathered breath is released from the depths of the brain toward the boundless outer space.

As we do this special breathing, we gradually cease our various thoughts, entering into a state of no-thinking. When we reach a non-thinking state, we develop the image that we are completely free, in the form of spirit or in a formless form as a part of space. Through imagination, we recognize that we are nothing but an empty space which is expanding in all directions toward the infinite distance.

If during this meditation any thought begins to disturb us, we repeat in our inner heart with voiceless voice, saying: "I am Infinity"—as if spring water is bubbling out from the innermost depths of our heart.

We continue this meditation for about ten to fifteen minutes, and then return our breathing to normal and our head to normal position. In this meditating posture, we reaffirm our infinite status which is far beyond all relative perception and thinking, in order to prepare to enter into usual daily activity with the purest mind.

SP. 8 (神拝) Shin-Pai: Spiritual Worship

In order to be harmonious with the environment, including our relationships with other people and the natural surroundings as well as vibrational and spiritual phenomena, it is absolutely essential to be freely adaptable to these changing external conditions. Especially in our relations with seniors and elders, and with the natural-spiritual phenomena influencing us, we should be modest and humble, surrendering our egocentric delusions. Unconditional surrender is another expression of complete freedom, because freedom can be achieved only through complete adaptation. When we surrender ourselves to the presence of seniors and elders, and to any natural forces including the infinite universe, God, we dedicate our respect to them.

Before we dedicate our respect to anyone or any being, we must purify ourselves by eliminating the delusional vibrations which are emanating from us in the form of confusing physical energies and mental vibrations. Therefore, in the way of respect, we must always keep a reasonably balanced dietary practice according to macrobiotic principles, and we practice the following exercise of Spiritual Worship.

Spiritual Worship can be practiced every morning and evening for our ancestors' spirits, extending our appreciation to them for making it possible for us to be here. We can also use this Spiritual Worship for the appreciation of any force of nature and the universe, as well as the force of infinity, to which we owe our existence.

We take the Natural Right Sitting Posture (as in DSE 1, page 131), facing in the direction toward which we wish to dedicate our respect. We breathe slowly and naturally through the nose, and make our various thoughts calm down into a peaceful, gentle state. In order to reach this state, we may lightly close our eyes.

Fig. 50   Fig. 51   Fig. 52   Fig. 53

Fig. 54

When our mind reaches a peaceful state, we raise both arms to the position of the heart, with the palms held together in the prayer position (Fig. 50). We further pacify our mind, keeping this position for a while.

Then, with the palms still lightly attached together, we slowly extend both arms toward the front, and slightly slide the right hand down (Fig. 51). Immediately afterward, open both arms, forming an angle of about sixty to ninety degrees (Fig. 52), and quickly clap both palms together (Fig. 53), producing a sharp, clear sound which can penetrate the surrounding atmosphere and wipe out the delusional vibrations surrounding us. We repeat this hand-clapping two times. Both times, the sound should be as sharp and clear as possible.

Fig. 55

Gently withdraw the arms, returning the palms to the prayer position. Then, place both hands on the lap as before, in the Natural Right Sitting Posture. Sliding the palms down the sides of the thighs, we place them before us on the floor, forming a triangle with the thumbs and index fingers (Fig. 54).

We bow, lowering the head toward the floor, the nose toward the center of the triangle but not touching the floor—about one inch above the floor (Fig. 55). This bowing motion should be done together with a natural inhalation of breath. When we bow, the eyes may be naturally closed. Keep the bow for the duration of about two breaths. During this time, breathe with natural, gentle inhaling and exhaling. Then, with an exhalation, we slowly raise our body, sliding our hands up the sides of the thighs and returning to the meditating posture, continuing our spiritual respect and mental state of selflessness for a while before we finally return to the Natural Right Sitting Posture.

Throughout the exercise, we keep in our mind complete respect for that to which we are dedicating our thoughts. Especially while we are bowing, we should totally abandon our ego, keeping an absolute state of selflessness.

SP. 9 (天舞) Ten-Bu: Heavenly Dance

Fig. 56

In order to release ourselves from the various confusions of daily life and to confirm our spiritual nature, the Heavenly Dance can be performed at any time. We have come from the infinite universe, realizing ourselves in this infinitesimal, ephemeral world through the process of creation. Creation has taken place by the harmonious working of antagonistic and complemental forces, yin ($\triangledown$) and yang ($\triangle$). From the relative, ephemeral manifestation in which we have been realized, we dissolve our physical appearance, returning to the infinite universe. Therefore, our genuine self is nothing but the infinite universe itself, and our genuine self is nothing but the will of the infinite universe.

The Heavenly Dance is a series of forms which represent the process of creation, together with our declaration of wholeness. It serves for remembering our genuine status as the infinite universe which is omnipresent, omnipotent, and omniscient, and it serves for the re-establishment of our faith in our eternal and universal life. When we repeatedly perform this Heavenly Dance, we are able to develop the invincible confidence as the One who is immortal.

During this Heavenly Dance, we utter the following declaration in a clear voice, as we proceed with each step:

Fig. 57

> "I am, I am.
> I am the One.
> I am the All.
> I am heaven and earth.
> I produce yin and yang.
> I combine them into one.
> Thus I create everything,
> And I destroy everything.
> Then I resurrect them again,
> And I destroy them again.
> I am eternal.
> I am universal.
> Yet, I am Nothingness."

| Fig. 58 | Fig. 59 | Fig. 60 |

Step 1: We stand straight, holding our hands at the level of the lower abdomen —*Tan-Den*, the center of the body—as in the posture of meditation, with the left hand placed lightly on the right hand, palms up, and both thumbs lightly attached (Fig. 56). The eyes are open, looking into the infinite distance. Breathe with the lower abdomen to develod firm confidence within ourselves. During this posture, our shoulders and elbows as well as all other parts of the body should be relaxed. We say the words, "I am, I am."

Step 2: We keep standing still and slowly raise our hands to the prayer position, keeping both hands lightly attached, at the level of the heart (Fig. 57). We pronounce, with unshakeable confidence, the words, "I am the One."

Step 3: Slowly raise both hands in front of the face, and upward to the heavens. Then, gradually open the arms, drawing the largest possible circle (Fig. 58), saying clearly, "I am the All."

Step 4: We slowly lower the opened arms, then make the form as illustrated in Fig. 59, with the right hand raised from the elbow, palm facing toward the front, and the left hand extended straight out from the waist toward the front, with the palm facing upward. During this motion, we say, "I am heaven and earth."

Step 5: Keeping the same posture as in Step 4, form circles by touching the thumb and index finger of each hand (Fig.60), saying, "I produce yin and yang."

Fig. 61

Fig. 62

Fig. 63

Fig. 64

Fig. 65

Fig. 66

Fig. 67

Step 6: Slowly join the left and right hands, juxtaposing the circles which have been formed in Step 5, the left circle on top, the right circle on the bottom, and attaching the other three fingers lightly (Fig. 61), saying, "I combine them into one."

Step 7: We gradually open the arms, and with the palms upward, raise both hands upward in a waving motion, two or three times (Fig. 62), saying, "Thus I create everything."

Step 8: We turn our palms downward, again waving them two or three times slowly (Fig. 63), saying, "And I destroy everything."

Step 9: We turn our palms again upward, waving them as if raising up two or three times (Fig. 64), saying, "Then I resurrect them again."

Step 10: Repeat Step 8, turning our palms downward and waving them slowly two or three times (Fig. 65), saying, "And I destroy them again."

Step 11: We slowly bring our hand toward the center, lifting them up to the level of the shoulders, palms facing to the front, then slowly extend them to the front, as in Fig. 66. While we are extending the arms, we say, "I am eternal." From that position, we slowly open our hands to both sides, forming the largest possible circle horizontally (Fig. 67). During this motion, we say, "I am universal."

Step 12: Then, slowly return to the original form as in Step 1, in the standing posture of meditation (Fig. 68), saying, "Yet, I am Nothingness."

Fig. 68

We repeat this entire process with each declaration two times, and we end the Heavenly Dance.

SP. 10　(霊視) Rei-Shi: Spiritual Sight

We use our eyes to distinguish objects which are normally in a state of solid and liquid, and in some cases, masses of gas. We are not used to seeing vibrations, waves, and rays, with the exception of the very narrow spectrum of wavelengths which appears as light and color to our eyes. However, during the early period of infancy, with the condensed constitution of the central region of the brain which tends to attract more varied stimulation, our eyes are able to see some vibrational phenomena. As we grow, together with the gradual loosening of the midbrain area, such ability gradually diminishes.

Spiritual Sight enables us to see vibrational phenomena, including the aura and electromagnetic radiations which form around the human body and other living beings. These also include the vibrational motion of the thoughts produced around our head, sometimes in the form of waves and sometimes in the form of mist, according to the nature of the thought. They further include vibrations and waves which we receive from distant living beings, and which gather around us either in the form of sparkling waves or as a series of massive vibrations. So-called ghosts, souls, and spirits, as well as personal radiations and various delusions, are not excepted.

In order to develop the ability to see through our eyes and to feel through our perception, our physical and mental conditions should be relaxed; but at the same time, our nervous system—especially the central part of our brain, the midbrain area, and the parasympathetic nervous functions—should be active. Such a state can be developed through our dietary practice, together with physical-mental exercises. At the same time, however, we are able to train our way of seeing, becoming accustomed to using our eyes without focussing upon certain objects, but rather looking at vibrations and space.

We sit with Natural Right Sitting Posture (Fig. 69), holding the back straight, with all other parts of the body relaxed. We breathe peacefully through the nose.

When we reach a state of tranquility, we raise one hand, holding it at the level of

Fig. 69

Fig. 70

Fig. 71

our eyes with the index finger standing straight up. Then, we look intensely at the tip of the standing index finger (Fig. 70).

We continue to focus on the tip of the finger, and suddenly move the finger out of sight, by rapid motion of that arm (Fig. 71); but we continue to look at the same point where the finger was, which is now empty. At that time, we may feel a slight dizziness and a cross-eyed sensation. We continue to see the same point in space, for more than one minute.

Then, we return our arm again to the same position in front, with the index finger standing. After we focus our sight on the tip of the finger for about ten seconds, we again move our finger out of sight, but continue to see the same point which is now again empty. We repeat this five times, and continue to do this exercise every day.

After we train our sight with this exercise for some period, about one or two weeks, we start to look at moving objects such as walking people, running animals, and the waving branches of trees with this same method. Then, we can start to see the vibrations which are surrounding these moving bodies, including their auras, radiations, and other movements of energy.

From that state, we further advance our ability of seeing to include all objects, looking at them but not focussing, trying rather to observe the whole view, including their surroundings. As we train ourselves in this way of seeing, we shall begin to see phenomena as solid material cores with vibrational peripheries. This shall reveal to us that matter is not material, but is nothing but a mass of vibrations and energy, having no boundaries as things independent or separate from their environmental space and the universe.

SP. 11 (霊動) Rei-Dō: Spiritual Movement

All of our body motions and mental activities, if they are arising naturally without special intention, are the natural progressive flow of energies which are constantly coming in toward us from the external environment, and constantly emanating from us toward the external environment. Under normal circumstances, they are causing our normal physical and mental movement; but when they are intensified, they produce extraordinary physical and mental activity.

Rei-Dō, Spiritual Movement, is unusual movement, produced without the participation of consciousness by the intensified charge of the energies which are interchanging between our body and the environment. There are many ways to induce Spiritual Movement, and they sometimes produce unexpected motions such as transportation, jumping to heights, floating in the air, rapid walking, and others. These motions arise only when our physical and mental attention is not in conscious control—in other words, in the state of unconsciousness or empty mind—at which time we are able to orient the degree and direction of the energies or forces which we receive and generate between our body and the environment.

The following is only an introduction, but we are able to develop from this stage toward the management of various spiritual movements.

Fig. 74

Fig. 72   Fig. 73

We either sit in the Natural Right Sitting Posture or stand straight, as in Fig. 72. We make all parts of our body completely relaxed. There should not be any rigidity remaining, except in our spine, which should be straight in order to actively receive the forces of heaven and earth. We keep our eyes either open or closed, whichever we feel is more conducive to calming our thinking, which should eventually be erased into a state of no-thinking. During this period, breathing should be done through the nose in the most natural and relaxed way.

Gradually, we take a form similar to the prayer position, by raising both hands and attaching the palms together reasonably tightly. The elbows are to be slightly to the front, and the hands are to be standing straight up, pointing toward the heavens (Figs. 73 and 74).

From our state of empty mind, we begin to image that heaven's and earth's forces, which are entering respectively from the head and the lower part of the body, collide harmoniously at the region of the heart, streaming rapidly down both arms toward the hands, and radiating out through the fingers toward heaven. Together with this image, we begin to make a rhythmical motion with our hands, up and down vertically. In the beginning, this motion is to be small, and should increase rapidly in its speed and vibration. As the motion increases, we erase our images of energy flow, entering into the state of empty mind, and allow our hands to move as their motion naturally increases in speed.

When this motion reaches a very high speed, our whole body begins to rise or jump. From this point, unconscious movement of the whole body occurs—repeated rising and falling, becoming increasingly higher. At that time, someone looking at us with Spiritual Sight (SP 10) would see that our whole body is radiating intense white light in all directions.

When we wish to stop this extraordinary movement, we separate our hands from each other.

Spiritual Movement serves not only for the understanding that very natural motion can be extraordinary if we do not control it with our consciousness, but also that all of our systems, our organs, and the trillions of cells of our body are charged by intensive currents of energy passing rapidly through our body through this movement, automatically dissolving all stagnation. Therefore, Spiritual Movement of any sort rejuvenates our physical, mental, and spiritual conditions. The repeated exercise of Spiritual Movement is desirable to regenerate our human abilities.

SP. 12　(地行)　Chi-Kō: Walking on the Ground

When we walk we usually rely on our experience of intuitive balance—left and right, front and back. However, in most cases, we do not fully utilize the energies coming from heaven and earth as well as from the surrounding environment to make our walking very smooth and effective. Physical imbalances, together with internal disorders and sicknesses, cause most of our walking to be inharmonious with the environment. Individual physical and mental habits also characterize each person's way of walking.

The human body does not grow from the ground; it extends vertically in both directions from the region of the mouth cavity and *medulla oblongata*—upward, forming the head, and downward, forming the body, arms and legs. In other words, the center of the body is floating in space and the lower periphery, the legs and feet, attach lightly to the ground. In Walking on the Ground, therefore, we should hold our body, especially its lower region, including the waist, thighs, legs, and feet, as lightly as possible. Briefly speaking, we should walk not with our legs and feet, but with our mind.

In order to familiarize ourselves with the real way of walking, the following exercises can be practiced every day, even for a short period like ten minutes, during daily walking.

Walking A: Ordinary Walking

We keep our posture straight, receiving the forces of heaven and earth in their maximum possible power, charging our body, then discharging through the arms and legs. We keep our sight straight forward as far as we can see, as if we are looking into the infinite distance (Figs. 75 and 76).

We breathe through the noss very naturally, with the exhalation three to five times longer than the inhalation. This longer exhalation is one of the important factors in walking and running in any circumstance. In fact, a longer exhalation in comparison to the inhalation is more effective to produce the smooth movement of our body, in walking with a peaceful mind.

We keep as the center of the body the region of the Third Chakra, the stomach region, always pushing it forward as if walking from that place. Both arms, if we are not carrying anything, should be held lightly and should move naturally front and back. We should not pay any attention to the legs and feet as we usually do, allowing them to move as freely as possible.

We find that with this way of walking we can walk twice as fast as in usual walking, while having a peaceful mind and lighter weight. At the same time, we are able to respond instantaneously when we need to change our direction, stop walking, or change our physical posture to meet new surroundings.

Walking B: Faster Walking

When we wish to walk faster or almost run for long distances we maintain our posture, as described in Walking A, to utilize effectively the forces from heaven and earth and the environment.

Fig. 75   Fig. 76

Fig. 77

Fig. 78

Breathing should be done through the nose and the slightly opened mouth, with the exhalation four to seven times longer than the inhalation. Our breathing is to be mainly exhaling, with the inhalation merely a reaction to the result of exhaling.

We keep the center of the body farther up than in the previous exercise, at the Fourth Chakra—the heart region—with all lower parts of the body completely relaxed, allowing them to respond freely.

When we walk with the shoulders, which we move slightly forward and back; and the arms and hands swing naturally, responding to the movement of the shoulders. While walking, we first put our body weight toward one side, either left or right, and we use that foot to support the body, using the foot of the other side to roll or move forward. After about 50 to 100 steps, we shift our body weight to the other side, and use the opposite side to roll or move. We alternate this way of using the legs every 50 to 100 steps. If we wish to walk more slowly, we alternate every 150 to 200 steps; and if we wish to walk faster, we alternate every 30 to 50 steps (Figs. 77 and 78).

The important point in this exercise is that although during the learning period we need our conscious attention to keep the proper posture and movement, we should eventually reach an unconscious state and keep an empty mind during this Faster Walking.

SP. 13 (降魔) Gō-Ma: Cutting Through Delusions

In our daily life, we produce various delusions in the form of mental-spiritual clouds of stagnation. We carry them around us as a misty mass of heavy vibrations. They may manifest as attachment, prejudice, jealousy, selfishness, greed, or anger, as well as seemingly inexplicable feelings of frustration, fear, and insecurity. Various Dō-In exercises serve to purify these clouds of delusion, but when they are heavily influencing us—in other words, when we are in confusion—we may need to cut through these massive surrounding delusions. The following method is one of several which we can use for this purpose.

It is not necessary to perform this exercise every day. It is to be performed only when we feel it is needed. This exercise is also to be accompanied with deep self-reflection, in respect to our way of eating and our way of thinking. Therefore, before and after this exercise, we may perform other Dō-In exercises to pacify and strengthen our physical, mental, and spiritual conditions.

Step 1: We sit in the Natural Right Sitting Posture (DSE 1, page 131). In the daytime, we sit with the sun at our back, and in the night we sit facing toward the South, having the Northern sky at our back. (In the Southern Hemisphere, we have the Southern sky at our back, facing toward the North.) We meditate, eyes closed, breathing through the nose quietly, in order to enter into a state of tranquility.

Fig. 79

Fig. 80

Fig. 81

Fig. 82

Fig. 83

Fig. 84

Fig. 85

Fig. 86

Step 2: We open our eyes, looking sharply toward the front. Holding our hands in front of our chest, we form the Seal of the Sword: we extend the first two fingers of the right hand, making the sword, and touch the tips of the other two fingers to the tip of the thumb. We place the extended fingers of the right hand across the left palm, folding the fingers and thumb of the left hand around them to make the sheath, except for the left index finger, which naturally extends (Fig. 79). (A left-handed person should reverse the hand positions.) We breathe with the Second Chakra—the lower abdominal region—to stabilize our confidence.

Step 3: We smoothly take out the sword from the sheath, pointing the right hand high above the head, while the left hand naturally points to the side (Fig. 80).

Step 4: We raise the right hand further above the head, ready to cut, and the right leg moves up and forward as we rise to our knee (Fig. 81).

Step 5: With a sharp voice, loudly uttering the sound "TOH," we cut quickly from the upper right toward the lower left (Fig. 82).

Step 6: Lift the sword hand (the right hand) back over the opposite shoulder (Fig. 83) (the left shoulder), and cut downward diagonally to the other side (Fig. 84).

Fig. 87 Order of Cutting Delusions in *Gō-Ma*

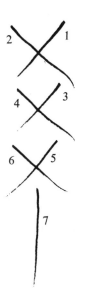

Step 7: Repeat steps 5 and 6 two more times, cutting right to left, left to right, right to left, and left to right.

Step 8: We hold the right hand pointing up straight (Fig. 85), and with a long, loud, sharp sound of "TOH," which comes from our *Tan-Den*, cut vertically straight down (Fig. 86).

Step 9: We then return to the meditating posture, making our breathing gradually calm down, until we return to a peaceful mind.

SP. 14 (言霊) Koto-Dama The Spirit of Words

In our daily conversation, we use various words and pronunciations to express ourselves. The sounds of these words are vibrations which are formed in the mouth, nasal and throat cavities in coordination with the vibrating uvula, the walls of the cavities, the teeth, the motions of the throat muscles, and the vocal cords, as well as respiratory movement. The forces which create these vibrations, however, are originally descending from heaven through the hair spiral in the center of the head, and ascending from the earth through the lower region of the body. Accordingly, when our physical and mental conditions are harmonious with the environment, through the daily practice of proper diet, thought and activity, the sound of our words is able to represent the powerful forces of heaven and earth, and our verbal expressions are able to carry the true vision of nature and the universe. Words or verbal sounds pronounced in such a healthy state, harmonious with the environment, represent the Universal Spirit, and give a powerful influence both to ourselves and to all beings surrounding us.

Fig. 88 Formation of Words

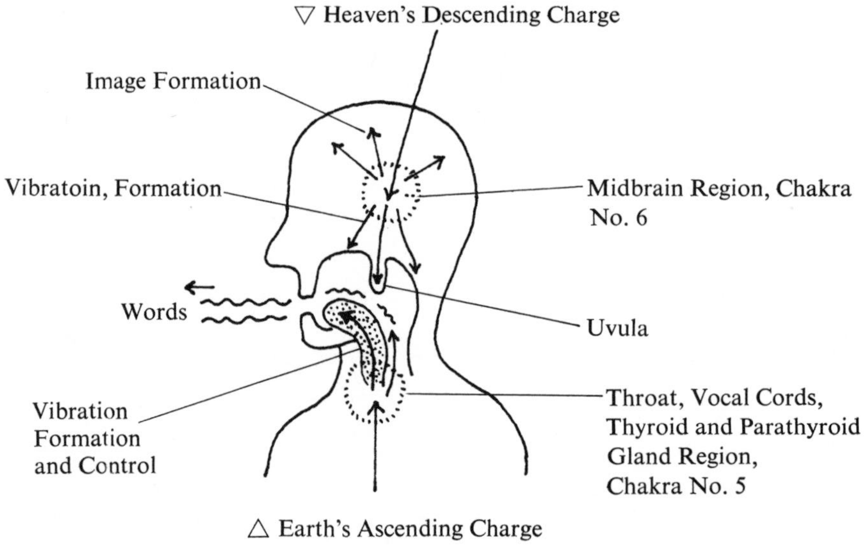

▽ Heaven's Descending Charge

Image Formation

Vibratoin, Formation

Midbrain Region, Chakra No. 6

Words

Uvula

Vibration Formation and Control

Throat, Vocal Cords, Thyroid and Parathyroid Gland Region, Chakra No. 5

△ Earth's Ascending Charge

Words and verbal sounds uttered in such a state are called *Koto-Dama*, the Spirit of Words. Each verbal sound which is pronounced when we are in a healthy condition carries its respective meaning and power, as well as its special effect to our physical, mental, and spiritual conditions. Among these sounds, some are pronounced with the mouth open—yin sounds—and others are pronounced with the mouth closed—yang sounds. There are many varieties in between. When our physical and mental conditions become more peacefully adaptable to nature through a dietary practice of vegetable quality, these sounds become more clear in pronunciation; while if our conditions become disharmonious with the environment through other varieties of food including heavy animal quality, our sounds become more rough.

The basic sounds which have been pronounced from ancient times in the Far East have been summarized into the following 50 sounds:*

A	KA	SA	TA	NA	HA	MA	YA	RA	WA
I	KI	SHI	CHI	NI	HI	MI	I	RI	I
U	KU	SU	TSU	NU	FU	MU	YU	RU	U
E	KE	SE	TE	NE	HE	ME	E	RE	E
O	KO	SO	TO	NO	HO	MO	YO	RO	O

1. The line of "A" sounds includes sounds representing various states of invisible forces.
2. The "I" line represents various sounds, forces and vibrations of life phenomena.
3. "U" and other sounds in that line show various states of harmony and balance.
4. "E" and the sounds of that line represent various states of art and creation.
5. The sound "O" and its line represent various states of physicalized form—the end of movement.

Fig. 89   *Koto-Dama*—Spirals of Sound

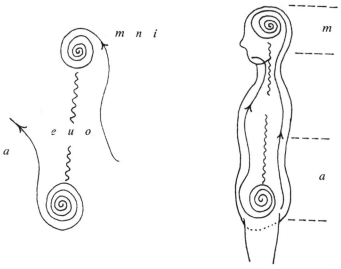

On the left are shown the spirallic patterns of the human body and the sounds corresponding to the major regions. On the right are shown the areas of the body corresponding to the sounds A-U-M, as described in the exercise below.

---

* The vowels are pronounced as follows: "A" as in "ah"; "I" as in "machine"; "U" as in "true"; "E" as in "grey"; and "O" as in "rose."

These 50 sounds vibrate respectively certain parts of the body, generating its activity: for example, "I" for the stomach and middle region of the body; "O" for the kidneys and back side of the middle region; "HA" more for the lungs and respiratory function. Therefore, the proper use of selected sounds can physicalize and spiritualize our daily activity. Some examples which we can use frequently in Dō-In exercises and physical, mental, and spiritual development are as follows:

1. The Prolonged Sound of "SU." This sound is for harmonization in peace between ourselves and all surrounding people and existences throughout the world. In our breathing, we sound "SU" in exhaling, with or without actually uttering the sound. Breathing is an interchange to harmonize ourselves with the surrounding atmosphere.

2. The Prolonged Sound "A-U-M." The sound "A," which is pronounced with the mouth open, represents the infinite universe, and physically it vibrates the lower part of our body. The sound "U" represents harmony, as we saw in the case of the sound "SU," and it physically vibrates the upper region of the body and the lower region of the head. The sound "M," which is pronounced with the mouth closed, represents the infinitesimal world and physically vibrates the most compacted area, the brain.

Therefore, if we pronounce "A-U-M," it is the expression of the whole universe, and vibrates our body and spiritual channel from the lowest part to the highest part, resulting in the active charge of vibrations and electromagnetic currents in our physical, mental, and spiritual functions. This sound, therefore, has been used in oriental countries for centuries to generate our life activity as well as to establish our existence as a part of the universe.

3. A Series of Sounds: "*HI-FU-MI-YO-I-MU-NA-YA-KO-TO-MO-CHI-RO.*" These sounds were universally used in prehistoric times by ancient people as the most basic and inspiring sounds for generating physical, mental and spiritual activity in their unified form. The series of these sounds also describes the creation of the universe. Each sound represents various specific meanings:

HI: Oneness or One; also, Universal Spirit, and fire.
FU: Two; differentiation or polarization, and the beginning of vibration and wind.
MI: Three; physicalization and materialization, or self.
YO: Four; direction and sphere. It also represents the world, as well as generation.
I: Five, and life phenomena. The most active relative intention or will; the center.
MU: Six. Phenomena of birth and motherhood. It also represents Nothingness.
NA: Seven. Identifiable relative existence or name. It also has the meaning

of vegetable quality, and the plant kingdom. The course to return to infinity.

YA: Eight. All directions and phenomena of radiation. It also represents infinity.

KO: Nine; infinitesimal being, as well as children or small things. It also represents the meaning of "here and now."

TO: Ten; accomplishment and construction; a building and gate. It also has the meaning of opening the gate toward infinity.

MO: One hundred; expansion, forming roundness. It also means harmony and further development, as well as mother.

CHI: One thousand. The variety of life phenomena and their common factor—blood, or energy. It also means father.

RO: Ten thousand. Harmony on a large scale; constant movement of spirals and circles. It also represents the central position.

Repeated pronunciation of these sounds as a series was practiced in prehistoric times in daily life, in the way of counting numbers, as well as to remind us of the process of creation of life phenomena within the one infinite universe. If we repeat these sounds in a positive and energetic way, as a physical, mental and spiritual exercise, it encourages us to lead a long and active life with a peaceful mind.

4. A Series of Sounds: "A-MA-TE-RA-SU-O-O-MI-KA-MI." In the prehistoric Far East, especially in ancient Japan, the series of these sounds was considered to have a secret powerful influence to protect our life and to elevate our physical, mental and spiritual quality. It has been called in traditional Shintoism, *Togoto-No-Kajiri*, or "Ten-Syllable Divine Words." As a whole, this pronunciation also represents the "Heavenly Shining Great Graceful Spirit," or God. Each syllable has its respective meaning, and the series of these combined syllables also represents the infinite universe and infinitesimal phenomena, and the harmony between them. For example, the first sound, "A," represents the sound of infinity; the last sound, "MI," represents the self; and the central sound, "SU," represents harmony, as mentioned before.

When these sounds are repeatedly pronounced in the form of meditation and prayer, which is done in the Natural Right Sitting Posture, active vibrations energize all parts of the body, and mental-spiritual vitalities start to arise, forming around us a shield of the aura or radiations, resulting in the performance of extraordinary abilities.

5. A Series of Sounds: "NAM-MYO-HO-REN-GE-KYO." This series of sounds has been used in one of the Buddhist sects as a chant and prayer. The meaning of this chant is: "Infinite Miraculous Law of the Lotus Flower Sutra," or "The Miraculous Order of the Infinite Universe," the teaching of which has been considered as the ultimate essential teaching of Buddhism.

The repeated pronunciation of these words energizes our physical and mental activity, producing our positive adaptability to the environment, resulting in beneficial contributions in our life. Together with this chanting, powerful vibrations wave out toward the surrounding space, which also give positive influences to the surroundings.

The above uses of the Spirit of Words in daily chanting or prayers are only a few examples. When we understand the influential power of each sound, we are able to freely produce certain combinations of sounds in the form of words and expressions for physical, mental and spiritual development. In fact, in the beginning of our life as human beings, we start to use the infant voice for our intuitive utterance of inner vibrations; these are produced physically and mentally, the human interpretation of the surrounding energies and vibrations that originate in the infinite universe.

Chapter 2

Daily Spiritual Exercises (DSE)

Introduction

When we wish to develop our physical, mental and spiritual constitutions as a harmonious unity with all surrounding people and environmental conditions, it is highly recommended that we practice the Spiritual Exercises daily, either alone or together with our family or friends.

As for the time of practice, it is most advisable to do them when the sun is rising from the horizon. However, these exercises can be practiced at any time, under any circumstances where the surrounding conditions are suitable. As for the place of practice, it may be anywhere, indoors or outdoors, though it is more suitable to practice them on the ground, in natural surroundings, especially on the higher level of a hill or mountain.

Clothing to wear for these practices should be simpler than the usual working clothing, and it is preferable to wear clothing made of vegetable quality materials such as cotton or jute, as far as they are directly in contact with the skin. Metallic or synthetic ornaments should be minimized in order to allow the harmonious circulation of physical, mental and spiritual vibrations which can achieve our adaptation to the environment.

These Daily Spiritual Exercises, if practiced regularly, can serve the development of the whole personality in physical strength, mental confidence and spiritual clarity. Some exercises have been known and practiced since ancient times and others have been recovered and developed by me according to the understanding of human nature physicalized upon the earth within the universe. These exercises have been specially refined and composed as one of several series of Dō-In exercises for anyone to practice easily, in the early morning at the time of sunrise. Each exercise should be performed like the smooth running of clear water in a gentle stream, and our performance of the entire series should be conducted with no interruption whatsoever from one exercise to another, as spring water bubbling out from under the bushes deep in the mountains forms a stream which runs down continuously, gathering water and becoming a river, and reaching the ocean at last.

The series of practices includes the following twelve exercises:

1. (正座) *Sei-Za:* Natural Right Posture and Natural Breathing
2. (瞑想呼吸) *Mei-So-Ko-Kyū:* Meditation and Breathing
3. (鎮魂) *Chin-Kon:* The Prayer of Oneness
4. (拍手) *Haku-Shu:* Purification by Hand Clapping
5. (阿吽) *A-Um:* Spiritualization by Sound Vibration

[129]

6. (天鼓) *Ten-Ko:* Beating the Heavenly Drum
7. (天露) *Ten-Ro:* Drinking the Heavenly Dew
8. (甘露) *Kan-Ro:* Tasting Nectar in Meditation
9. (天楽) *Ten-Gaku:* Listening to the Heavenly Music
10. (光明) *Kō-Myō:* Seeing the Inner Light
11. (和音) *Wa-On:* Sounding Harmonization
12. (平和) *Hei-Wa:* Pacification of the World

The Daily Spiritual Exercise 1 (DSE 1), Natural Right Posture and Natural Breathing, is the basis of the practice of all spiritual exercises, by which we prepare ourselves in a peaceful state.

DSE 2 is for generating the physical, mental and spiritual vibrations actively in a harmonious state by gradually changing our breathing.

DSE 3, the Prayer of Oneness, is the standard exercise for most prayers, using an intensive image. It especially enables us to become absorbed in our image of oneness.

DSE 4, Purification by Hand Clapping, is a traditional practice, especially in Shinto worship, for any spiritual phenomenon as well as the Universal Spirit, by wiping out any heavy stagnated vibration of delusion.

DSE 5, Spiritualization by Sound Vibration, has been practiced widely in India, originated by the ancient Vedanta philosophy which began at a further ancient time in the Far East.

DSE 6, Beating the Heavenly Drum, and DSE 7, Drinking the Heavenly Dew, are traditional practices for rejuvenation and longevity from an unknown age in *Shin-Sen-Dō* (see page 39), the way of life to develop into free man with natural and spiritual powers.

DSE 8, Tasting Nectar in Meditation, DSE 9, Listening to the Heavenly Music, and DSE 10, Seeing the Inner Light, are all arts to understand the universe through sensory and emotional experiences, and have also originated from *Shin-Sen-Dō* from an unknown age.

DSE 11, Sounding Harmonization, is the art of using the power of the sound of spirit and pronunciation, and has been simplified into a universal sound which is common for all people as a symbol of the universe. The sound particularly used here as well as in the following practice, DSE 12, symbolizes the center of the universe as well as the harmony among all phenomena.

DSE 12, Pacification of the World, is the art to universalize a particular image throughout the world by sending certain vibrations in all directions.

This series of Daily Spiritual Exercises is a harmonious combination of personal development for well-being and world development for universal peace, through actively using the forces of heaven and earth which are the origin of all relative manifestations on this earth, including ourselves. When these forces are flowing through our body vertically between the spirallic center of the head and the genital area of the body, they are respectively rejuvenated in different ways, through each of these twelve exercises. This series of Daily Spiritual Exercises as a whole develops our oneness with the infinite universe by developing our boundless consciousness.

DSE. 1 (正座) Sei-Za: Natural Right Posture and Natural Breathing

Face the rising sun.

Keep natural posture, either standing straight or sitting straight on a chair or on the floor or ground, as illustrated (Figs. 90–95).

Completely relax all parts of the body, including all muscles of the face, neck, chest, abdomen and back, as well as all joints of the shoulders, elbows, wrists, and other places, but keep the spine straight.

Breathe naturally and peacefully through the nose, with the exhalation three to five times longer than the inhalation.

Keep the mouth lightly closed and the eyes looking into infinite space toward the rising sun. If clouds, trees, houses, walls and windows are sheltering the sun, we keep our sight toward the infinite distance beyond them.

Fig. 90   **Fig. 91**

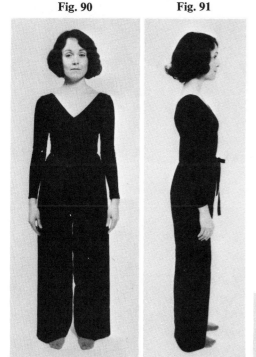

Fig. 92   **Fig. 93**

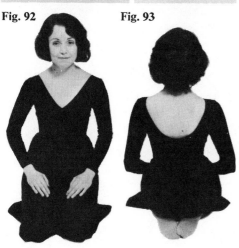

Fig. 94   **Fig. 95**

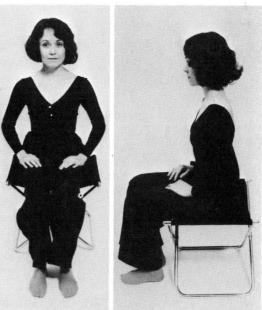

DSE. 2　(瞑想呼吸)　Mei-Sō-Ko-Kyū: Meditation and Breathing

Keep the posture as in DSE 1.

Gently move both arms and hold both hands together, palms upward, placing the left hand lightly on the right hand (in the case of a left-handed person, place the right hand on the left hand). Lightly attach the inner side of the tips of both thumbs in order to join together the spirals of the thumb tips. Place the hands naturally on the lap, close to the body (Fig. 96).

Begin the Breathing of Selflessness, steadily developing into the Breathing of Harmony, every few minutes; and then the Breathing of Confidence (page 43), the Breathing of Action, finally reaching the Breathing of Spiritualization (page 44), continuously performed about ten times.

Fig. 96

Then gradually return to normal and natural breathing, the Breathing of Harmony, which is maintained in a relaxed manner.

DSE. 3　(鎮魂)　Chin-Kon: The Prayer on Oneness

Keep the posture as in DSE 2, eyes looking into the infinite distance, with natural breathing. Gently dissolve the position of the hands, which have been on the lap, and lightly attach both palms with natural space between them. Gradually lift the

palms so that they are held at the level of the heart region—the posture of praying (Fig. 97). Keep this praying posture for about two minutes with the intensive image of our being as one with nature and the universe—the image of oneness.

See far away, but do not see any particular object. Receive all sounds freely, but do not listen to any particular sound. Accept unconditionally all of what we are feeling, but do not pay any attention to any particular feeling. Let our consciousness be absorbed completely into the unlimited ocean of one endless tranquility.

Fig. 97

DSE. 4 (拍手) Haku-Shu: Purification by Hand Clapping

Continuing to keep our consciousness in the unlimited ocean of tranquility of oneness we have achieved in DSE 3, and beginning with the same posture (Fig. 98), slowly extend both arms, holding both palms together, and stretch them with a natural curve, having no tension.

Then slightly slide off the right hand diagonally (Fig. 99), at an angle between fifteen and thirty degrees to the left hand. At the next moment, open the arms wide, about forty-five degrees (Fig. 100), and rapidly close them with the sharp clapping of hands (Fig. 101). The sound arising by the clapping of hands should be natural but clear and sharp, penetrating and echoing into the surrounding atmosphere, to the far distance. Repeat this clapping of hands only two times, representing heaven and earth, male and female, or yin and yang, which are primary differentiations of one infinite universe.

Fig. 98

The purpose of clapping hands with the clear and sharp sound is to swiftly wipe out any heavily stagnated vibrations manifested in delusional thought around our head, in unbalanced motion around our body, and in unharmonious movement in surrounding environment.

After two clappings of the hands for purification, return the slanted right hand to meet the left hand (Fig. 99), and then slowly return both stretched arms to the praying position (Fig. 98). A while later, gently return them by placing them on the lap, holding both hands in the meditating posture as described in DSE 2.

Fig. 99

Fig. 100

Fig. 101

DSE. 5 (阿吽) A-Um: Spiritualization by Sound Vibration

In the posture of meditation as described in DSE 2, lightly close the eyes, breathing in the beginning with natural breathing—the Breathing of Harmony (page 43)—with a gentle exhalation three to five times longer than the inhalation, entering into the imagination that we are one with the infinite universe (Fig. 102).

Then, deeply inhale through the lightly opened mouth and slowly exhale, five to seven times longer than the inhalation. During this long exhalation, pronounce the sound "A" (*ah*) with the widely-opened mouth, in the first period of exhaling; changing to the sound "U" (*u*) with the slightly opened mouth in the middle period of exhaling; and further changing to the sound "M"(*m*) with the lightly closed mouth

Fig. 102

and teeth. These continuous sounds "A-U-M" should be pronounced as naturally and as long as possible, and one sound should flow into the next as smoothly as possible, as if they are one continuous sound.

During the beginning part of exhaling, when "A" is pronounced, vibrate deeply inside the middle and lower regions of the body; and during the middle part of exhaling, when "U" is pronounced, vibrate deeply inside the upper region of the body as well as the lower region of the head, including the throat region. Finally, during the last part of exhaling, when "M" is pronounced, vibrate the whole head including the inner depths of the brain.

In other words, the purpose of this exercise is to clear our inner spiritual channel from any stagnation and blockages to allow much smoother passing of the forces of heaven and earth, letting them fully charge all cellular organizations throughout our body. It also actively energizes all digestive, respiratory, nervous, as well as circulatory and excretory functions.

After repeatedly exercising this Breathing of Spiritualization by the sound vibration A-U-M about ten times, return to normal and natural breathing.

DSE. 6 (天鼓) Ten-Ko: Beating the Heavenly Drum

Continue the posture of meditation (DSE 2), as pictured, keeping the eyes either continuously closed as in the previous exercise (DSE 5), or naturally open, looking straight into the distance (Fig. 103).

Begin the Breathing of Physicalization (page 44), and repeat it deeply about five times. Then, begin what is traditionally called "Beating the Heavenly Drum":

that is, strongly knocking the upper teeth and the lower teeth together by the rhythmical motion of opening and closing the mouth.

Strong sounds naturally occur as the lower teeth attack the upper teeth—sharp sounds of beating teeth against teeth—"ka, ka, ka." By actively moving the lower jaw, perform this drumming of the teeth in the following order:

First, the front part: beat about ten times.
Second, the left side: beat about ten times.
Third, the right side: beat about ten times.
Fourth, all teeth: beat about ten times.

This exercise has the effect of actively energizing the electromagnetic charge, together with the acceleration of blood flow, in the entire brain region. It also has the effect of inducing active metabolism among all systems, organs and glands, since each tooth represents a certain part of the physical constitution; as well as representing each vertebra of the spine, in the nervous system.

Fig. 103

DSE. 7　(天露)　Ten-Ro: Drinking the Heavenly Dew

Fig. 104

Upon the completion of the exercise of Beating the Heavenly Drum, keeping the same posture, return to natural breathing in order to begin the exercise of Drinking the Heavenly Dew. The eyes are to be kept either lightly closed or naturally open, looking into the far distance.

Using the tongue, collect the liquid in the mouth and the saliva from the inner, upper region of the mouth, the area of the palate. After gathering a mouthful of liquid and saliva, drink it down deeply, as if we are able to hear the sound of drinking, and we feel it going down through the esophagues toward the stomach. At the time of drinking, if we bend the head slightly downward and then lift it slightly upward, this can be more properly exercised (Fig. 104).

Repeat this drinking of liquid and saliva three times, each time collecting a mouthful of liquid and saliva by using the tongue.

The effect of this exercise is to activate the digestive function, normalizing the activities of those organs, together with the stimulation of various hormonal glands throughout our body.

DSE. 8 (甘露) Kan-Ro: Tasting Nectar in Meditation

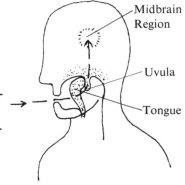

After the exercise of Drinking the Heavenly Dew (DSE 7), Tasting Nectar in Meditation naturally follows. The purpose of Tasting Nectar in Meditation is to experience the sweetness of breathing air, when it is charged by the force of heaven entering through the spirallic center of the head, charging the inner region of the midbrain and descending to the hanging uvula which is located in the inner mouth. (See Figs. 105 and 106.)

Fig. 106 Breathing Nectar in Meditation

Fig. 105 Location of the Uvula

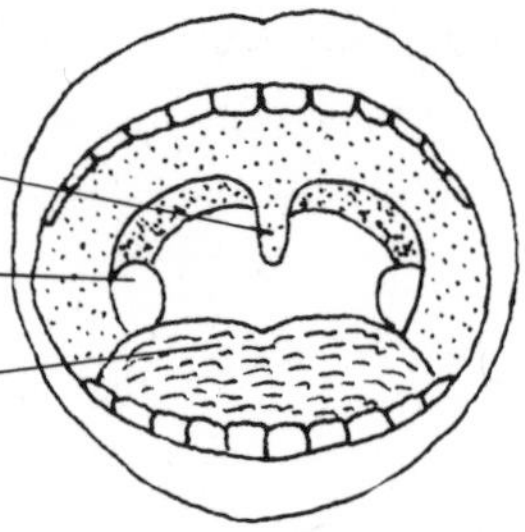

Keeping the same posture of meditation, hold the tongue slightly tighter and withdraw it toward the inner region, lightly attaching it to the inner upper jaw—the palate region (Fig. 107). Then, begin the long inhalation of breath through the slightly opened mouth, with the exhalation which naturally occurs as the result of inhaling. Repeat this breathing about ten to fifteen times.

Fig. 107

During the long inhalation, regularly performed, we experience a sweet taste at the area of the root of the tongue on both sides, which gradually spreads, covering the whole tongue and mouth cavity. At its most intense degree, we experience a taste as sweet as honey, or even much sweeter.

Together with our tasting of sweet breath, we meditate that the grace of nature and the infinite universe is far sweeter in spiritual nature than we can possibly imagine.

The experiencing of the sweet taste in Tasting Nectar in Meditation depends delicately upon the technique of managing the tension and location of the tongue, as well as the intensity of inhaling. Those who may not taste the sweetness in the beginning will be able to experience it as they repeat the exercise.

DSE. 9　(天楽)　Ten-Gaku: Listening to Heavenly Music

Keeping the Natural Right Sitting Posture as in the previous exercise, dissolve the hands from the meditating position on the lap, and lift them toward the ears. Deeply insert each thumb into each ear and fix them to prevent any external sound from entering from the surroundings. The four fingers of each hand should lightly hold the forehead, which is slightly bending down toward the front. (See Fig. 108.)

Fig. 108

Together with the Breathing of Harmony (page 43), repeated as slowly and gently as possible, listen to the musical sounds which are arising in the inner and front regions of the brain as well as deep in the inner ear. The musical sounds vary, including the sounds of drums beating in the air, the music of ocean waves coming and going along the shore, the stream of flutes sharply echoing in the sky, the melody of harps singing harmoniously in the clouds—all of which are composing the heavenly orchestra.

By listening to these musical sounds and melodies, we meditate in the understanding that nature and the universe are nothing but musical vibrations of an orderly nature, composing a grand orchestra which is beginningless and endless, infinitely complex. All phenomena appearing and disappearing in this universe are something like musical notes specifying certain sounds arising within the grand orchestra of the infinite universe.

DSE. 10　(光明)　Kō-Myō: Seeing the Inner Light

Sitting in the Natural Right Posture (DSE 1), and practicing the Natural Breathing of Harmony (page 43), slowly lift up the right arm (the left arm for a left-handed person) and place the index finger at the area of the third eye or at the center of the forehead with the thumb at the outer edge of one closed eye and the middle finger

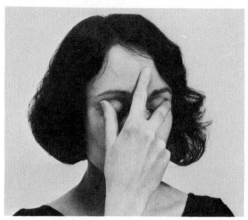

Fig. 109

(the third finger) at the outer edge of the other eye. Begin to gently squeeze the thumb and middle finger toward the inner corners of both eyes, with pressure slightly applied toward the inside (Fig. 109).

As the pressing of the fingers gradually increases, bright light starts to shine, covering the whole inner darkness. Lightening may illuminate all directions from the center, or may circle out spirallically. Dazzling brightness may form a ring-like circle with colors changing beautifully. Let your consciousness be absorbed into the fullness of bright light, meditating that the creation of the universe has begun with the light, and the light of creation endlessly continues. When we look up slightly, seeing far under the covered eyelids, the brightness of light would become increasingly intensified.

After the experience of Seeing the Inner Light for a few minutes, gently loosen the pressure applied by the fingers and finally detach the fingers from the eyes and forehead. Continue to keep both eyes closed and continue to meditate with the remaining light until it completely fades away.

Physically, this exercise for Seeing the Inner Light gives an intense stimulation in the area of the midbrain, gathering nervous activities together; and spiritually, it enables us to experience the world of radiations, the basic forces of all phenomena.

DSE. 11　(和音)　Wa-On: Sounding Harmonization

Fig. 110

With the Natural Right Sitting Posture, holding the hands in the meditating form on the lap (as in DSE 2), begin to breathe deeply through the slightly opened mouth with the eyes either fully closed or half closed, seeing far, without focussing upon any particular object. The duration of exhaling should be four to seven times that of inhaling (Fig. 110).

During the exhalation, pronounce naturally the sound SU ("su-u-u"), the sound of peace and harmony (SP 14, page 124), as long as possible. It is not necessary to make the sound loudly, but it is necessary to make the sound peacefully. At that time, let the sound echo, spreading its vibration through the inner regions of the chest, throat, and face.

At the time of inhaling, intensively have the image that we are inhaling the whole universe deeply within us, and that it is being distributed into all the billions of cells, to all corners of our body. At the time of exhaling, keep the image intensively that we are distributing the inner universe to the external infinity, toward the boundless space of the universe.

Repeat this breathing with the sound of peace and harmony (SU) four to eight times, in order to harmonize ourselves with all environmental conditions including the people and human affairs which are surrounding us.

DSE. 12 (平和) Hei-Wa: Pacification of the World

From the previous exercise, Sounding Peace and Harmony, keep the peaceful state of mind in the meditating posture (Fig. 111). Slowly raise the hands to the level of the heart in the prayer position (Fig. 112), and then again raise them slowly to the level of the mouth (Fig. 113). Then gradually extend both arms with both palms naturally opened toward the front, sitting or standing in order to send out peaceful waves of harmonious vibration through the palms, especially from the centers of the palms (Fig. 114).

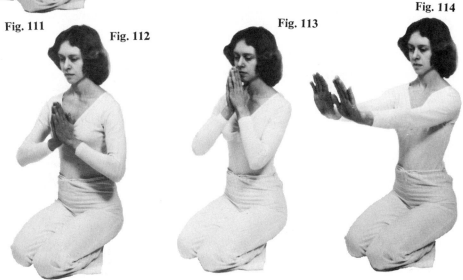

Fig. 111 Fig. 112 Fig. 113 Fig. 114

Fig. 115

Fig. 116

Together with one long sound of peace and harmony (SU), uttered with the intensive image of sending peace to all beings and to the world, gradually open and move the arms horizontally until they make a straight line with the shoulders (Fig. 115).

Then, with the next long sound of peace and harmony, gradually move both arms toward the original center position, continuously keeping our intensive image, radiating peace waves in all directions (Fig. 116).

Repeat this exercise several times, slowly.

Upon the completion of this practice for the Pacification of the World, slowly return both extended arms to the ordinary praying position (Fig. 117), and then place the arms and hands back in the meditation form (Fig. 118), and return to normal and natural breathing.

Fig. 117

Fig. 118

Chapter 3

Daily Exercises

1. (早朝修法) Sō-Chō-Shū-Hō: Morning Exercises

Introduction

Morning is the beginning of new life. The quality of the physical, mental and spiritual life we experience during the day depends largely upon our condition in the morning, especially at the time of leaving bed to begin our activity. It is essential to completely refresh our physical and mental conditions by releasing all stagnation which may have arisen during sleep and during the previous day.

During the daytime, we tend to form certain postures and develop certain physical and mental habits more than others, through our engagement in certain occupations and activities. Similarly, during the night while we are sleeping, we tend to develop certain physical conditions due to our way of sleeping, the condition of the bed, and the surrounding circumstances in the room, including the conditions of atmosphere and temperature. Our condition is also influenced by what we consumed in the previous day as our food and drink, together with our physical and mental experiences.

In order to begin our life anew every morning, to meet any circumstance which may arise during the coming hours of the day, it is necessary that we adjust our physical condition so that all our energies and the electromagnetic flow running through our body are energetic to perform our activities, and harmonious to meet any surroundings.

Accordingly, it is advisable that every morning we perform exercises for our physical adjustment. The following series of exercises can be performed as morning exercises after we awake and leave the bed, and finish elimination. Windows should be opened to allow free circulation of air between the indoors and the outdoors.

This series of exercises is to be performed on the floor or on a hard mattress, in a completely relaxed manner.

The performance of these exercises is not necessarily limited to early morning; they can also be done before eating lunch. However, we should avoid performing them immediately after taking meals.

The series consists of ten progressive steps, bringing the whole physical and mental conditions—including ki flow through the meridians and the circulation of blood and other body fluids—into a uniformly energetic state. It also releases tension of the joints and muscles.

Step 1: Massage of the feet and toes

[141]

Step 2: Extending and flexing the ankles
Step 3: Extending and flexing the knee joints
Step 4: Vertical movement of the leg joints
Step 5: Horizontal movement of the leg joints
Step 6: Extension of the thighs
Step 7: Pressing massage on the abdominal region
Step 8: Extending and flexing the waist region
        A. Front and back motion
        B. Left and right motion
        C. Left and right motion
Step 9: Extension of the arms
Step 10: Extension of the neck region

All the steps of this exercise should be performed in a smooth continuity, like a waterfall streaming down.

Step 1: Massage of the Feet and Toes (more than one hundred times)

Purpose: Circulation of blood in the feet and legs becomes active, preventing hardening of the legs, feet and toes. The stomach, intestines, liver, spleen, bladder, and kidneys are energized by the electromagnetic currents generated through meridians running in the feet and toes.

We lie down with complete relaxation, the arms separated by about three feet, palms up. Holding the thumbs toward the middle of the palms, lightly wrap the other four fingers over the thumbs. The knees are bent and held about three feet apart. Slightly raise the feet and rub them together strongly, as illustrated (Fig. 119)—the soles of the feet, the tops, and the toes—using the first or second toes to perform the massage. We massage rapidly in this way more than one hundred times, until both feet feel very warm.

Then, we extend the legs. With the first toe, cover the second toe of the same foot and push, making a flicking sound. We may do this with both feet at once, or one

Fig. 119

foot at a time. Repeat about ten to twenty times. Then, raising the second toe, do the same upon the third toe.

After the completion of these exercises, completely relax the legs and feet and the whole body, resting still for a while before proceeding to Step 2 of the exercise.

Step 2: Extending and Flexing the Ankles (right, three times; left, three times)

Purpose: To keep the ankles very flexible, softening the joints and muscles. It also prevents weakening of the legs and feet by the extension of the muscles of the back of the entire leg, together with the acceleration of energy flow along the bladder and stomach meridians.

Fig. 120

Fig. 121

We continue to lie down in complete relaxation.

We place the left foot on the right foot and, extending the left leg, strongly rub the right foot four or five times; then exchange feet, the right foot strongly rubbing the left foot.

Next, we raise the legs a few inches off the floor, as illustrated, and extend, then flex the ankles, repeating about five to ten times (Figs. 120 and 121).

Then, completely relax and rest for a while.

Step 3: Extending and Flexing the Knee Joints (right, three times; left, three times)

Purpose: To generate the activity of intestinal digestion by extending the muscles on the sides of the legs, together with accelerating the functions of the liver and gall bladder, as well as the lungs, through their meridians.

We continue to lie down with the arms separated about two feet from the body. We bend the right knee ninety degrees. Bend the left knee so that the outside of the ankle is resting on the outside of the right knee (Fig. 122). With the mouth open, we breathe out, as the left leg pushes the right leg over to the ground (Fig. 123).

Repeat three times; then, repeat three times with the opposite leg, again with a long exhalation through the open mouth.

Then, stretch the legs and relax.

Fig. 122

Fig. 123

Step 4: Vertical Movement of the Leg Joints (right, three times; left, three times)

We continue lying down.

With the foot held straight (but not pointing the toes), raise the right knee up above the stomach, lightly clasping it with the hands (Fig. 124). Exhaling strongly through the open mouth, pull the leg up with the hands so that it almost touches the chest. At that time, we stretch, extending the left leg as much as possible (Fig. 125).

Repeat three times, then change legs and repeat three times with the opposite leg.

Then, relax completely.

Step 5: Horizontal Movement of the Leg Joints (right, three times; left, three times)

Purpose: To accelerate intestinal digestion, releasing stagnation in the abdominal region by the extension of the muscles in the region of the buttocks and abdomen, as well as the side of the body. It also energizes, through the meridians, the functions of digestion and respiration.

We continue lying down.

Place the right hand on the floor about two feet away from the body, palm down. Raise the right leg. With the left hand, hold the outside of the right knee (Fig. 126). While breathing out through the open mouth, we use the left hand to push the

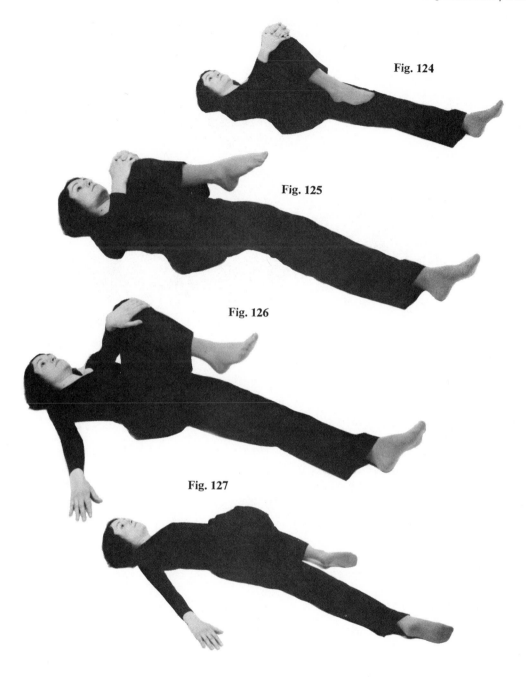

Fig. 124

Fig. 125

Fig. 126

Fig. 127

right knee down to the floor (Fig. 127). Repeat three times. Then, repeat three times with the opposite leg.

Then, extend the legs and relax.

Step 6: Extension of the Thighs (right, three times; left, three times)

Purpose: To prevent arthritis and hardening of the arteries, by maintaining flexibility in the condition of the muscles and blood circulation, through the extension of the muscles of the thighs, the sides of the body, and the rib-cage. It also generates the functions of digestion and breathing as well as the excretory functions by activating the related meridians.

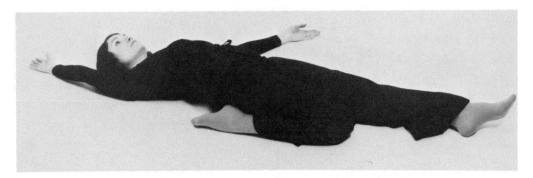

Fig. 128

We continue lying down in a relaxed posture, on the back. We bend the right leg under, and extend the right arm upward relaxedly. The left hand is out to the side about two feet, palm up. (See Fig. 128.)

In this posture, the right leg tends to be slightly off the floor. Then, exhale, and push the right knee down, touching it to the floor as much as possible; and the right arm extends upward as much as possible. At the same time, we extend our left arm and left leg downward as much as possible. Then, relax.

Repeat three times. Then, change sides, and repeat three times. Then extend the legs, return to the original position and completely relax.

Step 7: Abdominal Massage (three times and sixteen times)

Purpose: To soften the abdominal muscles and accelerate the activity of all organs in the abdominal region. It also serves to improve digestive and excretory functions. For longevity, it is essential to keep the abdominal region soft and flexible.

We keep our reclining posture, with the knees bent, keeping the abdominal muscles relaxed as much as possible. Then, with the left hand, hold the right wrist. Using the four fingers of the right hand, slowly but deeply push down into each part of the abdominal region, in the following order:

A. The left region, from the bottom upward along the ascending colon.
B. The upper part of the abdominal region, from right to left along the transverse colon. (See Fig. 129.)

C. The right side of the abdominal region, from top to bottom along the descending colon. (See Fig. 130.)
D. The lower abdominal region, left to right.
E. The central abdominal region, from top to bottom: (1) across the position of the navel; (2) about two inches to the right of the navel; (3) about two inches to the left of the navel. (See Fig. 131.)

Fig. 129

Each of these pressing motions is to be done together with an exhalation, and upon finishing each press, the hand should be released suddenly and rapidly.

Repeat the entire massage, steps A through E, three times.

Fig. 130

Then, hold the right hand over the left hand on the abdominal region. Slowly and deeply massage around the navel, making circular motions with the entire palm of the right hand, repeating about sixteen times. (See Fig. 132.)

Then, completely relax.

Fig. 131

Fig. 132

Fig. 133 Abdominal Region

Important Points

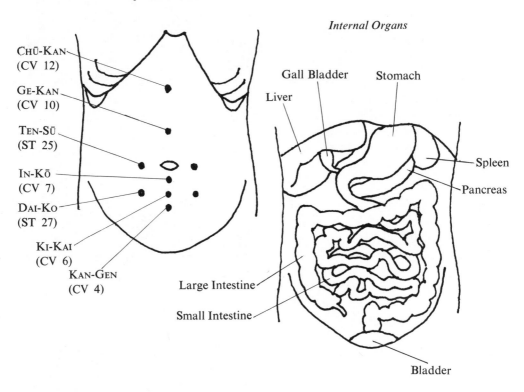

Internal Organs

CHŪ-KAN (CV 12)
GE-KAN (CV 10)
TEN-SŪ (ST 25)
IN-KŌ (CV 7)
DAI-KO (ST 27)
KI-KAI (CV 6)
KAN-GEN (CV 4)

Gall Bladder
Stomach
Liver
Spleen
Pancreas
Large Intestine
Small Intestine
Bladder

Lines of Pressing in Dō-In Exercises

Regional Diagnosis by Pressure

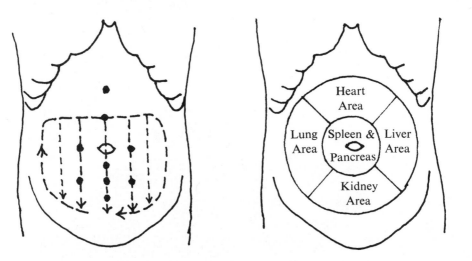

Heart Area
Lung Area
Spleen & Pancreas
Liver Area
Kidney Area

In the illustrations above are shown the important organs, meridians, points, and diagnosis areas influenced by the abdominal massage.

Step 8: Extending and Flexing the Waist Region

Purpose: The following three movements are to correct dislocations of the spine and soften all muscles of the back and waist regions, preventing back hardening and various waist disorders. They also serve to improve the respiratory, digestive, excretory, and nervous functions, as well as clarity of consciousness, by accelerating energy flow through the related meridians and muscles.

A. Front and Back Motion (three times): Hold the upper portion of the body upright, with the legs stretched to the front, and the feet straight, ninety degrees (Fig. 134). Hold the fingers in back of the head and neck region, and while breathing out through the mouth, bend over to the extent that both elbows touch the floor (Fig. 135). (If the elbows cannot touch the floor at first, it becomes possible in time as we continue practicing the exercise.) Then, return the body to the upright position.

We repeat this exercise three times.

Fig. 134

Fig. 135

B. Left and Right Motion (*left and right alternately, three times*): We keep the same posture as in Step A. As we exhale through the mouth, we twist and bend our body to the left, lowering the right elbow to the extent that it touches the floor at the right side of the right knee (Fig. 136). Return to the upright position.

Then, change sides and bend to the left (Fig. 137).

Repeat the exercise three times, alternating left and right.

Fig. 136   **Fig. 137**

C. Left and Right Motion (*left and right alternately, three times*): Taking the same posture as in the previous step, we twist and bend our body in the same way—this time, the right elbow touching the left knee (Fig. 138). Return the body upright, then twist and bend to the other side, the left elbow touching the right knee (Fig. 139).

Repeat this movement three times. When we bend and twist our body, we breathe out through the mouth; and when we lift our body upright, we inhale.

Fig. 138   **Fig. 139**

Step 9: Extension of the Arms (center, three times; right, three times; left, three times)

Purpose: To soften various muscles of the arms, shoulders, and back, by releasing stagnation in the shoulder, back, and elbow regions. This exercise also generates our respiratory, digestive, and circulatory functions by energizing the related meridians.

We sit upright as in the previous exercise, with the legs extended and the feet standing vertically.

Fig. 140

Fig. 141

Fig. 142

We hold our hands in front of our body, palms together, bending both elbows about ninety degrees (Fig. 140). Then, breathing out through the mouth, we bend our body forward, extending both arms as far as possible. Our hands should reach the feet. We try to keep our legs straight, and attached to the floor (Fig. 141).

While inhaling, we return our body to the upright position. We repeat this movement three times.

Then, we hold our right hand palm up, and grasp it with the left hand from below (Fig. 142). Exhaling through the mouth, we bend our body forward and extend both arms toward the right foot. At that time, the left hand twists the right palm so that it faces out toward the right side (Fig. 143).

Together with inhaling, we return our body to the upright position. We repeat the same movement three times. Then, changing hands, we again bend our body three times —this time, the left hand is twisted by the right hand.

Fig. 143

Step 10: Extension of the Neck Region (right and left alternately, three times)

Purpose: To activate the functions of the parathyroid and thyroid glands, as well as the respiratory functions. It also serves to soften the neck region, and accelerate energy flow and blood circulation in the regions of the shoulders, neck and head.

We take the Natural Right Sitting Posture, as in DSE 1. We apply the left palm to the bottom of the face, and the right palm to the upper left side of the head. Together with exhaling through the mouth, the right palm pulls the head down toward the right, while the left palm pushes the jaw up toward the left (Fig. 144).

Fig. 144

Fig. 145

Then, return the head to normal posture. Repeat three times.

Change hands and push in the opposite direction, bending the head to the left (Fig. 145). Repeat three times.

Conclusion to the Morning Exercises: After practicing the above series of exercises, we may proceed to practice the General Exercises (page 171), to further vitalize each part of the body.

After this series of exercises, it is also advisable to stand with straight posture and breathe deeply several times, before we begin our daily activity.

2. (均整修法) Kin-Sei-Shū-Hō: Evening Exercises

Introduction

Our daily life tends to create certain tendencies in our physical, mental and spiritual conditions, due to the standardized way of life in modern civilized society—which is not necessarily in balance with the natural order. It is important for everyone to recover a harmonious relationship with the natural environment at the end of daily activities. In order to keep such balance we should, of course, maintain our macrobiotic way of life, including the proper dietary practice; but also, physical and mental adjustment at the end of the day will be very helpful for physical health, mental peace, and spiritual awareness.

The exercises introduced below are to recover our physical and mental balance for the establishment of our well-being. It is desirable to practice this series every night before sleeping. It may also be performed before the evening meal. However, we should avoid practicing these exercises with a full stomach, immediately after the evening meal.

This series of exercises has been practiced among people seeking rejuvenation and longevity since unknown ancient times, as their daily habitual exercise. The exercises are simple and practical enough for anyone to perform. At first, some of us may feel difficulty in doing certain exercises well, but we shall become able to perform them smoothly as we continue our practice. These exercises should be performed successively, as if each exercise is a part of one entire movement.

The Morning Exercises aim to generate our energies physically, mentally, and spiritually; but these Evening Exercises aim more to harmonize them into a peaceful state, to achieve a balance of relaxation. Therefore, our mind as well as our body should be relaxed when we perform these exercises.

The exercises can be done on the floor or on a hard mattress, in twenty steps, as follows:

Step 1

Begin by standing straight (Fig. 146), facing toward the South or Southeast if in the Northern Hemisphere; North or Northeast if in the Southern Hemisphere. We keep our spine straight, but all other parts of the body should be relaxed, including the shoulders, elbows, and all joints. Put the body weight at the lower abdominal region —the Second Chakra, the physical center—breathing naturally and slowly.

Step 2

We raise the arms above the head as far as we can, leaning back and stretching the front part of the body—chest, abdomen, thighs and legs (Fig. 147). The eyes are looking up toward the heavens. We hold that posture for a while, about ten to fifteen seconds.

Fig. 146

Fig. 147

Fig. 148

Step 3

Together with a long exhalation, we bend forward, touching our hands to the floor (Fig. 148). At that time, we try to keep our knees and legs straight rather than bent. We keep this posture for a while, about ten to fifteen seconds, then again repeat Step 2, stretching our body, followed by Step 3. Repeat three times.

Step 4

We sit on the floor, keeping the legs extended straight forward, with the feet standing straight vertically.

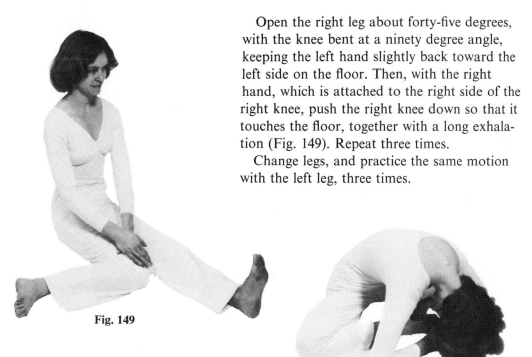

Open the right leg about forty-five degrees, with the knee bent at a ninety degree angle, keeping the left hand slightly back toward the left side on the floor. Then, with the right hand, which is attached to the right side of the right knee, push the right knee down so that it touches the floor, together with a long exhalation (Fig. 149). Repeat three times.

Change legs, and practice the same motion with the left leg, three times.

Fig. 149

Fig. 150

Step 5

Open the legs, and attach the soles of the feet together, holding the toes with both hands, the thumbs crossed on top. Then, bend the head down to touch the feet, with a long exhalation (Fig. 150). The forehead should touch the thumbs. If we can do this exercise perfectly, the knees and legs do not rise from the floor; however, if we are unable to do this, we practice to the extent that we can, as nearly as possible.

We repeat this exercise three times.

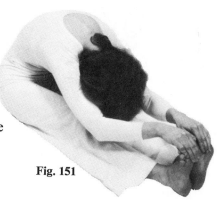

Fig. 151

Step 6

Sitting upright, we extend both legs straight to the front, then stretch the arms forward and hold onto the toes with the fingers. We bend the head forward to touch the knees, if possible (Fig. 151). At that time, we try to keep the legs attached to the floor. This may be difficult for some people.

Step 7

We take the same posture as in Step 6. The right hand is applied to the back of the head, and the left hand to the side of the left knee. We bend, touching the right

Fig. 152 Fig. 153

elbow to the floor at the outside of the right knee. At that time, the head and upper portion of the body face slightly toward the left (Fig. 152). This exercise is done with long exhaling. In the same manner, we do this with the left hand (Fig. 153).

Repeat these movements alternately, three times.

Fig. 154

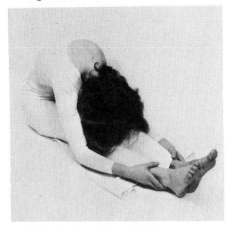

Step 8

We sit upright as in Step 6. We bend over, holding the ankles from the sides with both hands and touching our forehead to the knees (Fig. 154). Then, return to the upright position. During this exercise we try to keep the back of the legs attached to the floor.

We repeat this exercise three times.

Step 9

From the previous posture, as in Step 7, the upper part of the body gradually falls back so that we are lying on the floor. We gradually raise both legs to touch the floor above the head (Fig. 155). Both hands should be stretched, with palms attached to the floor in order to maintain balance. We hold this posture for ten to fifteen seconds. Then, we return to the original posture, and completely relax the whole body in a reclining posture.

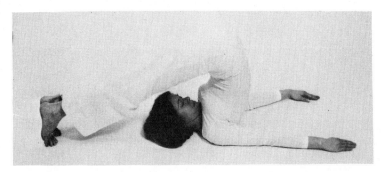

Fig. 155

Step 10

We sit in the Natural Right Posture, with the hands clasped at the back of the head. Together with a long exhalation, we bend our upper body toward the right side, slightly to the front (Fig. 156). At that time, our head faces slightly to the left, stretching the opposite side of the body. Then, return upright, and bend to the other side.

We repeat this exercise alternately left and right, three times.

Fig. 156

Fig. 157

Fig. 158

Step 11

We continue to sit in the Natural Right Posture, knees touching together. As we make a long exhalation, we bend our body as much as possible toward the front. In the perfected movement, the head touches the floor in front of the knees (Fig. 157). Then, return to upright posture and stretch the whole body backward, looking at the center of the heavens (Fig. 158).

Repeat this exercise three times.

Fig. 159

Step 12

We take the Natural Right Sitting Posture and bend the right knee, clasping it with both hands. We bend our head, touching the right eyebrow to the top of the knee (Fig. 159). Repeat three times, then exchange legs, bending the left knee and attaching the left eyebrow to the top of the left knee, again repeating three times. This exercise appear very simple, but some people are unable to do it.

Fig. 160

Step 13

We sit in the Natural Right Posture, attaching the knees together, applying the left hand to the right side of the right knee, and applying the right hand to the left side of the left buttock region, from the back (Fig. 160). Keeping our face straight toward the front, we turn the upper part of our body to the right as far as possible, with a long exhalation of breath. Repeat three times, then change sides and again perform the exercise three times.

Step 14

Continuing to sit in the Natural Right Posture with the knees attached together, we bend the right arm back and down over the right shoulder to grip the left hand, which is reaching upward in back (Fig. 161).

We change arms, and grip in the opposite way. Repeat this exercise three times. Some people may not be able to make their hands meet the first few times they try.

Fig. 161

Step 15

From the Natural Right Sitting Posture, with the knees attached together, we bend our body back until the shoulders touch the floor. Together with a long exhalation, we extend both hands straight, with the palms attached together (Fig. 162). While we are doing this exercise, we try to keep our knees touching the floor. Those who are unable to do this exercise may practice by bending only one leg.

Fig. 162

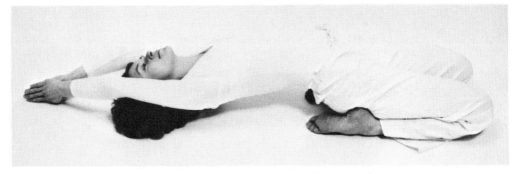

Step 16

We sit with both legs stretched forward, the feet pointing up vertically. Exhaling slowly through the mouth, we gradually lift our feet and bend the upper part of the body back, keeping the arms extended straight toward the feet (Fig. 163). The head is up, the eyes looking at the feet. In this exercise, we maintain our center of balance at the buttock region. We keep this posture for ten to fifteen seconds.

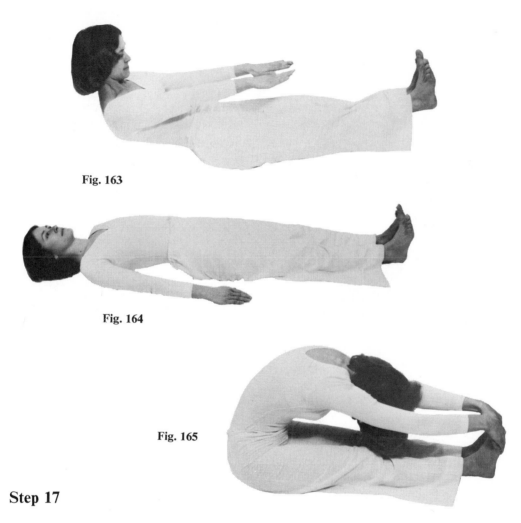

Fig. 163

Fig. 164

Fig. 165

Step 17

We lie down with the legs extended and the feet straight vertically (Fig. 164). From this posture, we slowly raise the upper portion of our body, using the power of the abdominal region, and bend the upper portion of the body toward the front as much as possible. With a long exhalation through the mouth, we extend both arms so that our hands reach and grip around the back of the toes (Fig. 165). We repeat this exercise three to five times. During the exercise, we should not bend our knees or lift our heels from the floor.

After we finish this exercise, we relax completely, in a reclining posture.

Step 18

We lie down on the stomach and apply both our palms to the sides of the waist, with the knees bent and the lower legs extended up straight. Together with a long exhalation, we raise our chest as high as possible (Fig. 166), then lower it again to the floor, relaxing and inhaling.

We repeat this movement three times, keeping the legs vertically straight throughout the exercise.

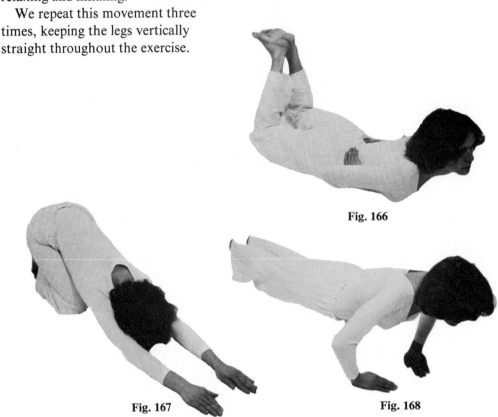

Fig. 166

Fig. 167

Fig. 168

Step 19

First, we kneel, with the bottoms of the toes on the floor. We extend the arms toward the front as far as possible, slipping the palms along the floor (Fig. 167).

Keeping the hands and toes in the same position, we move our body toward the front, raising the knees from the floor. The body is raised off the floor, supported by the hands, in a form similar to the push-up. We slowly bend our arms, with a gradual exhalation, and keep that posture as long as we can (Fig. 168).

When we can no longer keep the posture, we place the knees down on the floor and withdraw the upper part of the body. Then, we again extend our arms in order to repeat the same exercise, three times altogether.

After finishing the exercise we completely relax, lying face downward for a few moments, with natural breathing.

Fig. 169

Fig. 170

Step 20

From the posture of the previous exercise, with the knees touching the floor, we extend the toes so that the tops of the feet are also attached to the floor. We stretch both arms and inhale, extending the chest. As we breathe out, we bend our head backwards as far as possible, extending our throat (Fig. 169). Then we lower the head, and inhale. Repeat three times.

Then, breathing out, we turn the head to the right, three times (Fig. 170). Repeat to the left, three times.

After finishing this exercise, we lie down on the back with complete relaxation, closing our eyes until our breathing returns naturally to the normal condition (Fig. 171).

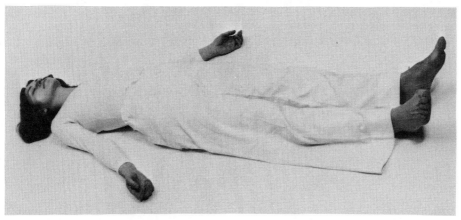

Fig. 171

Although the number of times for repeating each step of the Evening Exercises is specified, as we become used to them, it is not necessary to adhere to the specified number. From Step 1 to Step 15, each motion can eventually be reduced to only one repetition.

After this exercise, we are able to fall asleep very easily. However, when it is necessary to enter into sound sleep as soon as possible, we may add the exercise for Peaceful and Sound Sleep as introduced on page 168.

3. (経絡調整) Kei-Raku-Chō-Sei: Meridian Exercise

Introduction

Among the Dō-In exercises for physical, mental and spiritual development, there are exercises for the meridians which we are able to use in our daily life to maintain our health and develop our well-being. Most Dō-In exercises are directly or indirectly related to energizing the flow of electromagnetic currents through the meridians, and in that sense it is not necessary to put special emphasis on exercises for the meridians alone. However, we can use certain exercises especially for the purpose of extending the meridians to activate and release energy flow from any stagnation which may be caused by improper dietary practice, improper posture, and various unnatural daily activities.

There are twelve major meridians, as described before, which can be divided into six pairs according to yin ($\triangledown$), quiet energies, and yang ($\triangle$), active energies. They are:

1. The Lung and Large Intestine Meridians
2. The Spleen-Pancreas and Stomach Meridians
3. The Heart and Small Intestine Meridians
4. The Kidney and Bladder Meridians
5. The Heart Governor and Triple Heater Meridians
6. The Liver and Gall Bladder Meridians

These six exercises are different from usual movement. During these Meridian Exercises we should hold the postures at their extreme point for the duration of two slow breaths, which serves for the extension of the meridians as well as the acceleration of energy flow, resulting in the release of stagnation and disorders along the meridians and muscles.

a. Exercise for the Lung and Large Intestine Meridians

We stand with our feet apart slightly more than shoulder width. The hands are behind the back, palms turned outward, with the thumbs hooked together.

In that posture, we raise the arms and simultaneously raise the head, looking up toward the ceiling (Fig. 172). Then, we bend forward as far as possible, keeping the thumbs hooked together (Fig. 173). At that time, we notice that the Lung and Large Intestine Meridians running on the arms and hands are well extended, and that the muscles covering the lungs and connected with the large intestine are also pulled. At the extreme point, we hold the posture for a while, breathing slowly two times in a relaxed condition, which results in the active flow of energy along the Lung and Large Intestine Meridians as well as the active circulation of blood along the related muscles.

If we change the hand position so the other thumb is on top, and we perform the same postures again, we notice which side of the meridians—the right or the left— is in a more disorderly condition, by greater feelings of pain or strong tension in one side.

Fig. 172

Fig. 173

b. Exercise for the Spleen-Pancreas and Stomach Meridians

We sit with Natural Right Posture and clasp our hands together. Raise the hands up and slowly bring them back over the head, as illustrated (Fig. 174). Gradually lower the body backward to the floor, to the extent the shoulders touch the floor. If we extend our body and both arms enough to attach to the floor, the Spleen-Pancreas and Stomach Meridians running vertically in the front part of the body are strongly extended, and we also feel stimulation to the region of the spleen, pancreas and stomach.

Fig. 174

Keeping the posture, we breathe deeply two times, which accelerates the smooth running of energy and blood along the meridians and muscles.

If we change our hands so that the other thumb is on top, we notice that one side has more abnormalities than the other.

c. Exercise for the Heart and Small Intestine Meridians

Fig. 175

We sit with the legs open wide, the knees bent toward the floor and the soles of the feet together. Hold the hands around the toes, and bring the feet in toward the body as much as possible. Then, slowly bend forward, trying to touch the forehead to the thumbs. (See Fig. 175.) In this posture, with all joints relaxed, we repeat slow breathing two times. During this breathing, we notice energy and blood streaming actively toward the heart and small intestine.

If either knee is higher than the other, we feel more tension in that side, and disorderly symptoms appear more in that side.

d. Exercise for the Kidney and Bladder Meridians

We sit on the floor, extending the legs, the backs of the legs touching the floor, the feet held straight up vertically. Then, extend the arms and grasp the toes with the fingers.

Slowly bend the upper portion of the body toward the front, making the head touch the knees. (See Fig. 176.)

Fig. 176

Keeping that bending posture, we breathe deeply and slowly two times. At that time, through the Kidney and Bladder Meridians, energy starts to flow more actively. If one of the knees tends to rise, or if more tension is felt along the back muscles of one leg, that side of the kidney function is more disordered than the other.

Fig. 177

Fig. 178

e. Exercise for the Heart Governor and Triple Heater Meridians

We sit in the Lotus Flower Posture (SP 1, page 100). Then, we cross the arms and hold each knee with the opposite hand, pressing down on the knees (Fig. 177).

We slowly bend forward as far as we can (Fig. 178).

Keeping this posture, breathe two times slowly, keeping all muscles relaxed. At that time, energy passes actively through the Heart Governor and Triple Heater Meridians, stimulating vertically the central region of the body and the back spinal region. If we change arms so that the other arm is crossed on top, and compare this posture, we may feel much more tension in one side of the body than in the other, which indicates that that side has more stagnation.

f.   Exercise for the Liver and Gall Bladder Meridians

We sit with both legs extended to the front, opened as widely as we can. Do not raise the knees, but keep them attached to the floor (Fig. 179). With the fingers extending forward, reach both arms toward one foot, bending forward as far as possible (Fig. 180). We slowly breathe two times in this posture, during which we can feel that the liver and gall bladder regions are being stimulated. Then, we raise our body and bend again toward the other foot.

When we alternate left and right, we notice that it is more difficult to reach the foot on one side. There are more disorders and stagnation in that side.

Fig. 179   **Fig. 180**

4. Additional Exercises

Introduction

Among Dō-In exercises, there are many exercises for special purposes. All of them are designed to adjust the flow of energy within our body, to establish either active relations or tranquil harmony with the environment.

Among these exercises, the following two are especially useful for daily life, and the first exercise, Breathing Energy, is to bring about active relations with the environment—physically, mentally, and spiritually—by taking in the atmospheric energies in the form of inhaling. The second exercise is for inducing peaceful, sound sleep by making all muscles and meridians relaxed, releasing us from various sorts of tension to realize tranquil relations with the environment.

a. (服気法) Fuku-Ki-Hō: Exercise for Breathing Energy

This exercise should be performed either at the time of awakening in the morning, or before taking lunch. It should not be practiced when the stomach is full, and also not after the sun starts to decline toward the West, that is, after noon.

Step 1: Sit in any Natural Right Posture as described in SP 1 (page 100), forming the hands in the meditation posture and keeping the mind as quiet as possible.

Step 2: We close our eyes lightly, make the spine straight, and pacify our delusions into peaceful silence. (See Fig. 181.)

Step 3: When our thinking becomes peaceful we raise the right hand (in the case of left-handed persons, the left hand) to the nose, lightly attaching the thumb and index finger to the sides of the nostril area. (See Fig. 182.)

Step 4: We close the right nostril by light pressure of the thumb and we gradually exhale through the left nostril. (See Fig. 183.) As we exhale, the abdomen gradually contracts, as if the upper portion of the body is slightly bending toward the front.

Step 5: After we exhale completely, we gradually begin to inhale through the left nostril. During each inhalation, we first bring our breath down to the lower abdomen at the Second Chakra. Then, we breathe into the stomach region, the

Fig. 181   **Fig. 182**    **Fig. 183**

Third Chakra; then further raise our breathing toward the heart region, the Fourth Chakra. During these three steps of the inhaling process, we keep our back straight, as if aiming it toward the heavens.

Step 6: After this inhalation, we hold the breath and close both nostrils with our thumb and finger. We tighten the anus, and tighten the throat by rolling up the tip of the tongue and attaching it to the upper palate.

Step 7: Continuing to keep the anus and throat closed, we bring our energy down toward the lowest part of the body—the prostate area in the case of man, or the ovarian region in the case of woman—and then center it in the lower abdomen, the region of the Second Chakra.

Step 8: We close the left nostril with our finger, and gradually breathe out through the right nostril. (See Fig. 184.)

Step 9: After we completely exhale, we begin to inhale through the right nostril and repeat the exercise, from Step 5, on the other side.

Step 10: We repeat this process of breathing three to five times, and then return to the original sitting posture. (See Fig. 185.)

Fig. 184   **Fig. 185**

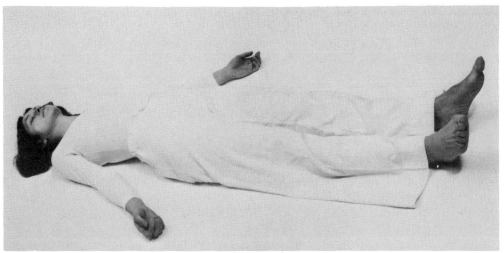

Fig. 186

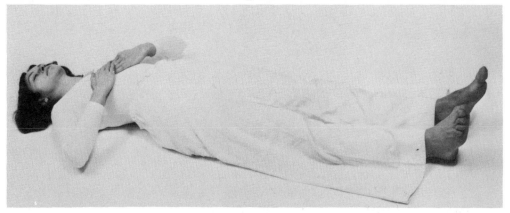

Fig. 187

B. (安眠法) An-Min-Hō: Exercise for Peaceful, Sound Sleep

To induce peaceful, sound sleep we need to release all tensions produced by physical activities and mental delusions. It is important to relax completely, softening all muscles and joints, and to forget our thinking, as if we make ourselves a part of the environment. The following exercise is very helpful for this purpose.

Step 1: We lie down in bed with complete relaxation (Fig. 186). At that time, if we put our head toward the North (toward the South in the Southern Hemisphere), we are able to sleep better.

Step 2: We slowly rub downward with both hands from the chest to the lower abdomen (Fig. 187). In this motion, we rub lightly in the chest region, slightly stronger in the middle region (around the stomach toward the upper intestines), and very strongly around the lower abdomen, as if almost pressing. Repeat this motion five times.

Fig. 188

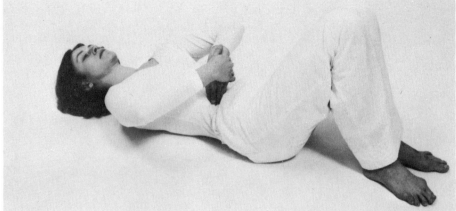

Fig. 189

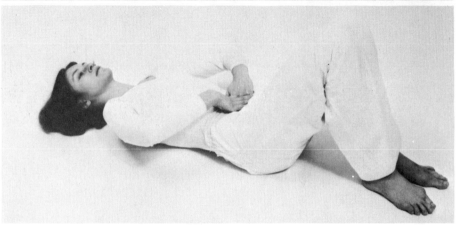

Step 3: We bend both knees up, and with our hands, press down into the abdominal region gently but deeply, along the ascending colon, transverse colon, and descending colon. Then, continue to press down vertically across the region of the navel, and down the right and left sides. (See Fig. 188.) After we repeat this three times, we rub the whole abdominal region in a circular motion about sixteen times, with the right palm attached to the abdomen, and the left palm covering the right hand (Fig. 189). This exercise is the same as that described in the Morning Exercise, Step 7 (page 146).

Step. 4: We lie in a relaxed posture with the arms crossed behind the neck as if pillowing the head. Our legs are extended and the toes pointing up vertically. Keeping the left leg stationary, we push the right leg downward, allowing the hips to naturally slant following this movement. Return the leg to the beginning position. Then, keep the right leg stationary and push the left leg downward, again allowing the hip area to slant naturally with the movement. Return to the beginning position. Repeat te.. times with each leg, alternating right and left, the hips moving back and forth.

Step 5: We extend the legs, lying in a relaxed posture with the arms about one foot out from the body on the floor, palms up. Twist both hands to face outward and extend the chest, lifting the back while inhaling. At the same time, the feet are held vertically straight, creating tension along the spine (Fig. 190).

Suddenly exhale and release the posture, turning the palms downward and relaxing the feet (Fig. 191).

Then again repeat the tensed posture, and again relax. Repeat five times.

Fig. 190

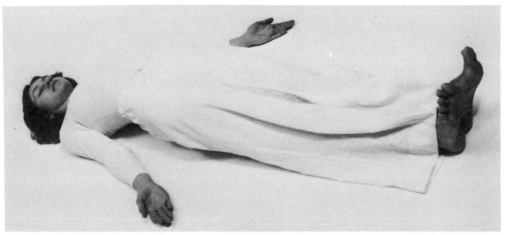

Fig. 191

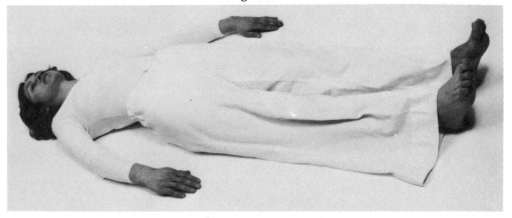

Step 6: Make the whole body—including the neck, shoulders, elbows, wrists, waist, knees, and ankles—completely relaxed, and enter into sleep.

Chapter **4**

General Exercises

Introduction

The General Exercises of Dō-In have been designed primarily to improve, maintain and develop our physical health, beauty, mental soundness and spiritual happiness. They can be practiced easily by anyone who is capable of maintaining a normal daily life, and can be practiced whenever we desire, without requiring any special effort. These General Exercises have been introduced in Western countries for the past ten years by me and my associates, for the purpose of self-maintenance and development of comprehensive well-being within an active daily life. Of course, the exercises should be accompanied by proper dietary practices following macrobiotic principles, enabling us to more efficiently develop our total happiness.

The General Exercises, unlike all other Dō-In exercises, cover all parts of the body. They are applied mainly through the use of our hands and fingers, and in that sense may be called "self-massage," although the techniques that are used are different from those employed in usual massage. We may summarize their effects as follows:

1. The General Exercises utilize the meridians to activate the flow of electro-magnetic current and energy throughout various parts of the body and the organs.
2. They also treat the tissues and muscles, releasing any stagnation and hardness and producing harmonious movement throughout the whole body.
3. They further influence the organs, directly or indirectly, according to the complementary relations between various parts of the body related to the organs. For example, by treating parts of the head, we stimulate and activate the inner organs of the torso. By treating the palms and feet, we also generate the functions of the internal organs.
4. In addition, these exercises deal with vibrational energy running within and surrounding our body, from head to toes, fingers to organs. This vibrational energy is also controlled by the use of various types of breathing, which naturally coordinate with the exercises.

The General Exercises should be performed like flowing air or streaming water, without pause from beginning to end. Although any one part of the series of exercises can be practiced independently to produce its special results to particular functions or organs, it is desirable to perform the whole series of exercises at one time, in order to develop our physical, mental and spiritual condition as a whole. During the exercises, we should keep natural posture as well as natural breathing, and we should maintain a peaceful mind by eliminating any delusions. The movement of our head, body, arms, legs, fingers and toes should be as natural as possible. We need not wear any special kind of clothing, but should dress lightly and simply so that we are comfortable during the exercises.

The General Exercises are presented in the following sequence:

A. Preparation: for pacifying our physical and mental condition
B. Face, head, neck and shoulder regions
 1. Cheeks
 2. Eyes
 3. Nose
 4. Mouth and jaw
 5. Ears
 6. Head
 7. Neck
 8. Shoulders
C. Arms and hands
D. Front, back, and sides of torso
E. Waist, legs, feet and toes
F. Completion

Following the General Exercises, two special series are introduced: Additional Exercises Especially for Facial Beauty, and Some Daily Practices for Health.

1. Preparation: for Pacifying Our Physical and Mental Condition

Fig. 192

Step 1: We sit in the Natural Right Sitting Posture (as described in DSE 1, page 131) with the sun at our back if it is daytime, or facing the South if it is nighttime. We take the meditation form, with the left hand on top of the right hand. (See Fig. 192.) The spine is straight, in order to have a smooth flow of the forces of heaven and earth through our spiritual channel.

We close our eyes naturally and breathe gently through the nose, making the images in our mind quiet and calm.

Step 2: After we feel more relaxed with a peaceful mind we slowly lift our hands to the level of our throat, with both palms applied together as in prayer. We lightly touch both thumbs to our throat. Our elbows should be slightly lifted, yet relaxed and without tension. (See Fig. 193.)

Step 3: Keeping this position, we begin breathing with long inhalations and exhalations repeated several times. We begin to pronounce the long sound of "SU" with each exhalation, which should be five to seven times longer than our inhalation. The exhaled breath should pass through the space between our palms. We repeat this long exhaling with the sound of "SU" about five times. This generates energy through our hands and fingers which we are going to use in the General Exercises that follow. After the palms and fingers are well charged, we gently detach our hands and proceed to the next part.

Fig. 193

2. Face, Head, Neck and Shoulder Region

These exercises generate active blood circulation throughout the body, together with strengthening the respiratory and breathing functions, as well as regulating active heart beating. They also serve to raise the body temperature.

a. Cheeks

Fig. 194

Step 1: We apply both palms to our cheeks—the right palm to the right cheek, the left palm to the left cheek—and breathe deeply at least three times. (See Fig. 194.)

Step 2: We rub our cheeks in an up-and-down motion with our palms until the skin becomes warm. (See Fig. 195.)

Fig. 195

Fig. 196   Major Points on the Face

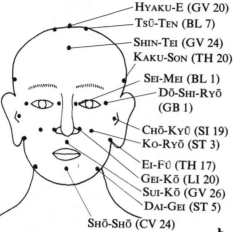

- Hyaku-E (GV 20)
- Tsū-Ten (BL 7)
- Shin-Tei (GV 24)
- Kaku-Son (TH 20)
- Sei-Mei (BL 1)
- Dō-Shi-Ryō (GB 1)
- Chō-Kyū (SI 19)
- Ko-Ryō (ST 3)
- Ei-Fū (TH 17)
- Gei-Kō (LI 20)
- Sui-Kō (GV 26)
- Dai-Gei (ST 5)
- Shō-Shō (CV 24)

Fig. 197   Areas on Face Corresponding with Areas of Body

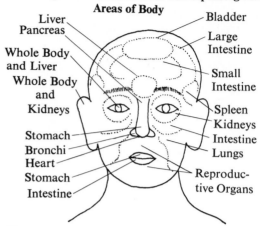

- Liver
- Pancreas
- Whole Body and Liver
- Whole Body and Kidneys
- Stomach
- Bronchi
- Heart
- Stomach
- Intestine
- Bladder
- Large Intestine
- Small Intestine
- Spleen
- Kidneys
- Intestine
- Lungs
- Reproductive Organs

Fig. 198

Fig. 199

Fig. 200

b.   Eyes

These exercises are to improve eyesight and to eliminate various disorders of the eyes including near- and far-sightedness, detached retina, glaucoma, astigmatism and other problems. These exercises also serve to control the rate of heartbeat and blood pressure, and to improve the circulation and the general mental condition.

Step 1:   We apply both palms over our eyes (see Fig. 198), keeping them there for a duration of several breaths, warming up the region around our eyes. This makes our blood circulation more smooth.

Step 2:   Using the index, middle and ring fingers, we press firmly on the bony edge of the upper eye socket, moving from the inside toward the periphery, and then press the bone underneath the eye. Repeat this process about three times.

Step 3:   With the same three fingers we press in above the eyeball, between the eyeball and the socket, as deeply as we can, giving a light vibrating stimulation. (See Fig. 199.) Release suddenly. Then, we press as deeply as we can below the eyeball, between the eyeball and the socket, giving a vibration and detaching suddenly. (See Fig. 200.)

Step 4: Using the tips of the same three fingers, with our eyes closed, we slowly and gently press upon the front of the eyeballs, and again detach suddenly. (See Fig. 201.) Repeat ten times. This exercise controls the beating of the heart and corrects the condition of the eyes and eyesight.

Step 5: We again apply our palms over our eyes, as in Step 1, and while our hands remain there, we slowly move our eyeballs, looking up and down as far as possible in each direction. Repeat ten times. Then, look to the left and right as far as possible, ten times. Then, we make a circular motion with our eyes, first counterclockwise and then clockwise repeating ten times in each direction.

Fig. 201

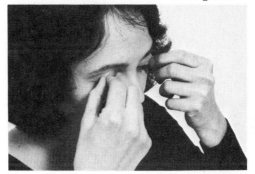

Fig. 202

Fig. 203

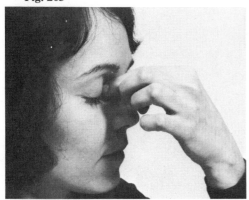

Fig. 204

Step 6: Picking up our upper eyelids with the thumbs and index fingers we vibrate the eyelids fifty to a hundred times. (See Fig. 202.) We begin to hear the sound of water, and excessive liquid is expelled in the form of tears. This exercise helps to correct the eyesight, as well as various disorders of the eye.

Step 7: With our index finger and thumb, we pinch the bridge of the nose and the corners of the eyes (see Fig. 203). This point is called *Sei-Mei* (晴明), which means "Clear Brightness." We push deeply for about ten seconds, and then suddenly detach, pulling our fingers away from our face (see Fig. 204). We repeat three to five times. This exercise makes our vision clear, and is especially helpful if the eyes are fatigued.

c. Nose

These exercises benefit the general functioning of the stomach, pancreas and lungs, as well as the improvement of thinking. They also stimulate the development of intellectual thought.

Fig. 205

Step 1: With the thumb and index finger, we strongly rub the sides of the nose, in an up-and-down direction, until it becomes warm. (See Fig. 205.) This exercise makes breathing activity more smooth, and also activates the condition of the stomach and its digestive function, together with the pancreatic function.

Step 2: With the thumb, index and middle fingers, we begin from the top of the bridge of the nose and squeeze the nose strongly along the sides and tip, and then suddenly detach our fingers. This exercise makes our thinking far more clear, and improves the heart condition and circulatory function.

Step 3: With one thumb, we press the side of the nose to close one nostril, and slowly breathe in and out, five to ten times, with long breaths. Then, we repeat on the other side, closing the nostril and breathing slowly and deeply five to ten times. This exercise promotes better respiratory functioning, as well as loosening and opening the nasal cavities and bronchi.

Fig. 206

d. Mouth and Jaw

These exercises strengthen the digestive activities, especially the circulation around the mouth and the secretion of saliva. They also improve physical strength and smooth excretory functions.

Step 1. With the four fingers of both hands, we press deeply around the mouth, and along the sides of the jaw from the chin to the ears. When pressing, we use circular motions of our fingers (see Figs. 206 and 207). Repeat five to ten times. Wherever there is soreness, press harder. This exercise improves the circulation in the jaws and gums around the teeth, releasing stagnation in that area.

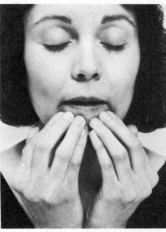

Fig. 207

Fig. 208

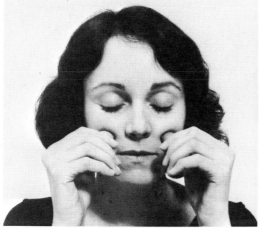

Step 2: Using one finger, we push underneath our cheekbone, about one finger's width away from the sides of the nose, with a circular motion (see Fig. 208).
This relieves tension caused by mucus accumulation in the nasal cavity.

Fig. 209

Step 3: Using our thumbs, we press deeply under the lower jaw, as if making deep indentations from underneath the ear to below the chin. (See Fig. 209.) Repeat three to five times. This exercise activates several glands related to the ears, saliva and lymph so that they function properly. As a result of this motion, the secretion of saliva becomes more active.

e. Ears

These exercises improve our hearing, and harmonize all circulatory functions and the coordination among various systems of the entire body. They also improve mental balance as well as kidney and excretory functions.

Step 1: With the thumb or index finger we press the indented point below the ear, between the jaw and the neck. Press deeply several times, releasing the finger rapidly. If we feel sharp pain, it indicates that mucus and fat have accumulated in the inner ear, causing increasing difficulty in hearing.

Fig. 210

Step 2: With the index, middle and ring fingers we press around the ear several times, to release any stagnation in the circulation around the ear (see Fig. 210). This also helps us to have clearer thinking, and especially improves our sense of balance.

Fig. 211

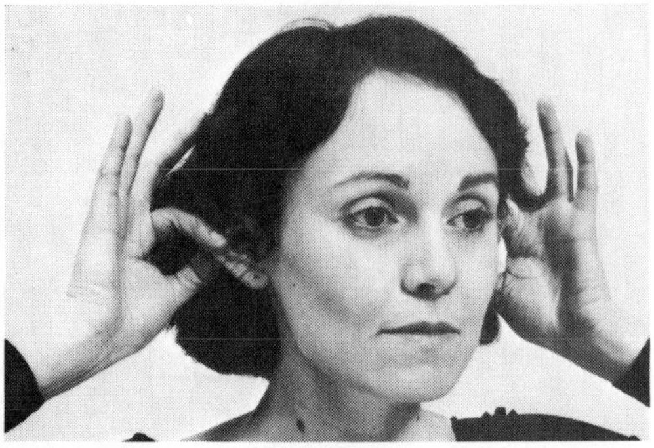

Fig. 212

Step 3: We massage our ears, using the thumb and index finger (and the middle finger, if desired). First, we rub the peripheral ridge of the ear in order to activate the circulation of blood and lymph throughout the body (Fig. 211). Second, we rub the middle ridge, with the thumb behind the ear and the other finger(s) in front, stimulating the nervous system (Fig. 212). Then, we rub the inner ridges and indentations, helping to activate the digestive functions (Fig. 213). Dur-

Fig. 213

ing all these processes, we may squeeze the earlobe hard, as well as all other areas along the ridges, in order to release all stagnation. This indirectly helps to release stagnation in other parts of the body.

Fig. 214

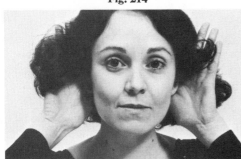

Step 4: With our fingers and palms, we vigorously rub the whole ear, up and down, until it becomes warm. This helps to make our whole mental and physical metabolism harmonious and active.

Step 5: Using our palms, we strongly bat our ears, with a brisk back-to-front motion (Fig. 214). Repeat about ten to twenty times. This strongly energizes our kidney and excretory functions, as well as our circulation.

Fig. 215

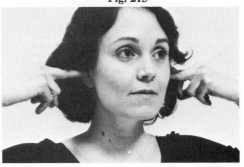

Step 6: We insert the middle fingers deeply into the ears, and gently vibrate them, as if giving a vibration to the eardrums. (See Fig. 215.) Then, suddenly remove the fingers, making a spirallic motion in the air. Repeat three to five

times. This exercise improves our hearing, and helps to strengthen the activity of the midbrain.

Step 7: We cover the right ear with the left hand and, with the first three fingers of the right hand, we tap briskly on the back of the left hand, sending sharp vibrations toward the inner ear. We tap in pairs—about ten pairs of taps. Reversing hands, we repeat this procedure upon our left ear. (See Fig. 216.) This exercise is helpful to improve our hearing ability, and to strengthen the activities of the midbrain and the functions of the kidneys and excretory system.

Fig. 216

f. Head

These exercises are to release physical stagnation and mental cloudiness, by accelerating the circulation of blood and lymph as well as the energy flow in the meridians. They are also helpful to overcome physical and mental fatigue.

Step 1: Using all our fingers we press and massage hard with circular motions, beginning from the forehead, moving down to the brows and temples. We then go along the sides of the head behind the temples and above the ears (Fig. 217), and continue down to the back of the neck. From the back, we massage up the center

Fig. 217   **Fig. 218**

Fig. 219   **Fig. 220**

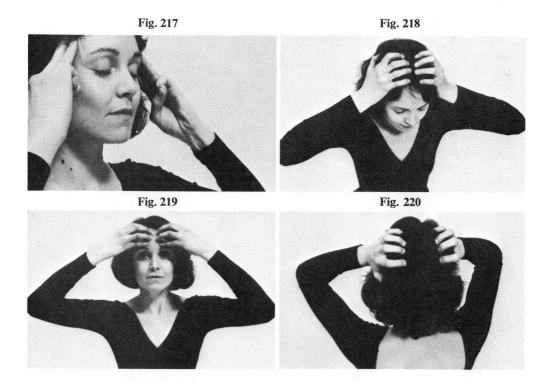

of the head toward the top, pressing hard down to the forehead (Fig. 218). Then, beginning at the forehead, we move our hands a little to the sides of center (Fig. 219) and press over the top of the head, down to the back of the neck. Beginning again at the forehead, we move our hands further to the sides, and press again (Fig. 220) over the top of the head down to the back of the neck. Repeat this entire procedure two or three times. This pressure and massage help to release stagnation in the circulatory and nervous systems as well as accelerating smooth energy flow in the related meridians.

Step 2: With our lightly-gripped fists, we bang the entire head region lightly—as if bouncing all over the head—covering the top, sides, front and back. (See Fig. 221.) We use the side of the fist at the little finger. This exercise is to stimulate all physical and mental activities and the coordination of various systems.

Step 3: With one palm covering the forehead and the other covering the back of the head, we breathe deeply three times. Then, with our palms covering the sides of the upper head (see Fig. 222), we again breathe deeply three times. Next, we cover the central sides of the head with our palms (see Fig. 223), and breathe deeply three times.

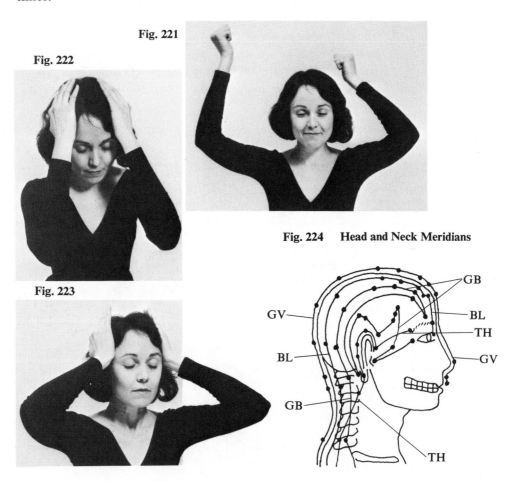

Fig. 221

Fig. 222

Fig. 223

Fig. 224   Head and Neck Meridians

Fig. 225   Face and Neck Meridians

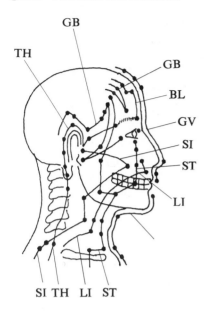

Fig. 226   Meridians and Points in the Back of the Head and Neck

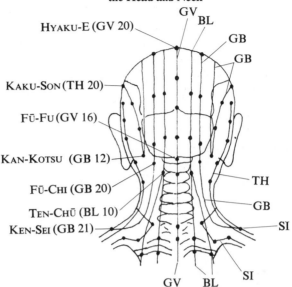

g.   Neck

These exercises are to unite our physical and mental activities together in a harmonious state and, at the same time, to generate our physical and mental energies as a whole, including the function of the stomach, pancreas, liver, and kidneys, and the regulation of blood pressure.

Fig. 227

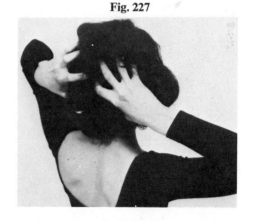

Step 1:   With our thumbs, we press the two points at the top of the back of the neck on both sides, holding our head with the other four fingers (Fig. 227). We tip our head up, in order to press underneath our skull. We release our thumbs quickly, and repeat this process three to five times. Then, we use our stronger thumb to press deeply the central point at the base of the skull, while the other hand holds our forehead, tipping our head slightly up and back. While pressing, we give a gentle vibration, then quickly release the thumb. Repeat three to five times. These exercises improve the functions of the middle region of the body, including the metabolism of the kidneys, pancreas, spleen and liver.

Step 2: On the back of the neck, we use our fingers to press along both sides of the upper spine, down to the shoulders, using a circular vibrating motion wherever hardness is found. Then, we repeat this process on the sides of the neck below the ears. Next, on the front of the neck at both sides of the vocal cords, we press down to the collarbone. Then, with one palm covering the throat and vocal cords, we press and massage around this region. These exercises are to release all stagnation in the related muscles and meridians, controlling blood pressure and harmonizing various systems.

Step 3: Folding our hands behind our neck, we tightly squeeze our neck with the heels of our palms, and release suddenly, repeating about five times (Fig. 228). This exercise releases any stagnation in that area, improving the circulation of blood.

Fig. 228

Fig. 229

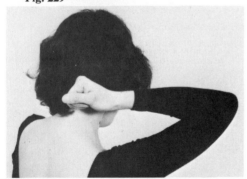

Fig. 230

Step 4: Tilting our head to the left, we bang the right side of the neck with the right fist (Fig. 229). Then, bang the left side of the neck with the left fist (Fig. 230). Tilting the head forward, we bang the back of the neck (Fig. 231). Next, we release stagnation and activate the circulation of blood and energy by tilting the head fully forward and back several times (Figs. 232 and 233), and side-to-side several times (Fig. 234). Finally, we rotate the neck counterclockwise about five times, and then clockwise about five times (Fig. 235). This exercise is to help release stagnation and accelerate active circulation and nervous functions, and to produce mental clarity.

Fig. 231

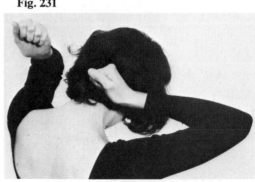

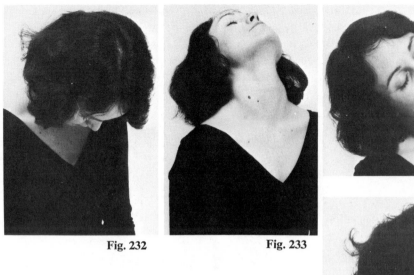

Fig. 232   Fig. 233

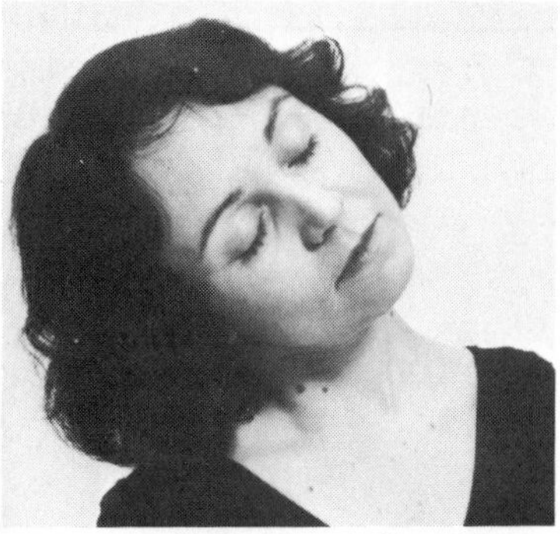

Fig. 234

Step 5: We apply our palms over both sides of the neck, and breathe deeply about three times. Then, we apply the palms over the back and front of the neck and again breathe three times.

Fig. 235

h. Shoulders

These exercises are to improve our circulatory and digestive functions by releasing physical and mental stagnation, and to regulate the respiratory and digestive metabolism. They also help to release fatigue by dissolving general tension in the shoulder region.

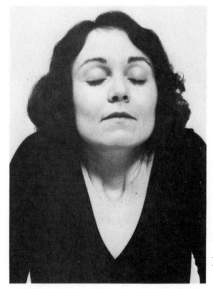

Step 1: We raise our shoulders, contracting our shoulder muscles as much as possible (Fig. 236). Then, we quickly release the contraction, completely relaxing these muscles as much as possible. Repeat five times. Then, tilting our shoulders, we contract the upper shoulder and relax the lower shoulder. Repeat three to five times, alternating shoulders. These exercises are helpful to release tension in the shoulder region, making the digestive function, especially in the intestines, smooth and active.

Fig. 236

Step 2: Using the four fingers of one hand, we press down upon and massage the opposite shoulder, tilting our head to the other side (Fig. 237). Repeat upon the other shoulder. Wherever we feel hardness or stiffness, we should massage with a circular motion. This exercise releases tension and stagnation, and accelerates circulatory and digestive activity.

Fig. 237

Fig. 239

Fig. 238

Step 3: Making a fist with one hand, we pound our opposite shoulder about ten to twenty times (Fig. 238). Repeat on the other shoulder. Wherever pain is felt, we should bang longer and harder. Also pound the top of the spine as well as the back of the neck, about ten to twenty times, using the stronger fist. These exercises are to achieve active metabolism throughout the body.

Step 4: Apply the palms upon the opposite shoulders (Fig. 239) and breathe in and out three times, slowly but deeply, to harmonize the functions of circulation and respiration. (If desired, the palms may be applied to the shoulders on the same sides instead.)

3. Arms and Hands

These exercises are to release stagnation arising in the bloodstream, tissues, muscles and joints, as well as in the energy flow along the related meridians, resulting in the harmonious activation of the various functions of the lungs and respiration, the heart and circulation, the intestines and digestion, and the coordination among all major organs through the Heart Governor and Triple Heater Meridians. These exercises also energize the functions of the various chakras, especially the second, abdominal and physical chakra, the third, stomach and power chakra, and the fourth, heart and emotional chakra.

Step 1: Holding our arms naturally at our sides, we turn and twist them, stretching them as far as we can, with the fingers spread wide open (Fig. 240). Repeat several times, twisting to the back and to the front. Then we lift up our arms to shoulder level and repeat the twisting motion, again as far as we can, several times (Fig. 241). Lifting our arms further (Fig. 242), at about a forty-five-degree angle, we twist them again. Finally, we lift our arms far over our head (Fig. 243) and twist them several times.

Fig. 240

Fig. 241

Fig. 242

Fig. 243

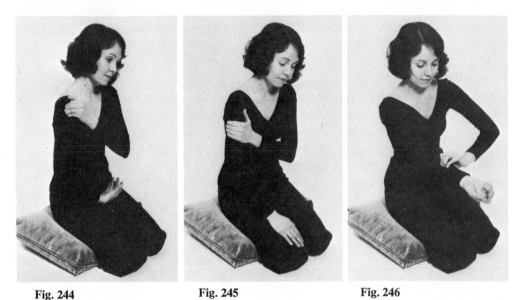

| Fig. 244 | Fig. 245 | Fig. 246 |

Step 2: Gripping the shoulder joint (Fig. 244), we thoroughly massage that area to release any muscular tension. Then, we massage down the arm (Fig. 245) toward the elbow, pressing all indented places around the elbow and releasing tension there. We further gradually go down toward the wrist, releasing tension in all areas (Fig. 246).

Step 3: We press from the shoulder to the wrist along each meridian running on the arm, namely the Lung, Heart Governor, Triple Heater, Heart, and Small Intestine Meridians. (See Figs. 247 and 248.) We may use four fingers to press these meridians, or the thumb, if it is more practical.

Fig. 247 Meridians and Points in the Outside of the Arm

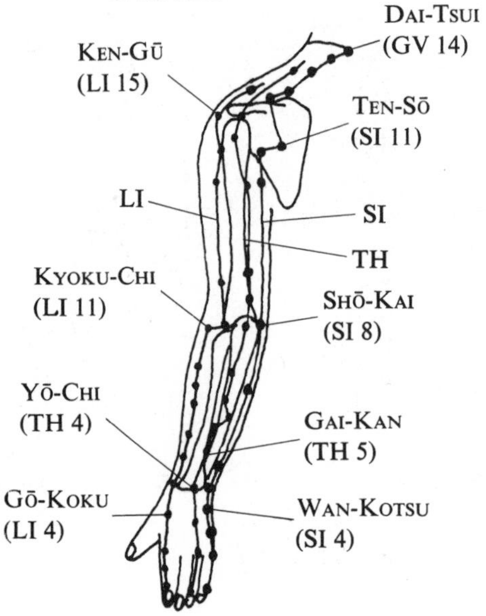

KEN-GŪ (LI 15)
DAI-TSUI (GV 14)
TEN-SŌ (SI 11)
LI
SI
TH
KYOKU-CHI (LI 11)
SHŌ-KAI (SI 8)
YŌ-CHI (TH 4)
GAI-KAN (TH 5)
GŌ-KOKU (LI 4)
WAN-KOTSU (SI 4)

Fig. 248 Meridians and Points in the Shoulder and the Inside of the Arm

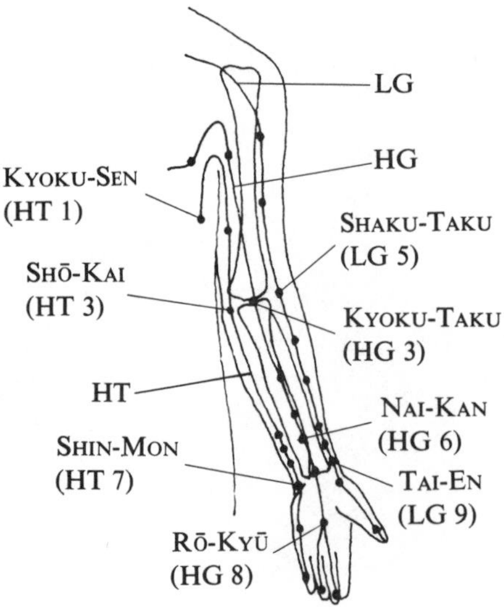

LG
HG
KYOKU-SEN (HT 1)
SHAKU-TAKU (LG 5)
SHŌ-KAI (HT 3)
KYOKU-TAKU (HG 3)
HT
NAI-KAN (HG 6)
SHIN-MON (HT 7)
TAI-EN (LG 9)
RŌ-KYŪ (HG 8)

Step 4: When we reach the wrist, we thoroughly massage all indented places in the area of the wrist (Fig. 249). Then, we press along the bones on the back of the hand (Fig. 250). We proceed to the fingers, using the thumb and index finger to massage each finger toward the tip, on the sides and then on the top and back (Fig. 251). This massage should proceed from one finger to another, slowly and carefully. It is especially important to strongly press and massage the tip of each finger, using the thumb and index finger to twist it back and forth (Fig. 252).

Fig. 249

Fig. 250 **Fig. 251** **Fig. 252**

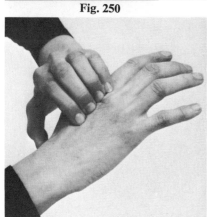
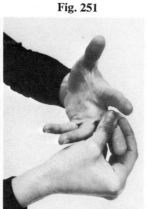
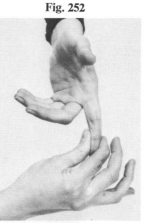

Fig. 253

Step 5: We pull and snap each finger. Then, using the thumb, we push down between the fingers. Or, we may press between the fingers by interlacing them and pushing down (Fig. 253).

Step 6: We press the palms very thoroughly (Fig. 254), first along the three major palm lines: the Life Line, the Line of Intellect, and the Line of Emotion. (See Part I, page 90 for detailed description of the lines on the palm.) Then, we thoroughly press all areas of the palm in a vertical direction. During this process, we press deeply with a circular motion. Two points especially should be strongly pressed: the center of the palm, the point *Rō-Kyū* (労宮), Heart Governor No. 8 (Fig. 255) and the point at the junction between the thumb and index finger, *Gō-Koku* (合谷), Large Intestine No. 4 (Fig. 256).

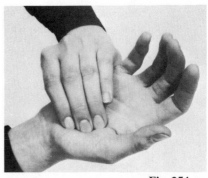

Fig. 254

After we complete the above process, we repeat the same exercises on the other arm, Steps 2 through 6.

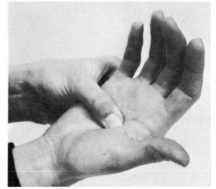

Fig. 255

Fig. 256

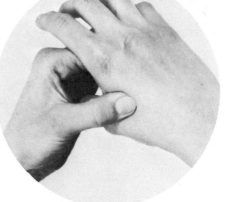

Fig. 257

Step 7: We shake the hands loosely and briskly (Fig. 257). Release any tension in the joints of the shoulders, elbows, and wrists as well as each joint of the fingers by strong shaking of the arms and hands.

Fig. 258 Corresponding Bodily Functions through the Meridians on the Hands

Fig. 259 Systems Corresponding with the Lines on the Palms

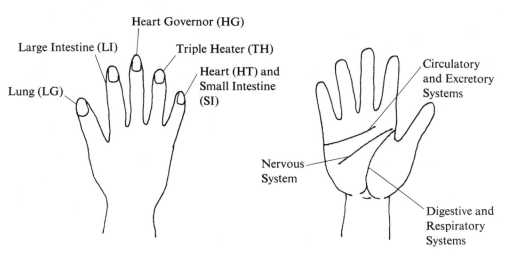

Fig. 260 Meridians on the Hands

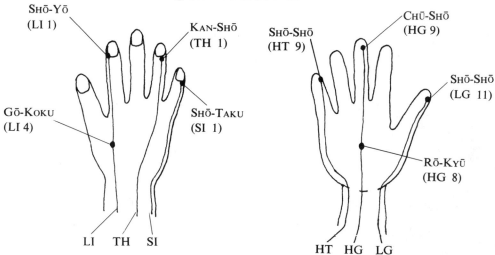

4. Front, Back and Sides of Torso

These exercises are to generate the active functioning of all major organs and glands located in the torso region. They also energetically activate the circulation of blood and other body fluid, and generate energy flow through all the meridians related to these organs and glands. Respiratory, digestive, circulatory, and excretory functions as well as nervous activities are harmoniously energized.

Fig. 261

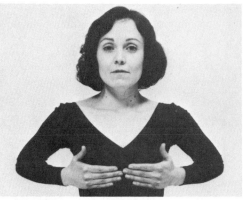

Fig. 262

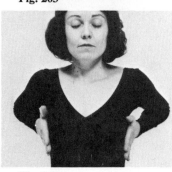

Fig. 263

Step 1: We apply both palms to the upper chest, and breathe deeply two to three times. (See Fig. 261.) Then, we apply our palms to the lower chest, and breathe deeply two to three times (Fig. 262). Next, we apply our palms to the middle (stomach) region, and then to the abdominal region (Fig. 263), in each case breathing two to three times.

On the sides of the torso, we first apply our palms to the upper chest (Fig. 264), then to the middle region next to the stomach, and then to the waist (Fig. 265), each time breathing two to three times.

On the back, we apply our palms on the middle region over the kidneys (Fig. 266), and again breathe deeply two to three times.

These palm applications are to harmonize the functional metabolism among the organs and glands.

Fig. 264

Fig. 265

Fig. 266

Fig. 267

Step 2: We begin a light banging or bouncing motion on the entire chest region (Fig. 267), including the sides of the rib-cage. This exercise strengthens the respiratory function, together with the acceleration of blood circulation and energy flow.

Using the same banging motion, we proceed farther down toward the stomach, and continue down to the region of the large and small intestines and the bladder. We should also pound the sides of the waist and pelvic region.

Fig. 268

On the back, we bang as high up as possible. We may sit up on our knees and bend our body forward (Fig. 268). Then, we bang down the back to the hips, including the middle and lower vertebral areas, the back muscles along the vertebrae, the bladder meridians running vertically on the back, as well as the muscles of the buttocks.

Fig. 269 **Areas of the Waist and Buttock Region Correlating with Areas of the Head and Large Brain**

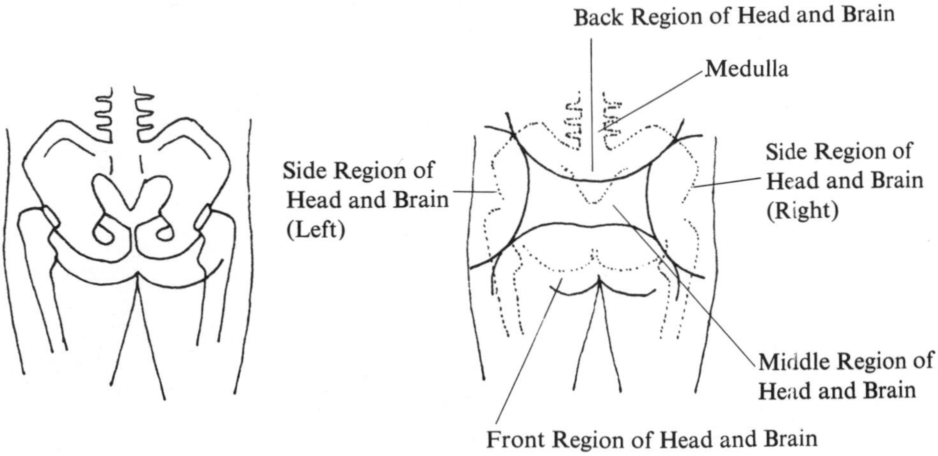

Back Region of Head and Brain

Medulla

Side Region of Head and Brain (Left)

Side Region of Head and Brain (Right)

Middle Region of Head and Brain

Front Region of Head and Brain

Step 3: Using the four fingers of both hands, we press the points and meridians on the front of the body as follows:

1. All along underneath the collarbones on both sides, two to three times.
2. Along the breastbone, pressing in a vertical line two to three times (Fig. 270).

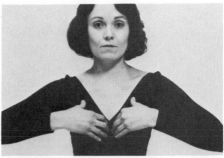

Fig. 270

3. From the top of the collarbone vertically down to the pelvic region, along the Kidney Meridian (Fig. 271).
4. From the collarbone downward along the Stomach Meridian (Fig. 272), to the pelvic region.
5. Using either four fingers or the thumb, press down from the indented place near the inside of the shoulder joint, along the Spleen Meridian, down to the pelvic region.

Fig. 271

6. On the sides of the body, press from the front of the armpit down along the Gall Bladder Meridian to the sides of the lower hips. To do this, it would be more practical to use the thumb rather than the fingers.

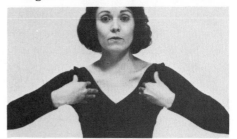

Fig. 272

7. Using the four fingers of both hands, press in and up under the edge of the rib-cage, as if pushing the rib-cage up (Fig. 273). Press all along the length of the rib-cage slowly and deeply. Two points should be pressed especially hard: *Ki-Mon* (期門), Liver Meridian No. 14 on the front of the rib-cage, and *Shō-Mon* (章門), Liver Meridian No. 13, at the bottom edges of the rib-cage.

Fig. 273

Fig. 274   Front Chest Region

Important Points

Lines for Massaging and Pressing in Dō-In Exercises

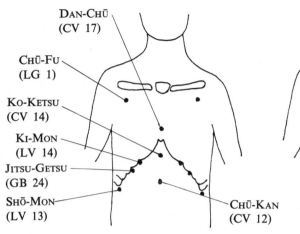

DAN-CHŪ (CV 17)
CHŪ-FU (LG 1)
KO-KETSU (CV 14)
KI-MON (LV 14)
JITSU-GETSU (GB 24)
SHŌ-MON (LV 13)
CHŪ-KAN (CV 12)

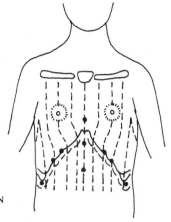

Fig. 275   Meridians on the Front of the Torso

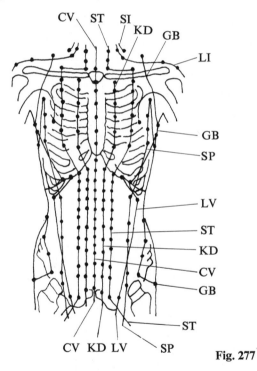

CV ST SI KD GB
LI
GB
SP
LV
ST
KD
CV
GB
ST
CV KD LV SP

Fig. 276   Meridians and Points on the Side of the Torso

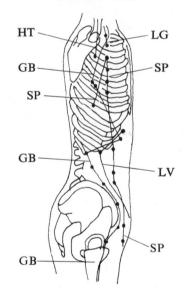

HT LG
GB SP
SP
GB LV
GB SP
GB

Fig. 277

Step 4:   Using our palms, we press and rub down the whole front of the body, covering the meridians from the top of the collarbone to the bottom of the pelvis (Fig. 277).

Step 5: On the back, press the indented area under the rib-cage, slightly arching the back to allow an easier grip (Fig. 278). Then, suddenly release. Repeat at least five times. (An alternative hand posture to the one pictured is to cross the hands in back, the thumb of the right hand on the right side of the spine and the fingers of the right hand on the left side of the spine, and the thumb of the left hand on the left side of the spine and the fingers of the left hand on the right side of the spine, and press using the thumbs and all fingers.)

Then, apply the hands on the region of the kidneys and adrenal glands, stretching backward to make the area softer and relaxed, and breathe deeply three times (Fig. 279).

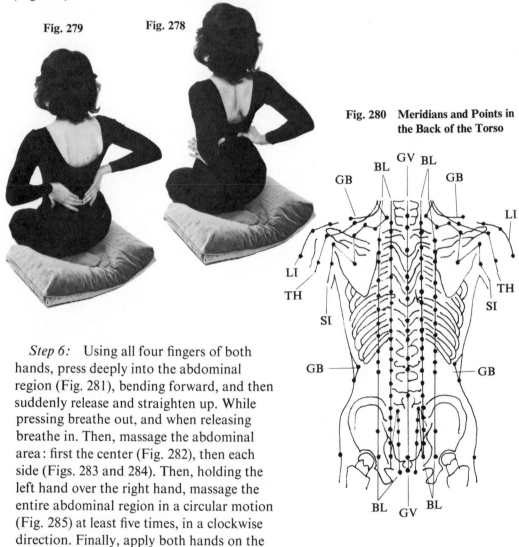

Fig. 279 **Fig. 278**

Fig. 280 Meridians and Points in the Back of the Torso

Step 6: Using all four fingers of both hands, press deeply into the abdominal region (Fig. 281), bending forward, and then suddenly release and straighten up. While pressing breathe out, and when releasing breathe in. Then, massage the abdominal area: first the center (Fig. 282), then each side (Figs. 283 and 284). Then, holding the left hand over the right hand, massage the entire abdominal region in a circular motion (Fig. 285) at least five times, in a clockwise direction. Finally, apply both hands on the abdominal region and breathe deeply in the lower abdomen (Fig. 286). During inhalation the abdomen should expand, and during exhalation it should contract. Repeat at least five times. This abdominal massage is very similar to that shown in the Morning Exercise, Step 7 (page 146).

Fig. 281

Fig. 282

Fig. 283

Fig. 284

Fig. 285

Fig. 286

Fig. 287

Fig. 288

Step 7: Twist the body left and right as far as possible, swinging the arms and keeping the head facing to the front. (Figs. 287 and 288.) This exercise activates and harmonizes the energy flow along all the meridians.

5. Waist, Legs, Feet and Toes

These exercises activate all body functions, especially the digestive, excretory and reproductive functions. Among the organs, the spleen-pancreas and stomach, liver and gall bladder, kidneys and bladder are especially affected through their meridians. However, the feet comprehensively reflect the entire body, including the functioning of the brain, and all body functions are activated by these exercises.

Fig. 289

Step 1: We take a position sitting up on the knees, the hands at our sides. We apply both palms to the pelvic region (Fig. 289) and breathe slowly three times. Next, we press and rub the hands down the front of the legs to the knees, four or five times (Fig. 290). Repeat this downward pressing on the insides of the legs, and then on the sides (Fig. 291), from the waist region down to thè knees, four or five times each. In back, we press down over the buttocks to the knees (Fig. 292). These rubbing motions are to smooth energy circulation and release muscular tension.

Fig. 290

Fig. 291

Fig. 292

Step 2: With lightly-gripped fists, we bang the front of the legs, moving up and down the legs more than five times (Fig. 293). Bang next on the insides of the legs, and then on the sides, moving up and down in each area. Then, bang up and down in back (you may need to bend over). This banging releases hardness and tension, and generates energy flow in the related meridians, such as the Spleen, Liver, Kidney, Stomach, Gall Bladder, and Bladder Meridians.

Fig. 293

Step 3: Sit cross-legged and then raise one leg, bending the knee and resting the foot on the floor. Squeeze the raised thigh, moving up and down the thigh, using both hands—the thumbs on the inside, the fingers on the outside. This motion not only releases muscular tension, but also generates energy flow along the Spleen, Kidney, and Gall Bladder Meridians.

Then, using the base of the palms of both hands, squeeze the thigh firmly, moving up and down. (This is the same motion as illustrated on the calf in Step 5, Fig. 296.)

Step 4: Apply the palms upon the knee for a while, warming that area. Then, using the fingers, press all indentations and tense muscles in the area of the knee (Fig. 294). Press and release many times, relieving stagnated circulation around the knee.

Step 5: Using the base of the palms, rub from the knee down to the Achilles tendon (Fig. 295), repeating five times. Next, squeeze and release, again using the base of the palms (Fig. 296), repeating more than three times, moving up and down the calf. This may be painful for many people. These exercises activate the intestinal and bladder functions.

Fig. 294

Fig. 295

Fig. 296

Fig. 297   Major Points and Areas on the Inner Leg
Corresponding to Bodily Regions

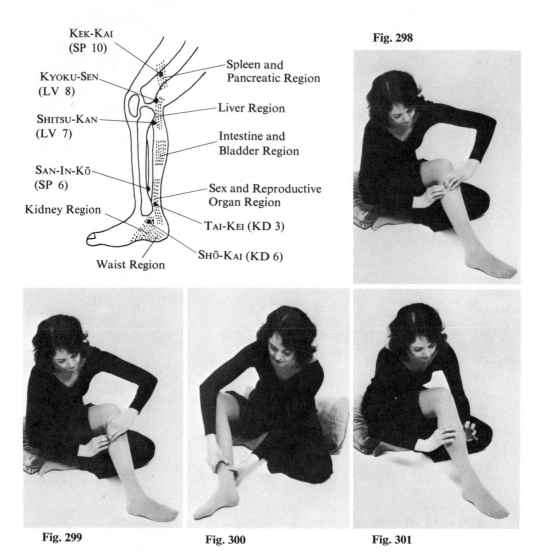

KEK-KAI (SP 10)

KYOKU-SEN (LV 8)

SHITSU-KAN (LV 7)

SAN-IN-KŌ (SP 6)

Kidney Region

Waist Region

Spleen and Pancreatic Region

Liver Region

Intestine and Bladder Region

Sex and Reproductive Organ Region

TAI-KEI (KD 3)

SHŌ-KAI (KD 6)

Fig. 298

Fig. 299   Fig. 300   Fig. 301

Next, press the Stomach Meridian (Fig. 298), from the knee to the top of the foot, using four fingers with the thumb on the other side of the leg for support. On the Stomach Meridian, the point San-Ri (三里), Stomach Meridian No. 36, should be pressed especially hard with circular motion. Then, press the Gall Bladder Meridian on the side of the leg in the same manner (Fig. 299).

On the inside of the leg, using both thumbs immediately behind the leg bone, with the other four fingers supporting on the other side of the leg, press the Spleen Meridian deeply, from the knee down to the ankle. The point San-In-Kō (三陰交), Spleen Meridian No. 6, should be pressed hard with circular motion (Fig. 300).

On the back of the leg, again using the thumbs, press deeply along the Bladder Meridian (Fig. 301), activating that meridian's energy flow.

Fig. 302 Meridians and Major Points on Leg

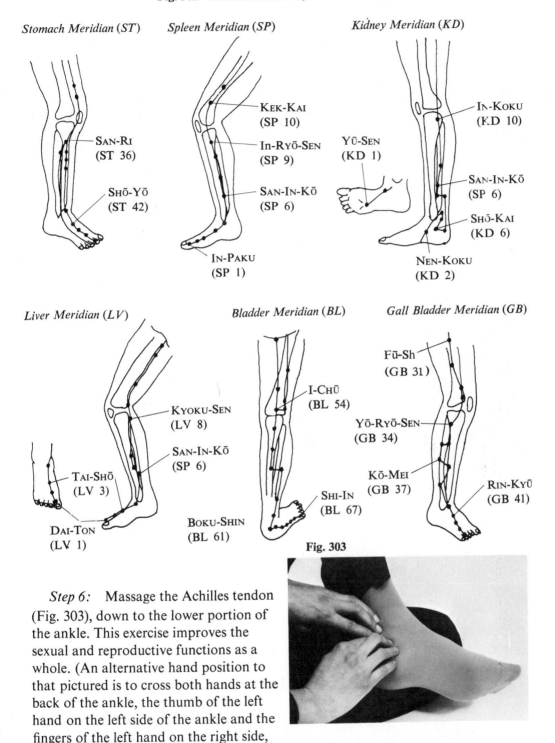

Stomach Meridian (ST)

SAN-RI (ST 36)

SHŌ-YŌ (ST 42)

Spleen Meridian (SP)

KEK-KAI (SP 10)

IN-RYŌ-SEN (SP 9)

SAN-IN-KŌ (SP 6)

IN-PAKU (SP 1)

Kidney Meridian (KD)

IN-KOKU (KD 10)

YŪ-SEN (KD 1)

SAN-IN-KŌ (SP 6)

SHŌ-KAI (KD 6)

NEN-KOKU (KD 2)

Liver Meridian (LV)

KYOKU-SEN (LV 8)

SAN-IN-KŌ (SP 6)

TAI-SHŌ (LV 3)

DAI-TON (LV 1)

Bladder Meridian (BL)

I-CHŪ (BL 54)

SHI-IN (BL 67)

BOKU-SHIN (BL 61)

Gall Bladder Meridian (GB)

FŪ-SH (GB 31)

YŌ-RYŌ-SEN (GB 34)

KŌ-MEI (GB 37)

RIN-KYŪ (GB 41)

Fig. 303

Step 6: Massage the Achilles tendon (Fig. 303), down to the lower portion of the ankle. This exercise improves the sexual and reproductive functions as a whole. (An alternative hand position to that pictured is to cross both hands at the back of the ankle, the thumb of the left hand on the left side of the ankle and the fingers of the left hand on the right side, and the thumb of the right hand on the right side of the ankle and the fingers of the right hand on the left side.)

Step 7: Holding the hands under the bottom or back of the foot, use the thumbs to rub downward along the top of the foot to the tips of the toes (Fig. 304). Since each area of the foot correlates to each region of the body and organs, giving stimulation and releasing stagnation in any part of the foot activates and improves the functioning of the corresponding regions of the body.

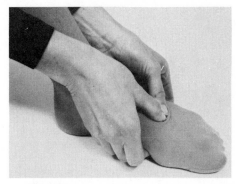

Fig. 304

Fig. 305   Lines for Foot Massage and Pressing in Dō-In

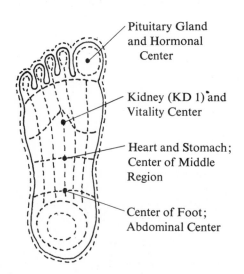

Pituitary Gland and Hormonal Center

Kidney (KD 1) and Vitality Center

Heart and Stomach; Center of Middle Region

Center of Foot; Abdominal Center

Fig. 306   Areas and Points on the Foot Corresponding to Bodily Organs

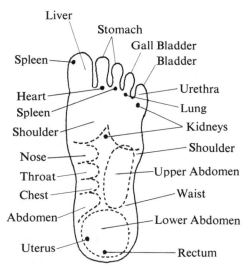

Liver
Stomach
Gall Bladder
Spleen
Bladder
Heart
Urethra
Spleen
Lung
Shoulder
Kidneys
Nose
Shoulder
Throat
Upper Abdomen
Chest
Waist
Abdomen
Lower Abdomen
Uterus
Rectum

Fig. 307

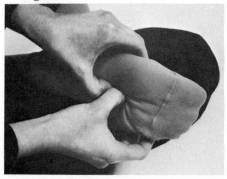

Step 8: We sit cross-legged with the sole of one foot turned up. Using the thumbs, we press the bottom of the foot (Fig. 307) in the following areas: first the inner side toward the large toe, moving up and down along the foot; then, starting from each toe, we press across the sole vertically, two or three times in each area. Next, we press across the sole sideways in three lines: near the heel, across the middle, and near the ball of the foot (see Figs. 305 and 306), two or three times. Finally, we press sideways along the fleshy region at the root of the toes, two or three times.

During this massage, if you find hard spots, press more firmly several times with circular motions, to release the stagnation.

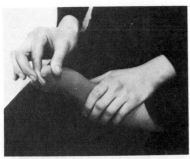

Fig. 308

Step 9: Pick up the large toe. Rotate the toe several times, and using the thumb and index finger, press the sides of the toe and the fleshy central region of the toe (Fig. 308). Then treat the other toes in the same way, one by one. The tip of each toe should also receive special stimulation by firm pressing.

Using the fingers, press between the toes (Fig. 309).

Step 10: Pull and bend each toe, trying to crack them, one by one. Then hold all of the toes and move them back and forth together several times (Figs. 310 and 311). Each toe has a meridian running along it, such as the Spleen, Liver, Stomach, Gall Bladder, and Bladder Meridians, and accordingly, stimulation given to each toe energizes and promotes the better functioning of the related organs.

Then, rotate the ankles with circular motion, several times in each direction.

Fig. 309　　**Fig. 310**

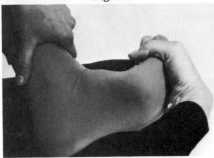

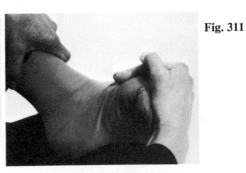

Fig. 311

Fig. 312　Meridians on the Bottom of the Foot

Fig. 313　Meridians on the Top of the Foot

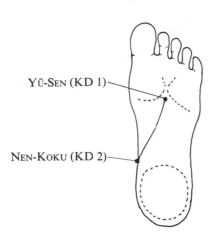

Yū-Sen (KD 1)

Nen-Koku (KD 2)

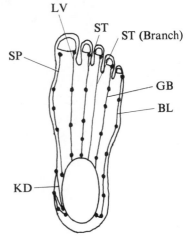

LV

ST

ST (Branch)

SP

GB

BL

KD

Step 11: Repeat Steps 3 through 10 on the other leg and foot.

Step 12: Sit with the soles of the feet together, holding the feet with the hands and breathing deeply three times (Figs. 314 and 315). This exercise comprehensively harmonizes the energy flow through all parts of the toes, feet, and legs.

Fig. 314

6. Completion

Throughout the series of General Exercises, each part of the body has been stimulated in its circulation of body fluid and energy flow, and the nervous response in each area has been activated as well. In the Completion, all of these bodily functions—in the muscles, organs, nervous systems, and energy—are harmonized as a whole unity, ready to meet any daily activity.

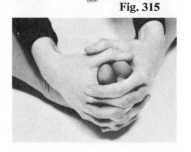

Fig. 315

Step 1: We stand with natural posture, and lightly jump (Fig. 316). Shoulders, elbows, wrists, and all other joints should be completely relaxed. Jump ten times or

Fig. 316

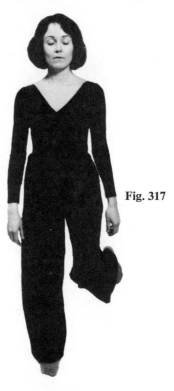

Fig. 317

more. Then, raise one leg and jump on only one foot (Fig. 317), ten times or more; then on the other foot.

Step 2: We stand with the feet shoulder-width apart, and twist side-to-side, swinging the arms (as in the Torso Exercise, Step 7, page 197). Shoulders, elbows, wrists, and all other parts of the body should be completely relaxed.

Step 3: Keeping the standing posture, we bend over, trying to touch the floor with both hands. Then, we stand up, spreading the arms wide, as if opening the chest. The shoulders and neck are to be very relaxed. Repeat twice.

Step 4: We stand straight, and lift the arms toward heaven, bending the body backward and inhaling deeply (Fig. 318). Then, we bend over and exhale, swinging the arms down (Fig. 319). We repeat this exercise at least three times, gradually slowing down.

Fig. 318

Fig. 319

7. Additional Exercises Especially for Facial Beauty

Although the General Exercises for the face, head, neck and shoulder regions serve well to maintain and develop beauty as well as health, the following exercises can be used especially for the development of beauty. These exercises help to balance the face, making the facial features more even, and making a loose face more tight and smooth.

Step 1: Tilt the head back, and use the heels of the hands to bang upward on the forehead. Alternate hands, or use both hands at once. Repeat ten to twenty times. This exercise serves to tighten the bone of the forehead, which tends to sag, as well as to tighten the muscles and skin of the forehead, eliminating wrinkles and making the blood circulation active.

Step 2: Using the fingers, smooth saliva along the eyebrows and around the eyes, both above and below. Repeat about ten times. This exercise makes the eyebrows grow beautifully and gradually eliminates wrinkles around the eyes. It also makes the eyesight more clear.

Step 3: Holding the cheekbones by the heels of the palms, push up, while opening the mouth. Repeat ten times. This exercise is to help the loose or sagging bones and muscles of the cheeks become tight and compact.

Step 4: With the thumbs at the back of the neck, and the fingers holding the head, tilt the head back. Drop the jaw, opening the mouth as much as possible. Then, suddenly drop the head forward and close the mouth. Repeat three to five times. This exercise helps to tighten loose vertebrae in the upper spinal region, and to strengthen and pull together the sides of the skull, thus enhancing the shape of the head. It is also good for circulation.

Step 5: Place the thumbs deeply in the indented area under the ears, tilt the head back and drop the jaw, opening the mouth wide. Then, close the mouth, bringing the jaw up. Repeat five times. This exercise tightens the mouth cavity as well as loose nasal cavities, and normalizes the coordination of the jaws in their left-and-right movement.

Step 6: With the middle fingers, push up hard on the bones of the middle region of the nose, squeezing in and up. The head naturally tilts back, and the mouth can be relaxed and slightly open. Then, release the pressure and drop the head back to its normal position. This exercise makes nerve action more alert and clear in the head region, including the eyes. It also causes the secretion of the pituitary gland to become more active, and breathing to become much smoother, and helps to discharge accumulated mucus from the regions of the forehead and nasal cavities.

Step 7: Inserting a finger in each corner of the mouth, stretch the mouth wide, and then release. Repeat about ten times. When releasing, it is very helpful to intentionally contract the muscles of the mouth. This exercise removes any wrinkles around the mouth and makes blood circulation better in the lips.

Step 8: Hold and vibrate the tip of the nose ten to twenty times. This exercise makes stagnated circulation in the nose more active, and corrects the shape of the nose.

Step 9: Thoroughly pull and stretch the ears: (1) up, (2) horizontally open, and (3) down, about five times in each direction. This exercise accelerates the circulation of blood, activating the kidney functions and the secretion of adrenal hormones, and improving the shape and angle of the ears if they have become loose and unbalanced.

Step 10: Rub and massage the cheeks about twenty to thirty times. This exercise is to make the circulation of blood and energy in the entire face region harmoniously active, and to eliminate wrinkles in the cheeks.

8. Some Daily Practices for Health

In addition to the daily Dō-In exercises for physical and spiritual development and for maintaining beauty, the following practices are also recommended for the development of health, and for the prevention of various physical disorders.*

1) For Headaches, including Migraine Headaches

In addition to the exercises for the head region given in the General Exercises, massage of the fingers and toes helps to relieve headaches. If the headache occurs in the front part of the head, give strong massage especially to the second and third toes. In the case of a headache arising in the side or back of the head, thoroughly massage the fourth and fifth toes. Massage the thumbs for a headache in the inside region of the head. These practices may be supplemented by strong massage on the middle and ring fingers, as well as on the thumbs and small fingers. These exercises should be repeated two to three times daily.

It is also helpful to rub grated ginger, onion or scallion into the afflicted area.

2) Baldness

For baldness in the peripheral regions of the head such as the front and side, it is advisable to practice the head massage exercises given in the General Exercises. In addition, apply saliva or salted water, strongly rubbing it into the bald area.

For baldness in the upper and central regions of the head, besides the exercises for the head region described in the General Exercises, apply daily the juice of grated ginger, *daikon*, red radish, onion, or scallion.

3) Red and Swollen Face

Every morning and evening, wash the whole face with cold salted water. Make an overnight buckwheat application: mix buckwheat flour with warm water to form a dough, and apply it at night to cover the whole face, removing it in the morning.

4) For the Health of the Eyes

Every morning and evening before sleeping, when we wash our face and hands, it is advisable to treat our eyes with the following care:

  a. We strongly rub all around our closed eyes with sea salt, which is applied to three dampened fingers of both hands.
  b. Wash the salt away, dipping and blinking our eyes in cold water.

---

* For a comprehensive explanation of recommendations for many other physical and mental conditions, please refer to *The Book of Macrobiotics* by Michio Kushi (Japan Publications, Inc., 1977).

c. Rub all around the eyes with plenty of saliva, applied to the fingers. Leave the saliva there for several minutes, allowing it to dry. Or, after several minutes, the eyes may be wiped with a towel.

These practices prevent any sort of eye trouble, including defective sight, cataracts, glaucoma, detachment of the retina, and other disorders. This exercise also helps to improve eye conditions resulting from these disorders, especially when practiced along with the eye exercises described earlier in the General Exercises, as well as with the use of eye drops of pure sesame oil applied once or several times daily. In some cases of eye disorders, applications such as the ginger fomentation, buckwheat plaster, or chlorophyll vegetable plaster may be needed also.*

5) For the Ears

In addition to the ear exercises shown in the General Exercises, it may be recommended to keep the ears clean by removing any wax accumulation. Use salted warm *bancha* tea, with or without a small amount of freshly-squeezed lemon juice, to wet a piece of cotton or tissue, and insert this into the ear, leaving it there for about two hours. Then, remove the cotton and use another piece of cotton or tissue to remove any remaining liquid from the ear. Repeat two or three times a day in cases of excessive wax accumulation.

The application of a ginger compress to the area around the ear also helps greatly to remove excessive wax. This may be done once or twice a day for several days.

6) For the Nose

For stagnation in the nose which causes difficulty in breathing, we can practice the exercises for the nose described earlier in the General Exercises. In addition, salted warm *bancha* tea or salted warm water can be sniffed into the nose and discharged through the nose without being swallowed; this can be done several times daily, and is also helpful in reducing and eliminating mucus accumulation in the nasal cavity and forehead.

In the event of nose bleeding, apply plenty of sea salt or dentie (the black powder of crushed, roasted eggplant) to damp cotton or tissue, and insert deeply into the nostril, leaving it in for five to ten minutes.

7) For the Teeth, Mouth and Jaw

Every morning and evening, the teeth can be brushed thoroughly with sea salt or dentie, both of which have been used traditionally in Far Eastern countries to strengthen the teeth and gums.

For inflammation of the gums and mouth, gargle with cold salted *bancha* tea several times daily.

---

* These and other applications are thoroughly described in *The Book of Macrobiotics* by Michio Kushi (Japan Publications, Inc., 1977).

8) For Congestion

Avoid mucus-forming foods such as dairy products, flour products, oily and greasy foods and various sorts of fat, as well as sugar, honey, and other sweeteners. Besides these dietary adjustments, regularly practice the Dō-In exercises shown in the General Exercise section, especially those for the chest and abdominal region. Strongly massage each hand and finger several times daily.

9) Constipation and Diarrhea

Practice the abdominal exercises regularly, as shown in the Daily Exercises (page 146) and in the General Exercises (page 196), together with regular eating following the natural, macrobiotic principles.

10) Leg and Foot Cramps

Eliminate the excessive intake of all sorts of liquid, as well as fruits and raw vegetables, sugar, honey, and other sweeteners. When a cramp arises, immediately apply one hand over the toes and the palm of the other hand to the place where the cramp is.

11) Dry Skin

Every day, massage the dry area well, applying the juice of grated ginger, radish, scallion or onion. Eliminate all fatty and oily products from the diet. It is also helpful to strongly massage the fingers and toes, especially those on which the meridians run that are related to the area where dry skin appears.

12) Freckles

Strictly avoid the excessive use of sugar, honey, chocolate, fruits and other sweeteners. Give a strong daily massage to the areas where freckles appear. Every day, apply and strongly rub in the juice of grated ginger, or rice vinegar, or lemon juice.

13) Moles, Warts, and Beauty Marks

Avoid over-eating, and especially avoid eating oily and fatty foods and rich sources of protein. Strongly massage the areas where moles or warts are found. It is also very helpful to regularly apply the juice of grated radish, or lemon juice. The warts and other marks may also be burned out using moxibustion (see page 69).

14) For Cuts and to Stop Bleeding

In order to stop bleeding, immediately apply dentie, sea salt or *miso*, spread upon either cotton cloth or tissue paper and held tightly in place with a bandage.

15)　For Fire Burns

Immediately soak the burned area in cold salted water, and continue to soak until the burning sensation disappears. Then, apply vegetable-quality oil such as sesame or corn oil with a tissue paper or cotton cloth. This can be held in place with a bandage and kept on the burned area for several hours. If necessary, the oil application may be changed every few hours.

16)　General Fatigue

For fatigue, which is universally experienced as a result of illness or physical and mental imbalances, besides the practice of Dō-In exercises, the following measures are recommended:

a. Regulate the way of eating in quality and volume moving more and more toward macrobiotic principles.
b. Wear cotton rather than synthetic clothing. At least, the underwear that is directly touching the skin should be cotton.
c. Rub and massage the whole body with a wet towel which has been tightly squeezed out, until the skin becomes red. This accelerates the circulation of blood and other body fluids, and generates nervous responses and energy flow along all the meridians. This may be done every morning or evening, or both.
d. Soak the feet in warm water (if in the cold season) or in cold water (if in the hot season) and clean all areas of the feet, including each toe, making the energy flow along the meridians very active. This may be done every morning or evening.
e. Before sleeping, practice Dō-In, especially the exercise *An-Min-Hō* (Peaceful and Sound Sleep), pages 168–171.
f. Sleep with the head to the North, in order to harmonize our physical, mental and spiritual conditions with the order of celestial motion, including the rotation of the earth and the stellular cycles of the Northern sky.

All of these exercises and practices for our daily life help greatly to maintain and develop our physical, mental and spiritual conditions. However, the foundation for our development is based upon what and how we eat and drink. Therefore, all of these exercises and practices should be accompanied with the proper way of eating following macrobiotic principles. If this is achieved in our daily life, our physical, mental, and spiritual development will be unlimited, and we will grow from our limited physical boundaries to eternal and universal consciousness, becoming aware that our life is beginningless and endless, and that our happiness is to continue to realize endlessly our infinite dream, which never perishes.

Appendix

Major Points for Diagnosis and Treatment Used in This Book

Page	Name of Point		Meridian and Point Number	Description
45	中脘	*Chū-Kan*	CV 12	Stomach *Bo*-Gathering Point. The center of the Middle Heater region and the Third Chakra. General stomach disorders, gastritis, morning sickness and nausea, stomach spasms, gastric ulcer, hyperacidity, descended stomach, diabetes, dyspepsia, abdominal pain, retroversion of the uterus.
61	肺俞	*Hai-Yu*	BL 13	Lung *Yu*-Entering Point. All lung disorders, asthma, shoulder stiffness, bronchitis, lung tuberculosis.
61	肝俞	*Kan-Yu*	BL 18	Liver *Yu*-Entering Point. Liver disorders, jaundice, gallstones, eye disorders, sciatica (waist pain), cystitis, facial paralysis, hepatitis, epilepsy, polio, vertigo, insomnia, half-body paralysis. Also for muscle disorders in general.
61	小腸俞	*Shō-Chō-Yu*	BL 27	Small Intestine *Yu*-Entering Point. General small intestine disorders, acute and chronic enteritis, lumbago, joint rheumatism, menstrual disorders, gynecological problems, sciatica (waist pain), cystitis, intestinal hemorrhage.
62	肺俞	*Hai-Yu*	BL 13	Lung *Yu*-Entering Point. All lung disorders, asthma, shoulder stiffness, bronchitis, lung tuberculosis.
62	厥陰俞	*Ketsu-In-Yu*	BL 14	Heart Governor *Yu*-Entering Point. Cardiac pain, anxiety, mental disorders, tachycardia, pleuritis, upper toothache.
62	心俞	*Shin-Yu*	BL 15	Heart *Yu*-Entering Point. Heart disease, cardiac pain, rheumatism, pleuritis, lung tuberculosis, half-body paralysis, strong headache, mental disorders, schizophrenia, hypertension, apoplexia, neurasthenia, night sweating, angina pectoris.
62	膈俞	*Kaku-Yu*	BL 17	Diaphragm *Yu*-Entering Point. Loss of appetite, gastralgia, esophagostenosis, gastritis, pleuritis, stomach atonia, hysteria, night sweating, tachycardia.

Page	Name of Point		Meridian and Point Number	Description
62	肝兪	*Kan-Yu*	BL 18	Liver *Yu*-Entering Point. Liver disease, jaundice, bitter taste in mouth, hepatitis, gallstones, lumbago, hemiplegia, polio, vertigo, epilepsy, eye disease, waist pain, facial paralysis, half-body paralysis, insomnia, dizziness.
62	胆兪	*Tan-Yu*	BL 19	Gall Bladder *Yu*-Entering Point. Gallstones, cholecystitis, jaundice, hepatitis, cholangitis, duodenal ulcer.
62	脾兪	*Hi-Yu*	BL 20	Spleen *Yu*-Entering Point. All stomach diseases, loss of memory, sinus congestion, gallstones, trachoma, diabetes, jaundice.
62	胃兪	*I-Yu*	BL 21	Stomach *Yu*-Entering Point. All stomach disorders, gastritis, hyperacidity, enteritis.
62	三焦兪	*San-Shō-Yu*	BL 22	Triple Heater *Yu*-Entering Point. Kidney fever, indigestion, waist pain, impotence, nocturnal enuresis, lumbago, fever (lung), nephritis, diabetes, dyspepsia, gallstones.
62	腎兪	*Jin-Yu*	BL 23	Kidney *Yu*-Entering Point. Kidney disorders, reproductive disorders, bladder disorders, nervous weakness, polio, impotence, lumbago, dysmenorrhea, sciatica, hemiplegia, hypertension, dyspepsia, diarrhea, vomiting.
62	大腸兪	*Dai-Chō-Yu*	BL 25	Large Intestine *Yu*-Entering Point. General intestinal disorders, enteritis, lumbago, sciatica, constipation, diarrhea, colitis, tenesmus, dermatitis.
62	小腸兪	*Shō-Chō-Yu*	BL 27	Small Intestine *Yu*-Entering Point. Joint rheumatism, intestinal hemorrhage, menstrual disorders, female organ disorders, enteritis, lumbago, hematuria, gynecological problems, sciatica, cystitis.
62	膀胱兪	*Bō-Kō-Yu*	BL 28	Bladder *Yu*-Entering Point. General bladder disorders, urinal function disorders, cystitis, lumbago, nocturnal enuresis, sciatica.
62	中府	*Chū-Fu*	LG 1	Lung *Bo*-Gathering Point, and beginning point of Lung Meridian. Lung disease, bronchitis, chest pain, asthma, coughing, tonsilitis.
62	膻中	*Dan-Chū*	CV 17	Heart Governor *Bo*-Gathering Point, central point of Upper Heater Region and Fourth, Heart Chakra. Cardiac and chest pain, breast pain, lack of breast milk production, depression, nervousness, pleuritis, asthma, vomiting, heart disease.
62	巨闕	*Ko-Ketsu*	CV 14	Heart *Bo*-Gathering Point. Heart disease, stomach spasm, gastritis, asthma, jaundice, rheumatism,

Page	Name of Point		Meridian and Point Number	Description
				inability to lift arms, diaphragm spasm, gastric ulcer.
62	期門	*Ki-Mon*	LV 14	Liver *Bo*-Gathering Point. General liver disorders, gallstones, bronchitis, excessive gastric acid, pleuritis, frequent coughing, diarrhea, hepatitis. Diagnosis point for the liver.
62	日月	*Jitsu-Getsu*	GB 24	Gall Bladder *Bo*-Gathering Point. Gallstones jaundice, pleuritis, gastric ulcer, chest pain, hypochondria.
62	京門	*Kei-Mon*	GB 25	Kidney *Bo*-Gathering Point. Kidney diseases, waist pain, pleuritis, stomach spasm, genital disorders, cystitis, kidney stones, intercostal neuralgia, lumbago.
62	章門	*Shō-Mon*	LV 13	Spleen *Bo*-Gathering Point. General spleen and liver diseases. Special point for water retention in the abdomen, descended stomach, chest arthritis.
62	中脘	*Chū-Kan*	CV 12	Stomach *Bo*-Gathering Point. The center of the Middle Heater Region and the Third Chakra. General stomach disorders, gastritis, morning sickness and nausea, stomach spasms, gastric ulcer, hyperacidity, descended stomach, diabetes, dyspepsia, abdominal pain, uterus retroversion.
62	天枢	*Ten-Sū*	ST 25	Large Intestine *Bo*-Gathering Point. Stomach disorders, large intestine disorders, dysentery, gastritis, enteritis, dysmenorrhea, pain control, diarrhea, nephritis.
62	陰交	*In-Kō*	CV 7	Triple Heater *Bo*-Gathering Point. Intestinal disorders, diarrhea, acute intestinal pain, kidney infection, impotence, nephritis.
62	関元	*Kan-Gen*	CV 4	Small Intestine *Bo*-Gathering Point. General physical fatigue, intestinal disorders, prolonging life, nocturnal emission, impotence, female diseases in general, arthritis.
62	中極	*Chū-Kyoku*	CV 3	Bladder *Bo*-Gathering Point. Bladder disorders, reproductive disorders, gynecological problems, menstrual disorders, headache, nephritis, enuresis, dysmenorrhea, urethritis and genital diseases, cystitis, leucorrhea, impotence.
72	気海	*Ki-Kai*	CV 6	"The Ocean of Electromagnetic Energy;" point representing the Second Chakra, the physical center. General physical weakness, nervous weakness, reproductive disorders, inability to conceive, kidney and bladder disorders, chronic appendicitis, diarrhea. Traditionally known as

Page	Name of Point		Meridian and Point Number	Description
				the "Ocean of Vital Energy" in the case of males, and the "Plate for Storing Blood Energy" in the case of females.
76	労宮	*Rō-Kyū*	HG 8	Center of the palm. Point for diagnosis and treatment of general fatigue. Rheumatism such as wrist joint pain and stiff fingers; cardiac pain, jaundice, nose bleeding, syncope.
148	中脘	*Chū-Kan*	CV 12	Stomach *Bo*-Gathering Point. The center of the Middle Heater Region, and the Third Chakra. General stomach disorders, gastritis, morning sickness and nausea, stomach spasms, gastric ulcer, hyperacidity, descended stomach, diabetes, dyspepsia, abdominal pain, uterus retroversion.
148	下脘	*Ge-Kan*	CV 10	General disorders of the Lower Heater Region. Gastritis, enteritis, kidney and bladder disorders, vomiting, genital disorders, lumbago.
148	天枢	*Ten-Sū*	ST 25	Large Intestine *Bo*-Gathering Point. General disorders of the large intestine, typhoid fever, dysentery, gastritis, pain control in the large intestine area, diarrhea, nephritis, enteritis.
148	陰交	*In-Kō*	CV 7	Intestinal disorders, diarrhea, acute intestinal pain, kidney infection, impotence, nephritis.
148	気海	*Ki-Kai*	CV 6	"The Ocean of Electromagnetic Energy;" point representing the Second Chakra, the physical center. General physical weakness, nervous weakness, reproductive disorders, inability to conceive, kidney and bladder disorders, chronic appendicitis, diarrhea. Traditionally known as the "Ocean of Vital Energy" in the case of males, and the "Place for Storing Blood Energy" in the case of females.
148	関元	*Kan-Gen*	CV 4	Small Instestine *Bo*-Gathering Point. General physical fatigue, intestinal disorders, prolonging life, nocturnal emission, impotence, female diseases in general, arthritis.
148	大巨	*Dai-Ko*	ST 27	Diagnosis point for liver and intestine, especially constipation. Large intestine disorders, uterus disorders, inability to conceive, menstrual difficulty, kidney disorders, respiratory disorders, leg disorders, hernia.
176	百会	*Hyaku-E*	GV 20	Headache, nervousness,, hypertension, rheumatism, stuffy nose, hernia, insomnia, hemorrhoids, constipation, hemiplegia.
176	通天	*Tsū-Ten*	BL 7	Effective point for migraine, headaches in general, constipation, anosmia, neck pain.

Page	Name of Point		Meridian and Point Number	Description
176	神庭	*Shin-Tei*	GV 24	Headache in general, hypertension, insomnia.
176	角孫	*Kaku-Son*	TH 20	Diagnosis point of mental fatigue. Deafness, all eye disorders, toothache, ear pain.
176	睛明	*Sei-Mei*	BL 1	Beginning point of Bladder Meridian. Diagnosis point for astigmatism. Cloudy vision, eye congestive trouble, headache, renitent keratitis, kidney and bladder disorders.
176	瞳子髎	*Dō-Shi-Ryō*	GB 1	Beginning point of Gall Bladder Meridian. Diagnosis point for eye disease. Conjunctivitis, atrophy of the optic nerve, keratitis.
176	聽宮	*Chō-Kyū*	SI 19	Deafness, tinnitus, conjunctivitis, ear ringing, mucus in sinus and inner ear, aphagia, headache.
176	迎香	*Gei-Kō*	LI 20	End point of Large Intestine Meridian. Toothache, facial paralysis, nose bleeding, trigeminus pain, mucus accumulation in sinus and nasal cavities, anosmia.
176	巨髎	*Ko-Ryō*	ST 3	Diagnosis point for nasal disorders. Facial nerve paralysis, empyema, toothache, gingivitis, keratitis, lip pain.
176	翳風	*Ei-Fū*	TH 17	Neuralgia, shoulder and neck paralysis of extremities, deafness, ear ringing, facial paralysis, tinnitus, hiccough, toothache, otitis media.
176	水溝	*Sui-Kō*	GV 26	Emergency care for shock. Facial paralysis, epilepsy, jaundice, syncope, trismus.
176	大迎	*Dai-Gei*	ST 5	Facial paralysis, lower toothache, neck pain, gingivitis, trismus.
176	承漿	*Shō-Shō*	CV 24	End point of Conception Vessel. Toothache, facial paralysis, epilepsy and madness, hemiplegia.
183	百会	*Hyaku-E*	GV 20	Headache, nervousness, hypertension, rheumatism, stuffy nose, hernia, insomnia, hemorrhoids, constipation, hemiplegia.
183	角孫	*Kaku-Son*	TH 20	Diagnosis point of mental fatigue. Deafness, all eye disorders, toothache, ear pain.
183	風府	*Fū-Fu*	GV 16	Influenza, headache, nervousness, hypertension, cerebral hemorrhage, dizziness, hemiplegia, mucus in sinus and nasal cavities.
183	完骨	*Kan-Kotsu*	GB 12	Migraine, tinnitus, hearing difficulty, headache, cerebral congestion, neck stiffness, facial paralysis, dizziness, mastoiditis.
183	風池	*Fū-Chi*	GB 20	Headache, migraine, influenza, hypertension, tinnitus, eye disease, nervousness, cerebral hyperemia, mucus in sinus and nasal cavities, rhinitis, empyema.
183	天柱	*Ten-Chū*	BL 10	Headache, head heaviness, insomnia, hypertension, cerebral hemorrhage, nervousness, spasm

Page	Name of Point		Meridian and Point Number	Description
				of neck and shoulder muscles, hysteria, eye disease, throat disorders, stuffy nose.
183	肩井	Ken-Sei	GB 21	Headache, cerebral hyperemia, neck and shoulder stiffness and pain, neuralgia of upper extremities.
188	肩髃	Ken-Gū	LI 15	All skin diseases, arm pain, shoulder stiffness, rheumatism, tooth pain, hemiplegia, headache, hypertension.
188	曲池	Kyoku-Chi	LI 11	All skin disease, hypertension, hemiplegia, fever caused by intestinal disorders, headache, toothache, eye disease accompanied by expansion of blood capillaries and fever.
188	合谷	Gō-Koku	LI 4	Gen-Source Point for Large Intestine Meridian. Diagnosis point for large intestine condition. Facial disorders, headache, nose bleeding, anemia, pain control, epilepsy, hemiplegia.
188	陽池	Yō-Chi	TH 4	Gen-Source Point of Triple Heater Meridian. Abnormal uterus position, tonsilitis, deafness, wrist joint arthritis, vomiting, nausea due to pregnancy, leucorrhea.
188	大椎	Dai-Tsui	GV 14	Intermittent fever, tonsilitis, headache, spasm of neck muscles, influenza, lung tuberculosis, malaria, vomiting.
188	天宗	Ten-Sō	SI 11	Chest pain, neck and shoulder stiffness, pleuritis, breast pain, inability to produce breast milk, disorders of bile secretion in the liver and gallbladder, inability to lift arms.
188	少海	Shō-Kai	SI 8	"Small Ocean of Energy." Elbow arthritis, neuralgia of shoulder and neck, radial neuralgia and paralysis.
188	外関	Gai-Kan	TH 5	Arm arthritis, rheumatism, hearing difficulty, influenza, headache, wrist and finger pain and paralysis, parotitis (mumps).
188	腕骨	Wan-Kotsu	SI 4	Gen-Source Point of Small Intestine Meridian. Wrist arthritis, headache, radial neuralgia, jaundice.
188	極泉	Kyoku-Sen	HT 1	Beginning of Heart Meridian. Cardiac pain, pain in the chest, hypochondria.
188	少海	Shō-Kai	HT 3	Ear ringing, sinus congestion, heart disease, elbow arthritis, schizophrenia, cardiac pain, tinnitus, empyema, rhinitis.
188	神門	Shin-Mon	HT 7	Various heart disorders, schizophrenia, nervousness, insomnia, constipation, wrist arthritis, epilepsy, amnesia, angina.
188	尺沢	Shaku-Taku	LG 5	Lung tuberculosis, asthma, coughing, tonsilitis, throat pain, eye disease, hemiplegia, quadriplegia,

Page	Name of Point		Meridian and Point Number	Description
				facial paralysis, dyspnoea, heart disease.
188	曲沢	*Kyoku-Taku*	HG 3	Bronchitis, frequent coughing, cardiac pain, elbow arthritis, brachial neuralgia.
188	内関	*Nai-Kan*	HG 6	Arm arthritis, palpitation, gastritis, brachial neuralgia, pain control, rheumatism.
188	太淵	*Tai-En*	LG 9	Wrist arthritis, rheumatism, insomnia, dyspnoea.
188	労宮	*Rō-Kyū*	HG 8	Diagnosis point for general fatigue. Physical and mental depression, syncope, foul breath, cardiac pain, wrist joint pain (rheumatism), jaundice, nose bleeding.
190	労宮	*Rō-Kyū*	HG 8	Center of the palm. Point for diagnosis and treatment of general fatigue. Rheumatism such as wrist joint pain and stiff fingers, cardiac pain, jaundice, nose bleeding, syncope.
190	合谷	*Gō-Koku*	LI 4	*Gen*-Source Point for Large Intestine Meridian. Diagnosis point for large intestine condition. Facial disorders, headache, nose bleeding, anemia, pain control, epilepsy, hemiplegia.
191	商陽	*Shō-Yō*	LI 1	Beginning point of Large Intestine Meridian. Intestinal fever, vomiting, diarrhea, tonsilitis, toothache, colds.
191	合谷	*Gō-Koku*	LI 4	*Gen*-Source Point for Large Intestine Meridian. Diagnosis point for large intestine condition. Facial disorders, headache, nose bleeding, anemia, pain control, epilepsy, hemiplegia.
191	関衝	*Kan-Shō*	TH 1	Beginning point of Triple Heater Meridian. Ear ringing, vomiting, laryngitis, emergency care, angina pectoris, headache, keratitis.
191	少沢	*Shō-Taku*	SI 1	Emergency care, headache, throat pain, heart constriction, stomatitis, pharyngitis, radial neuralgia.
191	少商	*Shō-Shō*	LG 11	End point of Heart Meridian. Emergency care, nervous excitement, layrngitis, fever, syncope, radial neuralgia, angina pectoris.
191	中衝	*Chū-Shō*	HG 9	End point of Heart Governor Meridian. Cerebral hyperemia, shock, mental disorders, emergency care, fever, finger pain.
191	少商	*Shō-Shō*	LG 11	End point of Lung Meridian. Tonsilitis, throat fever, throat tuberculosis, emergency care, pharyngitis, psychosis, apoplexia, heart disease.
191	労宮	*Rō-Kyū*	HG 8	Center of the palm. Point for diagnosis and treatment for general fatigue. Rheumatism such as wrist joint pain and stiff fingers. Cardiac pain, jaundice, nose bleeding, syncope.
194.	期門	*Ki-Mon*	LV 14	Liver *Bo*-Gathering Point. Diagnosis point for

Page	Name of Point		Meridian and Point Number	Description
				the liver. General liver disorders, gallstones, bronchitis, excessive gastric acid, pleurisy, frequent coughing, diarrhea, hepatitis.
194	章門	Shō-Mon	LV 13	Spleen Bo-Gathering Point. General spleen and liver diseases. Special point for water retention in the abdomen, descended stomach, chest arthritis.
195	膻中	Dan-Chū	CV 17	Central point of the Upper Heater Region and Fourth, Heart Chakra. Cardiac and chest pain, lack of milk production, depression, nervousness, breast pain, pleuritis, asthma, vomiting, heart disease.
195	中府	Chū-Fu	LG 1	Lung Bo-Gathering Point, and beginning point of the Lung Meridian. Lung disease, bronchitis, chest pain, asthma, coughing, tonsilitis, dyspnoea.
195	巨闕	Ko-Ketsu	CV 14	Bo-Gathering Point of the heart. Heart disease, stomach spasm, gastritis, asthma, jaundice, rheumatism, disability to lift arms, diaphragm spasm, gastric ulcer.
195	期門	Ki-Mon	LV 14	Liver Bo-Gathering Point. Diagnosis point for the liver. General liver disorders, gallstones, bronchitis, excessive gastric acid, pleuritis, frequent coughing, diarrhea, hepatitis.
195	日月	Jitsu-Getsu	GB 24	Gall Bladder Bo-Gathering Point. Gallstones, jaundice, pleuritis, gastric ulcer, chest pain, hypochondria.
195	章門	Shō-Mon	LV 13	Spleen Bo-Gathering Point. General spleen and liver diseases. Special point for water retention in the abdomen, descended stomach, chest arthritis.
195	中脘	Chū-Kan	CV 12	Stomach Bo-Gathering Point. The center of the Middle Heater Region and the Third Chakra. General stomach disorders, gastritis, morning sickness and nausea, stomach spasms, gastric ulcer, hyperacidity, descended stomach, diabetes, dyspepsia, abdominal pain, retroversion of the uterus.
200	三里	San-Ri	ST 36	Well-known as the point for moxibustion for health and longevity. General digestive diseases, hemiplegia, abortion, delivery problems, stomach disorders, nose disorders, arthritis, all chronic diseases.
200	三陰交	San-In-Kō	SP 6	All disorders of reproductive system and genital organs. Kidney and bladder disorders, cleansing of blood, menstrual irregularity, amenorrhea, vaginal discharge, cystitis, pain control. (Tradi-

Page	Name of Point		Meridian and Point Number	Description
				tionally prohibited to use this point by acupuncture and moxibustion in pregnant women.) Meaning is "Three-Yin-Meridian-Junction."
201	三里	*San-Ri*	ST 36	Well-known as the point for moxibustion for health and longevity. General digestive diseases, hemiplegia, abortion, delivery problems, stomach disorders, nose disorders, arthritis, all chronic diseases.
201	衝陽	*Shō-Yō*	ST 42	Gastritis, toothache, headache, facial paralysis, psychose. *Gen*-Balancing Point of the Stomach Meridian.
201	血海	*Kek-Kai*	SP 10	Cleansing of blood, menstrual irregularity, knee arthritis, dysmenorrhea, incontinence of urine, eczema, endometritis.
201	陰陵泉	*In-Ryō-Sen*	SP 9	Knee joint arthritis, paralysis of lower extremities, eschuria, asthma, lumbago, dyspepsia.
201	三陰交	*San-In-Kō*	SP 6	All disorders of reproductive system and genital organs. Kidney and bladder disorders, cleansing of blood, menstrual irregularity, amenorrhea, vaginal discharge, cystitis, pain control. (Traditionally prohibited to use this point by acupuncture and moxibustion in pregnant women.) Meaning is "Three-Yin-Meridian-Junction."
201	照海	*Shō-Kai*	KD 6	Mental disorders, pharyngitis, tonsilitis, dysmenorrhea, nephritis, otitis.
201	然谷	*Nen-Koku*	KD 2	Hypertension, pharyngitis, nocturnal emission, tetanus, night sweating, female genital diseases.
201	大敦	*Dai-Ton*	LV 1	Beginning point of Liver Meridian. Emergency care for heart pain, epilepsy and convulsions; headache, hordeolum (sty), syncope, genital pain.
201	太衝	*Tai-Shō*	LV 3	*Gen*-Balancing Point of Liver Meridian. Liver disorders, foot pain, gastritis, muscular spasm, headache, thumb pain, colic, bedwetting.
201	曲泉	*Kyoku-Sen*	LV 8	Knee arthritis, rheumatism, gonorrhea, frequent urination, nocturnal emission, hemiplegia, urethritis, cystitis, peritonitis.

Index